LITERATURE AND SOCIETY

LITERATURE AND SOCIETY

by

CHARLES I. GLICKSBERG

MARTINUS NIJHOFF / THE HAGUE / 1972

ISBN 90 247 1216 5

PRINTED IN THE NETHERLANDS

To Herbert Neuman

TABLE OF CONTENTS

PART III:

THE LITERATURE OF SOCIAL COMMITMENT   189

PART IV:

CONCLUSION   241

INTRODUCTION

1. Prolegomena

The purpose of this book is to examine anew and from a number of different perspectives the highly complex and controversial relation between literature and society. This is not meant to be a study in sociology or political science; the analysis of literature – its structure, content, function, and effect – is our primary concern. What we shall try to find out is how the imaginative work is rooted in and grows out of the parent social body, to what extent it is influenced in subject matter as well as form and technique by the dominant climate of ideas in a given historical period, and to what degree and in what manner literature "influences" the society to which it is addressed. The stream of literary influence is of course difficult to trace to its putative source, for here we are not dealing, as in science, with isolated physical phenomena which can be fitted precisely within some cause-and-effect pattern. The relationship between literature and society is far more subtle and complex than social scientists or cultural critics commonly assume.

Obviously literature does not operate in a vacuum; it is preeminently a social act as well as a social product. A book must be brought out under the aegis of some publishers, unless it is paid for and printed by the author himself, as Whitman did when he issued the first edition of *Leaves of Grass* in 1855. It is as a rule judged by a group of professional reviewers, critics, and, the author fondly hopes, by a host of readers, though it sometimes happens that a book is stillborn, unnoticed and consigned to the limbo of oblivion. All this is not meant to imply that the writer deliberately sets out to please his audience, even if he knew how, though some writers may consult the public taste of the day and labor hard to produce a best seller. The writer as artist struggles to preserve his integrity; he must satisfy himself first in his work and in releasing his deepest powers of imagination create what is of urgent importance to himself; only then does he discover that by probing his own obsessions and embodying his private vision, however singular in expression or rebellious in content, he has spoken for others as well. In the words of James Joyce, spoken through his *persona*, Stephen Dedalus:

I will not serve that in which I no longer believe, whether it call itself my home, my fatherland, or my church: and I will try to express myself in some mode of life or art as freely as I can and as wholly as I can, using for my defence the only arms I allow myself to use, silence, exile and cunning.[1]

And yet in the end Joyce goes forth to encounter "the reality of experience and to forge in the smithy of my soul the uncreated conscience of my race." [2] Whatever the writer as artist produces, be it a testament which will be released only years after his death, he is in effect engaged in an act of communication, conducting a dialogue between himself and other men.

In reviewing the variegated and copious mass of literary material, confined chiefly to fiction and the drama, issued during the modern period (beginning approximately in the second half of the nineteenth century and continuing till the present), we are faced at the outset with the formidable task of selectivity, of deciding which books are truly "representative" of their time. Frequently an inferior book like *Exodus* or *Peyton Place* may prove immensely popular and reach a wider audience than a novel of genuine distinction, whose importance is appreciated only by a small body of the intellectual elite, and sometimes not even by them.[3] *Moby Dick* created only a mild stir in its day, many contemporary critics regarding it as but another adventure story of the sea. The best seller, however, is a social phenomenon that must be seriously taken into account as reflecting the popular taste,[4] but our major concern is with literature as an art, aside from its "success" as measured by sales figures.

The delicate matter of definition remains to be taken up. What is society and how does literature react to and act upon the social process? Every novel, every play, however experimental or avant garde its technique, makes a contribution to society, even though the segment of the reading population or the theater-going audience that responds to it is small. Even if it is presented as a fable, a fantasy, a madman's confession, an allegory, a junkie's autobiography, it has definite social implications. Literature, as Harry Levin contends, is clearly a social institution, but the fact that society functions as the all-inclusive container tells us little or nothing about the way in which literature deals with the social theme. Though literary art is personal in its

[1] James Joyce, *A Portrait of the Artist as a Young Man*. New York: The Modern Library, 1928, p. 291.

[2] *Ibid.*, p. 299.

[3] See Henri Peyre, *Writers and Their Critics*. Ithaca: Cornell University Press, 1944.

[4] See Frank Luther Mott, *Golden Multitudes*. New York: R. R. Bowker Co., 1947.

origin, it represents the socialized working out of some personal problem. It must transmute the emotions seeking release "into some socially meaningful pattern." [5] It can do so only in terms of objective correlatives and individualized characters. But the struggle for selfhood that is the identifying mark of much of twentieth-century literature, from the time of the Expressionists to the sixties, is in itself a social manifestation. Society constitutes a second nature. As Max Stirner, the philosopher of anarchism, perceptively remarks, not being alone, "but society is man's original state." [6]

Once it is acknowledged that society is actually our state of nature or second nature, we are in a position to show why writers recurrently rebel against those institutions of society they consider repressive. Many writers introduce heroes who are not only alienated but in full revolt against their social order. As twentieth-century society grows more centralized and efficient, the individual comes to feel that he is stripped of personal autonomy. The development of mass society, together with the philosophy of determinism that science supports, reinforces his sense of helplessness. He sees himself as the victim of gigantic impersonal forces – atomic energy, for example – that he can in many cases neither comprehend nor control. He becomes not only the unheroic hero but, like Meursault in *The Stranger* or the protagonists of Samuel Beckett's novels, the anti-hero. Like Lieutenant Frederick Henry in *A Farewell to Arms,* he withdraws from a society that is mad with the rage to kill and destroy, but his retreat into the self is also a form of revolt or a symbolic gesture of rejection.

The gesture of rejection is generally marked by indifference to the play of politics. The asocial hero turns a deaf ear to the rhetoric of ideology; he ceases to believe in the beguiling promises of liberalism or to harbor any utopian aspirations; he abandons entirely the ideal of social reform or the messianic hope of revolution. Disillusioned, he lives in society as if he were not a part of it. This asocial anti-hero is often the reflected image of the writer's own attitude toward life, as is true of the work of Ionesco, Samuel Beckett, and Jack Kerouac.

Opposed to this apathetic and impotent anti-hero is the revolutionary saint who finds the true meaning, justification, and fulfillment of life in the sphere of history. Since there is no Kingdom Come, since God is absent or has never been present save in the consciousness of deluded men, since the assurance of immortality does not safeguard man against the terror and

---

[5] Ralph Ellison, *Shadow and Act*. New York: Random House, 1964, p. 39.
[6] Max Stirner, *The Ego and His Own*. Translated by Steven T. Byington and edited by James J. Martin. New York: Libertarian Book Club, 1963, p. 305.

finality of death, the revolutionary must become the architect of his own destiny and the conqueror of his own world. He stands ready to sacrifice everything, even his own life, for the sake of the social ideal. This ethic of commitment is the only way of salvation open to him: the transcendence of his finite and ephemeral self by means of dedication to a higher collective cause. He embraces a mystique of action even though, like Malraux's intellectual heroes, he may suspect that the ideology of commitment is but another species of illusion. The individual, as Bazarov knew, is unimportant. Society is God, society is immortal. Hence the death of the individual is of no consequence.

If all literature is social in content, the poles between which literature as a social institution oscillates are those of extreme individualism and collectivism. The first is represented by what we call asocial literature, which views the human condition *sub specie aeternitatis* or from the vantagepoint of the withdrawn and alienated self. The second produces the literature of commitment, written by those who wish to utilize their talent for the achievement of positive political ends. They may be Socialists like Upton Sinclair or Communists like Mayakovsky and Bertolt Brecht. The third type, what we call the literature of social criticism and social protest, is not hostile to the idea of society but only to those aspects of society that are unjust, decadent, oppressive, inimical to life. If writers of this persuasion attack the social order, they have as a rule no desire to overturn the applecart. Though these three categories will be treated separately, they are actually interrelated and overlap. A militant asocial movement in its inception, Surrealism led some members, including its founder, André Breton, to Marxism. Richard Wright, an ex-Communist, later turned to the writing of Existentialist fiction, whereas Sartre, after publishing *Nausea*, attempted the impossible task of reconciling Existentialism with Marxism. Then, too, there is the paradox that asocial writers like Proust produce some of the most devastating assaults on the existing social order and are thus more "revolutionary" in their impact than the mechanical, formula-ridden showpieces of Socialist realism in Soviet Russia.

If literature is social in its orientation even when it voices a defiant spirit of opposition, it must be remembered that society, like Nature, is an omnibus term. Just as "the unnatural" is comprised within the sphere of "the natural," so are asocial manifestations fundamentally an expression of social energy. But if everything is social to begin with, then the term "social" becomes virtually meaningless. It is necessary to make the proper semantic distinctions. The writer cannot give a picture of society as a whole, though Romains tried it in the twenty-seven volumes of *Les Hommes de bonne volonté,* which make society itself the hero. He can present it only from a number of interconnected but strictly limited points of view in time.

For he must portray the life of society in terms of the actions of his individual characters. Nor does his protagonist, whatever role he plays, confront Society as a personified abstraction. Like Bazarov he fights against the effete Russian aristocracy and the lie of romanticism. Like Jordan in *For Whom the Bell Tolls,* he participates in the battle against Fascism in Spain. Invariably and of necessity he sets himself a limited if urgent objective; it is always a present evil that he combats. Even epic novels like *The Sleepwalkers* or *The Man without Qualities* cover only a small sector of social life. To overcome this handicap, which is imposed by his search for a unified form, the novelist may enlarge his canvas, introduce a vast gallery of characters drawn from all walks of life, and even, like Tolstoy in *War and Peace,* interpolate chapters of pure exposition in which he logically disposes of mistaken philosophies of history and then proceeds to defend his own conception of the historical process. No matter which devices he uses – excerpts from contemporary newspapers, biographical summaries of important historical personages of the time, direct social commentary – to capture the complex reality of the life of the past, basically he must depend on his individual hero or heroes to reflect selected aspects of the social macrocosm. Through his cast of characters, which serve as his embodied dramatic agents, he weaves different patterns of acceptance or rejection, virtue and vice, history and society.

Thus the novelist or dramatist, whatever else he may include in his work, concerns himself of necessity with some selected phase of the social world. Whether he deals with the war between the two sexes or the Strindbergian motif of the inferno of marriage or the Brahmin vision of the illusion of reality (in *The Serpent and the Rope* or *The Root and the Flower*), every theme he handles is essentially social in nature. No character delineated, be he hero or anti-hero, outcast or schizophrenic, can help but offer an image, however distorted, of the social structure in which he has his being.

Since this is the case, it would be out of the question to examine the whole range of modern literature as a social institution. We shall confine ourselves to three broad approaches to the problem, which will focus attention on a number of illustrative literary specimens. First, there is asocial literature, metaphysical or absurd or anarchistic in content. Second, we take up the literature of social criticism, including the literature of moral protest, which for a variety of cogent and compelling reasons attacks the social order. The third section analyzes the contribution made by the literature of commitment. Obviously, the three groups all overlap. Revolutionary literature is certainly critical in its condemnation of capitalism, and we shall observe later how in the Soviet Union after the death of Stalin satires are written which, without repudiating the Communist ideal, constitute a scathing moral protest against the doctrinaire excesses of Socialist realism. As for asocial literature, that is not to be interpreted literally. There is, strictly speaking, no such thing. All three types – the asocial, the literature of social criticism, and the committed – shadow forth different versions of the life of man in society.

A man, in short, has no character apart from his being in the social world. He is both individual and social in nature. Indeed, the flowering of his very individuality is rendered possible by his place in society. But the first group of writers, the asocial, sees man as vastly more than a social creature, a conditioned unit in the social machine, identified with his role as citizen, worker, husband, father, nationality, race. His inner self is not summed up by these functional categories. They fail to do justice to his unique individuality, his dreams and anxieties and longing for transcendence, his personal attitude toward death, his relation to the universe at large. Hence writers in this group are as a rule concerned predominantly with the human condition. History for many of them is a nightmare, a desert of lost causes and buried empires. But this disillusioned stance can give way in some cases to a humanistic affirmation. The pure absurdist hero, however, spurns all mystiques. He carries on the tradition inaugurated by Kafka which projects a solipsistic dream-universe that is as irrational and fantastic as the social world he rejects. The writer as social critic, on the other hand, suffers from no qualms of doubt; he feels thoroughly justified in his moral protest against a world that is dehumanized, oppressive, downright evil. It is the socially committed writer who occupies, in his own eyes at least, the least equivocal position; he takes his stand. In behalf of exploited mankind he launches an impassioned literary crusade that will hasten the advent of the social millennium.

However nobly motivated in his intentions, the socially committed writer – a Bertolt Brecht for example – is mistaken in his assumption that literature can be instrumental in effecting social change. Poets are not, as they sometimes proudly assert, the unacknowledged legislators of mankind. Practically negligible is the value of their work as *direct* instigations to reform or revolution. The test of effectiveness is measured by the degree to which a book succeeds in changing the attitude of its readers on a particular social or political issue. Literary works that produce such results are hard to find. If poets have nevertheless exalted their calling and looked upon themselves as prophets whose utterances were divinely inspired, that is because they suffered from occupational delusions of grandeur. Without these vital delusions, the creative activity of artists would lose much of its sustaining force.

The spectre of the artist arose as a kind of being elevated above the rest of mankind, alienated from the world and answerable in thought and deed only to his own genius: the image of the Bohemian took shape, fostered as much by the ideology and conduct of the artists as by the reaction of the society on the fringe of which they lived.[7]

It is clear that the poet (a term that includes both the novelist and dramatist) does not wish to consider himself merely a singer of idle lays, a purveyor of entertainment, a worshiper of beauty for its own sake. He must try to justify his vocation by magnifying the constructive social value of his contribution. Behind every aesthetic of commitment there lurks a socio-ethical imperative. Logos is the all-powerful God who will enable the writer to be not only a music-maker but a shaker and shaper of the world. Through the incantation of language, the romantic apotheosis of the Word, he hopes to awaken the slumbering imagination of men and lead them to establish the Kingdom of Heaven on earth.

Fallacious as this aesthetic turns out to be when judged empirically by the fruit it bears, it is evident that literature must of necessity produce some social effect. Otherwise, why would rulers in the course of history have been so hostile to the work of the poets? Plato wished to banish them from his ideal commonwealth. The Puritans under Cromwell closed the theater as a pernicious corrupter of morals. Through the ages as their influence grew, writers have been persecuted, their books banned or burned. The roll call of refugees from Nazi Germany, as well as those intellectuals thrust into concentration camps where most of them perished, includes some famous writers. Thus we get the paradox that literature, on the one hand, is condemned as a form of make-believe with words, a kind of verbal game or species of enchantment, while, on the other, it is supposed to exercise a potent influence, whether for good or evil, on the course of world events. There is the further paradox that the writer, however favorably disposed toward the vision of society redeemed, jealously safeguards his independence, fearful of being conscripted for ideological ends alien and inimical to the art he practices.

If literature exerts any appreciable social influence – and it assuredly does – it functions thus by virtue of its imaginative power, by revealing the problematical character of social as well as individual existence. Obviously the social world constitutes an important part of reality, but it is not, as the

---

[7] Rudolf and Margot Wittkower, *Born Under Saturn*. New York: Random House, 1963, p. 95.

Marxists contend, the only reality, with the individual reduced in significance to the role of an epiphenomenon. The modern novel comes to grips with the leading psychological and socioeconomic conflicts of its time: labor disputes, strikes, revolution, the bitter struggle to rise in the world, anti-Semitism, homosexuality, the cruel warping effects of heredity and environment, racial discrimination, the corruption of big business, the venality and irresponsibility of politicians, the apocalypse of war, the threat of nuclear annihilation. But it also discloses numinous heights and depths of being which are not included within the naturalistic framework; it seeks to explore the spiritual destiny of man, his religious yearnings, his metaphysical nostalgias, his confrontation of the mystery of birth and death. Consequently the influence of literature is never direct. It may arouse discussion and debate and stir the conscience of its readers, but it does not produce immediate tangible "results." The universal works of the imagination – *Hamlet*, *The Adventures of Don Quixote*, *The Magic Mountain* – furnish no solution. Literature is not properly a medium for social reconstruction or moral uplift.[8]

We can certainly accept that literature can never be divorced from the world of which it is a part, and that the best literature will in various ways both reflect and create images of the best life in a society of which it is a part, without holding that judgment is entirely a matter of these effects.[9]

Nevertheless, numerous writers in our time continue to practice their profession as a form of sympathetic magic, convinced that it is precisely these practical effects on the life of society which identify the essential value of their work.

The purpose of literature as magic is to arouse emotions or reactions which can then be deflected into channels of socio-political reform. This type of aesthetic consciousness is by no means new, though it has in Soviet Russia been converted into a prescriptive Party dogma. The Marxist critic instead of concentrating on the writer's treatment of his material, his struggle to achieve unity of form, holds that he must choose the right subject and interpret it in the right manner. Here is a militant orthodoxy that exploits art as propaganda and sets up desired social "truths" as criteria of excellence. The value of a literary work, however, must always be sought in the work itself and not outside of it. Whatever a poem means can be legitimately

---

[8] This will be taken up in detail in the section dealing with the literature of commitment.

[9] William Righter, *Logic and Criticism*. London: Routledge and Kegan Paul, 1963, p. 14.

expressed only in terms of the poem itself, which comprises a universe of discourse that is "independent, complete, autonomous." [10]

Writers have temperamentally revolted against what they disparagingly call the cult of art for art's sake. Concretely, what does this pejorative label mean? No writer, however eccentric in his behavior or bizarre in his views, is completely withdrawn from the conflicts of his age. If we consider briefly the intellectual temper of writers in France during the nineteenth century, we observe immediately that there is no unanimity in their aesthetic outlook or creative purpose. The Bohemians of the age vent their hatred of the bourgeoisie. Gautier, in his preface to *Mademoiselle de Maupin*, attacks the official custodians of morality, the carping righteous critics of his day and their crusade for purity in literature. Gautier maintains that it is culture which shapes books, not books culture. The reformist critics want literature to be useful and edifying, whereas Gautier upholds the doctrine of art for art's sake.

One of the most influential and eloquent pioneers in exploring the relationship between society and literature was Madame de Staël, a leader in the field of the sociology of literature. She was particularly interested in examining the close relationship between politics and literature and, in addition, the impact of national character on expression. A descendant of the Age of the Enlightenment, she undertook in *Literature in Its Relation to Social Institutions* (1800) to reveal all literature as a function of social institutions. Literature and political life, she believed, were intimately interconnected. A social scientist rather than a literary critic,[11] she took it entirely for granted that literary forms corresponded to the needs of the social institution out of which they arose.

The political novel *par excellence* is *La Chartreuse de Parma*, but it is neither partisan nor prejudiced in tone. Stendhal was too civilized and sophisticated a novelist to be either a reactionary or utopian. In the case of Balzac, a Catholic royalist, we see how literature becomes a productive business. The novelist courts public taste, though he does not always succeed in his aim. Balzac composed his *Comédie humaine*, with its gallery of ambitious characters, each one striving to get ahead in the world. Though he produced over a hundred novels and tales and created over two thousand characters and brought a whole society into being, he never completed his grandiose project. He diagnosed the social diseases of his day, though politically he upheld the sanctity of the throne. Conservative in his instincts, he was hostile to the

[10] A. C. Bradley, *Oxford Lectures on Poetry*. London: Macmillan, 1934, p. 5.
[11] *Madame de Staël on Politics, Literature, and National Character*. Translated and edited by Morroe Berger. New York: Doubleday & Company, Inc., 1963, p. 66.

revolutionary ideal. Society was necessary not only to hold selfishness in check but also to provide the individual with opportunities for growth and development. The immoral impulses in man could be brought under control only by the monarchy and the rule of Catholicism. If evil plays such a preponderant share in his fiction, it is because he is roundly condemning a society which places no curbs on the vicious tendencies of its members. Individualism carried to excess presents a clear danger to social unity. Because he paints a repellent picture of social life in nineteenth-century France, both Marx and Engels cite Balzac as a prime example of the artistic conscience overriding conscious political sympathies. The point is, his sweep is so comprehensive that almost anything can be proved by reference to his work. He does not enunciate principles or dogmas or articles of belief; he portrays how men actually behave. He can be interpreted as a reactionary, an unreconstructed artist, a Catholic, a radical critic of capitalism. He remains, like every genuine artist, a bundle of contradictions.

If we study the career of Flaubert, we behold a man who, despite his radical disenchantment with life, dedicated himself austerely to the religion of art, a commitment that allowed of no compromise. This was the call of destiny, a sacred vocation like a priesthood, but if he gave himself wholeheartedly to his writing, he was too much the ironist not to laugh at his quest for perfection. There was always the spectacle of life to deflate his pride as an artist and mock his pretensions. Life, however much a cheat, was after all more engrossing and precious than literature. But whatever he may have said scoffingly of his own creative activity, he never scanted it; he continued to write.

The discipline Flaubert imposed on himself called for solitude, the absence of sentimentality, the elimination of illusion or feelings of pity. He himself resisted all efforts to confine him within a school or movement. The genuine artist, he believed, kept his objectivity, untrammeled by current opinions or systems of thought. He is not required to be a philosopher or sociologist or reformer; his task is to portray life and people as they are, not as they ought to be. The writer runs the serious danger of distorting or falsifying the truth if he ventures to obtrude his own convictions. Every work of literature conveys its own moral effect, but this is inherent in its structure and content, not something imported from without. Truth is the highest standard of morality. The artist becomes God in his own right. And Flaubert is the God who perceives and records the ironies present in the life around him; he is the observer whose all-seeing eye permits no blemish of ugliness, no touch of the grotesque, to escape him. He is the incorruptible artist, undistracted by the social, political, and economic crises of his age. Though he

was not without strong political and social convictions of his own, he opposed the sociological interpretation of literature.[12]

The leading French writers of the embattled nineteenth century were at
least fairly consistent in their determination to cherish their freedom of expression; they refused to be dragooned into conformity of thought or to
subordinate themselves and their art to the needs of some political party
or social movement. Toward the end of the century the naturalistic novelists
evinced a growing interest in contemporary themes. Zola's *Germinal* (1885)
marks an historical turning point in France in the emergence of socially
aroused fiction. Until that time Zola had betrayed little or no interest in social questions. In *Germinal*, the class conflict plays a crucial role. By 1897
Zola's socialist sympathies are powerfully expressed in his novel, *Paris*.

The *fin-de-siècle* artists confronted the same social problems that led
Zola to become an outspoken Socialist. They were not unaware, even as they
devoted themselves to their art, of the evils of their day – the misery of the
poor, the flagrant contradictions of their society, the persistent efforts being
made to carry out sweeping reforms. As the process of social change gathered
momentum, they found themselves in an anomalous position, alienated from
or in opposition to the society of their time. But here again there was no
aesthetic to which all could subscribe. Just as there were artists who desired
to keep the old order intact, so were there many who were interested only
in preserving the purity of their art.[13] The French decadents toward the end
of the last century hated society but they formulated no social evangel.
Asocial in temper, negative in attitude, many were uncompromising individualists. Their decadentism was a vigorous protest against giving their
"unconditional allegiance to an abstraction: State, Party, or society." [14]

If we jump to the nineteen twenties in the United States, we witness a not
too dissimilar process of conflicting loyalties and shifting aesthetic perspectives. This decade came to represent the spirit of rebellion against all that
the First World War stood for, as proclaimed by the propaganda issued by
the Allies. Before 1914 the American intellectuals had hoped to promote
social betterment through a change of government, through the eventual
establishment of Socialism, and through the effects wrought by an artistic
renaissance. The aftermath of the war brought on a mood of bleak and bitter
disillusionment. Ezra Pound fled to Europe, Eliot to England, and a band

[12] See Edmund Wilson, "The Politics of Flaubert," in *The Triple Thinkers*. New
York: Oxford University Press, 1948, pp. 72-87.
[13] See Eugenia W. Herbert, *The Artist and Social Reform*. New Haven: Yale
University Press, 1961.
[14] Herbert Read, *The Forms of Things Unknown*. New York: Horizon Press, 1960,
p. 105.

of disgruntled literati followed their example and went into exile abroad. There was, they felt, no freedom or opportunity for creative fulfillment in this land of cultural darkness. Though the major writers of the period were apolitical, they indulged in violent criticism of their country. America, they complained, was fabulously wealthy but intellectually anemic and spiritually impoverished. But industrialism continued to advance steadily and big business flourished while the literati acted out their drama of alienation, exile, and revolt. Then, when the financial crash occurred and the foundations of capitalism seemed to be temporarily shaken, the expatriates perforce had to return home.

The literature of the thirties set itself the task of combating the conception of man as the helpless victim of industrialized society. The individual was treated as a ghostly fiction and the self looked upon as a function of the social order. Leaving behind him the Waste Land and the aesthetic faith that nourished him there, the writer took seriously his role as social prophet, the inspired spokesman of the Marxist evangel of redemption. In an age of poverty, mass unemployment, economic dislocation, and the ominous spread of Fascism, the writer, it was urged, could no longer afford to remain in his ivory tower dedicated to the sterile cult of art for art's sake. Novelists, poets, and dramatists, many of whom joined the Communist Party or became devout fellow travellers, turned their attention to the social problem. To improve the living condition of the masses, to fight oppression and injustice on all fronts, to reveal the truth about social reality – the truth which is to be found in the economics of the class struggle: that was the professed aim of the embattled writers on the left. Unfortunately the didactic stridency of the revolutionary motif militated against the artistic effectiveness of the work produced in this vein. The themes chosen – strikes, labor exploitation, the Scottsboro case – were generally topical in nature. The contemporary issues, however urgent they seemed at the time, soon became dated. Who nowadays remembers, much less reads, the so-called "proletarian" novels published during the decade of the depression? The principal difficulty the radical writers faced was how to utilize their art for the promotion of their social ideals.

2. The Retreat into the Self

For a time the frenetic agitation in behalf of social justice and social improvement rendered suspect, if not absurd, the role of pure or politically uncommitted art. The unconditioned imagination, which had been discredited by such Marxist critics as Garaudy in France, Christopher Caudwell in England, and Granville Hicks in the United States, was during this period virtually driven out of business. Not that the writer is satisfied with either alternative: the belief that his creative faculty is autonomous, essentially asocial in character, or that it is completely at the mercy of historical circumstances. He wants to believe – perhaps he needs to believe – that his imagination has in some ways the power of "influencing" the world he lives in. The perplexing question is, how this influence is to be made effective?

Gradually, in a world in which Russian Communism had not lived up to its promise, a world given over once again to the senseless slaughter of war and the use of atomic bombs, the writer was forced to re-examine and revise his relation to social reality. Art as magic gave way to a journey into the interior. Now that the old utopian dreams had turned to radioactive ashes, he embraced art not as a redemptive social religion but a compulsion of the inner self. The American fiction of the forties bore witness to the disintegrating effect of two world wars, not to mention the traumatic impact of the depression of the thirties. Lost once more, the new generation of writers retreated within the fastness of the self and abandoned as illusions the social ideals of the recent past. The novels produced during this period are concerned predominantly with the quest for identity, with the search for personal values that would ensure survival in an age of crisis and catastrophe. The writer, rejecting the older schemes of social and political reform, had to start at scratch. He turned his gaze inward; there was no point in rebellion. Radicalism was virtually dead. Politics was, after all, not the province of the writer. During this decade the writers turned out fiction that testified to their alienation from society.[15]

The search for experimental forms of expression to capture the new emergent sensibility went hand in hand with an intrepid exploration of deeper levels of reality. The modern mind, having caught this profoundly disturbing vision of a world in process, dug into psychic areas that had hitherto been unplumbed, probing the fantastic world of the unconscious, stripping aside the veils of convention and throwing off the tyranny of ideology. It sought to communicate glimpses of a mysterious reality, which was no longer stable and knowable through the evidence of the senses. The objective confrontation of reality, the ideal of science, realism, and naturalism – that was no longer feasible. The senses could not reach to the subatomic universe that Einsteinian physics had disclosed. As the aesthetic of the new French fiction proclaimed, the world we behold is an anthropomorphic projection; we read our subjectivity into our observations of the physical universe. What fol-

[15] Charles E. Eisinger, *Fiction of the Forties*. Chicago and London: The University of Chicago Press, 1963, p. 20.

lowed as a result was a loss of confidence in the cult of objectivity, an increasing attitude of skepticism toward the truth of ideology. In the field of literature, the realistic and naturalistic method of portrayal was brought into question. As Eric Kahler pointed out:

It has become clear to us that reality is something very relative, something that depends on the capacity of our perception, on the degree of power, sharpness and rarity of perception. It has become clear to us that the "reality" of the sixteenth, eighteenth and twentieth centuries is by no means the same reality. Actual reality seems to be just the last frontier to which our perceptive capacity has progressed. Seen in this aspect, "realism," in the old conventional sense of the word, is not valid at all; it is – rendering as it does crude reality, the reality of our sheer surface experience – a very shallow and obsolete realism.[16]

Though naturalism persisted in some works of fiction, many novelists turned away from it, since it furnished only a limited view of reality.

3. Science and Mechanization

Thus the progress of science intensified in many quarters, both in Europe and America, the quest for self and was responsible in part for the withdrawal from a society that had become a technologically efficient nightmare. The fourth dimension, the discovery of the electron and the proton, the enigmatic conceptual reality that the twentieth century had brought to light, forced the writer to question the nature of the real, the relation between mind and universe as well as that between self and society. The growth of technology hastened the process of depersonalization. Under the domination of the machine, the individual became a thing, desensitized, incapable of feeling, alienated, held fast in the grip of external compulsion. The age of individualism is passing, if it is not already dead, but this obliteration of the individual self caused a reaction to set in: a reaction against conformity, regimentation, and collectivism. It is largely the asocial writer, together with the writer who criticizes society, who brings out the full force of the paradox that the machine, the fruit of organized intelligence, may be used to wipe out the human race. Science cures disease, prolongs life, and enlarges man's sense of freedom and power, but this sense of freedom is neutralized by his awareness that he is helpless in the face of conformist pressures all around him. A functional part of the social apparatus whose commands he must obey, he feels that his individual self is swallowed up in the collective whole.

Civilization moves forward, society advances, but at the expense of the

---

[16] Eric Kahler, *The Tower and the Abyss*. New York: George Braziller, Inc., 1957, p. 152.

development of the individual. Jung makes the point that collective culture is hostile to the flowering of the individual self.[17] The accelerated mechanization of the social process results inevitably in the dehumanization of man. The machine serves as an effective instrument for the integration of mankind as a whole. As Roderick Seidenberg remarks in *Posthistoric Man:*

By and large the direction of man's psychic orientation, at least within the span of history, has moved from a more subjective, introverted position to an increasingly objective, extroverted one. . . .[18]

This does not apply to the contemporary world of literature. For those who resist the deadly effects of depersonalization, those who refuse to become passive objects being manipulated by outside forces, take refuge more and more within the inner life; the flight into subjectivity is their only way out. The literary rebel places the accent on spontaneity, on freeing and fulfilling his "real" self. Yet his revolt seems doomed to failure in modern industrialized society. The industrialization of life led to the death of the hero. The anti-hero who appears on the literary scene today is an insignificant cog in a vast social and economic complex. He goes underground; he becomes extremely introspective in his rebellion against the oppression of society. His retreat within the self is, he suspects, a form of social infidelity, for how can he hope to achieve a true sense of identity apart from the society in which he lives?

[17] C. G. Jung, *Psychological Types*. Translated by H. Godwin Baynes. New York: Harcourt, Brace & Company, Inc., 1926, p. 94.

[18] Roderick Seidenberg, *Posthistoric Man*. Boston: Beacon Press, 1957, p. 235.

PART ONE

ASOCIAL LITERATURE

CHAPTER I

THE ASOCIAL WRITER

1. The Self and the World

By confirming the Newtonian picture of a mechanical universe determined in all its parts and operations, the Darwinian revolution made necessary a drastic revision of man's conception of the self and its relation to Nature and society. Hardy, whose novels sharply criticized the repressive conventions of Victorian society, also focused attention on cosmic alienation. Many writers in the twentieth century delineate the character of man as conditioned by his social environment but at the same time voice their awareness of the hopelessness and absurdity of the human condition. Dreiser who in *An American Tragedy* brought capitalism before the bar of justice and held it guilty of "the crime" that Clyde Griffiths committed and for which he was sentenced to death, formulated a stark mechanistic fatalism in his early fiction. Joyce, though his epiphanies capture intimations of something behind the veil, essentially "religious," if negative, glimpses of the numinous, is grimly naturalistic in his portrayal of the human quest for ultimate meaning. Lawrence, too, perceived the truth – and the danger – of the nihilistic *Weltanschauung* and tried to counter it by sounding his hope for instituting a better, less acquisitive society. He hated the England of his day, puritanical, materialistic, worshipful of Mammon, and periodically sought to affirm the animistic faith that sustained more primitive people, but he was not a primitivist at heart and he continued until the last to nourish his dream – it was only that – of a more perfect and organic social order.

All this supports the thesis that the asocial writer need not be hostile to his society. Just as the novelist as social critic – a Dickens, say, or a Thackeray – may expose the inhumane contradictions of his society without desiring to destroy it, so the asocial writer may, in his relentless exploration of the deeper dimensions of the self, draw a devastating portrait of the corrupt life of his society. He may like Kafka – the asocial novelist *par excellence* –

throw an ironic and cruelly revealing light on our modern bureaucratic, superorganized social institutions.

Who, then, besides Kafka, are some of the modern writers who might, in our sense of the term, be called asocial? Offhand we might mention such names as Maeterlinck, Strindberg during his Expressionist phase, Proust, Samuel Beckett, Ionesco, Henry Miller, Genet, and Jack Kerouac. Generally speaking, the asocial writer presents a hero who is an "outsider," homeless, uprooted, suffering from "nausea" or metaphysical vertigo. In order to counteract this oppressive vision of the void, he often plunges into the vortex of history, takes up a cause, commits himself to a political party or revolutionary movement. Like Malraux's "conquerors," he continues, secretly, to be haunted by the specter of total meaninglessness. The night of nothingness is always near that will nullify all human endeavor and make an end of the *hubris* of Promethean revolt. Sartre, for all his bold pronunciamentos in behalf of Communism, has never convincingly reconciled, as he himself confesses,[1] his Existentialism with what he calls his Marxist humanism. Similarly, Camus made an attempt to go beyond the myth of the absurd imaginatively set forth in *Caligula* and *The Stranger* and proclaim an ethic of human and social responsibility. For this reason, both these writers, though they never repudiated the myth of the absurd but simply went beyond it, are to be classified as socially committed spokesmen.

Whatever the nature of the literary production, the social motif cannot be kept out; a constitutive element in the creative work, it is present in the very structure, history, and development of the language used. The only force that militates against the exclusive domination of the social metaphor is the writer's apprehension of existence *sub specie aeternitatis*. The eye of vision beholds the vanity of human wishes, but even this perception must be situated, if it is to be communicated at all, within a specific social frame of reference. Everything that surrounds the writer – schools, colleges, factories, skyscrapers, prisons, courts of justice, cathedrals – are expressions of the social will. And the literature he creates, whatever the theme he chooses to deal with, is a contribution to his native culture. Fundamentally, by virtue of his calling, he is addressing other men, and it is the nature of his appeal that determines whether or not he belongs to the asocial category.

The asocial writer, whatever his professed aim, is engaged like the sa-

---

[1] "We were convinced *simultaneously* that historical materialism supplied the only valid interpretation of history and that existentialism remained the only concrete approach to reality. I do not pretend to deny the contradictions in this attitude...." Jean-Paul Sartre, *Critique de la raison dialectique*. Quoted in Victor Brombert, "Sartre and the Drama of Ensnarement," in John Gassner (ed.), *Ideas in the Drama*. New York and London: Columbia University Press, 1964, p. 174.

tirist in a "moral" crusade. Jarry's pataphysics, the militancy of the devotees of Dada in uncovering the cultural bankruptcy of the West, the anti-rationalist aesthetic formulated by the Surrealists, these were all battles fought in the name of "truth," of "sincerity." The principal function of asocial literature is that it articulates needs of the personality not comprehended within a particular social perspective. The asocial writer may, of course, go beyond the social framework and take for his central theme the relation of man to the universe. At this point, however, some distinctions must be drawn.

If we assume that all of literature is a social institution, then there is no such thing as asocial writing. Brecht is at one with Samuel Beckett and Ionesco. A few examples will perhaps drive home the distinction we are trying to make. In *Baal*, an early play, Brecht was nihilistic in outlook, but after his conversion to Communism he labored to create the kind of epic theater that would rouse the audience to a critical awareness of social conditions and move them to take appropriate revolutionary action. The asocial writer – a Kafka, a Borges – is not interested in social themes *per se* but in exploring deeper dimensions of being – modes of anguish and anxiety, dreams and fantasies and obsessions – which disclose the radical paradoxes of the human condition. But even in these extreme states of *Angst* and alienation, the characters are not cut off from their social roots. Their life must go on in the finite world of time even while they are searching the darkened skies for some glimmer of redemptive meaning.

For the private and the public, the individual and the social, the self and the community of which it is a part, are interdependent. Literature projects a social world to which everyone, though in different ways, is related. The social is not an external process to be objectively studied; it is the very stuff of human existence. Society is there before we are born. It is therefore not surprising that the social metaphor pervades all of literature. The portrayal of the self, however solipsist or mystical in character, is at the same time a symbolic expression of society in action. The protagonist is pictured as free or determined, enslaved by or triumphant over his environment. The novel, like the drama, acquires a new lease on life when it abandons the naturalistic conception of character as governed ineluctably by the combined influence of heredity and environment. The scientific synthesis reveals a great deal about the nature of man as he is observed reacting to his socioeconomic milieu, but it sheds no light on his potentialities of becoming. Asocial literature dwells on the complexities of the inner world of man; it traces a symbolic pattern of experience that involves a quest for authenticity of self, but this quest reveals not only the universe of self but also the social order in which the self must work out its destiny.

The asocial hero struggles to preserve the balance between inner and outer reality, society and solitude; he recognizes that the chief danger he faces stems from his tendency to ignore the mandates of the self, to merge with the lonely, anonymous crowd, to accept as absolutes the contingent values of his community. Though he tries to resist the pressures that make for conformity, the anti-hero in asocial literature is no rebel. Knowing that he stands no chance against his formidable adversary, the Goliath of society, he frequently fights to save himself by consenting to defeat as measured by the world's standards. In endeavoring to know himself, he must challenge the conventions of his society; they are not the heart of reality as he experiences it and he has the courage to throw them off, to rebel against the laws, the philosophical presuppositions, and ethics of his age. When the writer views life primarily from the aesthetic perspective, then social reality in all its vicissitudes is seen as but a dream in the mind of God, a passing episode in the sempiternal flow of time. If God is the supreme artist, then he is both asocial and amoral, "recklessly creating and destroying, realizing himself indifferently in whatever he does or undoes, ridding himself by his acts of the embarrassment of his riches and the strains of his internal contradictions." [2]

2. Strindberg and Expressionism

Strindberg rightly deserves the place of honor in the historical development of modern asocial literature. A pioneer dramatist who in his early naturalistic plays portrayed man as trapped by his instinctual compulsions and his neuroses, Strindberg in his later work explored the irrational, guilt-laden world of subjectivity. In those of his plays that highlight the obsessions of the unconscious, he emerges as the forerunner of the theater of the absurd. In his Expressionist dramas the emphasis is placed on the inner self, the phantoms haunting the subjectivized universe. The personality of the protagonist takes on a surprising variety of incarnations; he is not himself; the world around him is transformed by the projection of his mental states. Hence he has no strictly defined character; he is protean, ambivalent, psychologically complex, full of internal conflicts and contradictions, as he struggles to discover the truth about himself and to penetrate the baffling nature of reality.

This disintegration of reality and the sequence of public time is seen most strikingly in *A Dream Play,* in which the logic of the dramatic form is

[2] Friedrich Nietzsche, *The Birth of Tragedy.* Translated by Francis Golffing. Garden City, New York: Doubleday & Company, Inc., 1956, p. 9.

broken up so as to suggest the fluid structure of a dream. Expressionist drama objectified inner states of being, the inchoate and uncanny experiences of the interior life. It is not concerned with the accidental details of a person, his class, occupation, income; instead it paints the landscape of the soul and presents abstract but eternal types. It relies on monologues, symbols, and asides to capture the spirit of the unconscious, the mysterious dynamism of dreams, the ecstasies and despairs of the soul. In its experimentation with universal types and symbols, it portrays the search of the hero for the absolute, his quest for authenticity, his search for God. Expressionist drama, says Dahlström, is "first and foremost engaged in searching for the essential reality in our universe; it is a Weltanschauung and not a program for the arts." [3]

Expressionism thus makes the ego the center of the universe; though it may be combined with other ingredients, subjectivity is of its essence. The Expressionist, like the dramatist of the absurd, does not apprehend reality intellectually; he seeks not a documentary or psychological or social realism but a vision of life that attempts to do justice to the incoherence of the mind. The connection with external circumstances and the refractory objective world of society is cut; we hear the primordial cry of man, we behold his lacerating internal conflicts, his feverish efforts to reach the absolute. In his quest for the essence of reality, the Expressionist discards not only the empirical knowledge of science but also the social and economic determinants of his age. In his delineation of the phenomenology of the untrammeled ego, he creates a virtual solipsistic universe of the imagination, though even in his most bizarre and delirious productions he does not altogether lose sight of social reality.

Strindberg represents an extreme case. When he was asked what power he would most like to possess, he replied characteristically that he wanted power to solve the riddle of the world and the meaning of life. An unstable, explosive personality, he swung between alternating extremes of depression and euphoria. As a young man he twice tried to commit suicide. Realizing in part what was wrong with him, he sought unsuccessfully to be admitted to a mental institution in Upsala. In *Strindberg und Van Gogh*, Karl Jaspers contends that Strindberg early in life exhibited definite symptoms of schizophrenia. His obsessions never completely left him. He was convinced that those he had hurt were secretly conspiring against him. In *To Damascus*, he describes the terror he felt at the prospect that he was losing his reason. As the result of the intense suffering caused by his persecutory mania, he might

[3] Carl E. W. L. Dahlström, *Strindberg's Dramatic Expressionism*. Ann Arbor: University of Michigan Press, 1930, pp. 80-81.

have become a theosophist were it not for his refusal to accept the doctrinal requirement that to become an initiate he must first deny his ego.

All that I know, little as that may be, springs from one central point, my Ego. It is not the cult but the cultivation of this which seems to me to be the supreme and final goal of existence.[4]

Strindberg's *To Damascus* (1898), the first genuine Expressionist play to be composed, is pre-Existentialist in its embodiment of subjective, visionary states. He left naturalism far behind, deploring its wasted and mistaken efforts to achieve photographic verisimilitude. Reform was not his aim. Essentially modern in his probing of the hidden sources of motivation, he was not deceived by conventional notions of good and evil. People, far from acting according to the noble motives they profess, are driven by unconscious forces; the characters he draws are inscrutable even to themselves, stricken with *folie du doute* and terrible seizures of guilt. Strindberg develops a method which enables him to rise above the limitations of naturalism and to create a form of drama wedded to a vision of truth that goes beyond the social theme.

The Ghost Sonata, another illuminating example of Strindberg's Expressionist drama, paints a gloomy picture of a gallery of characters bound together by their crimes. Strindberg strips them of their mask and exposes the ugly lie they are living, the shameful secret of their past. All are seated in a circle but remain strangely silent. What shall they talk about? The Old Man says:

Talk of the weather, which we know? Inquire about each other's health, which we know just as well? I prefer silence – then one can hear thoughts and see the past. Silence cannot hide anything – but words can.[5]

The clock keeps ticking, marking the inexorable passage of time. According to the Mummy in the play, the crimes of the past can be wiped out through suffering and repentance.

We are miserable human beings, that we know. We have erred and we have sinned, we like all the rest. We are not what we seem, because at bottom we are better than ourselves, since we detest our sins.[6]

The Ghost Sonata is poles removed from a tragedy like *Ghosts* or a problem play like *Major Barbara*. Whereas Ibsen excoriates the moral weakness of

[4] August Strindberg, *Inferno*. Translated by Mary Sandbach. London: Hutchinson & Co., Ltd., 1962, p. 81.
[5] Otto Reinert (ed.), *Drama*. Boston and Toronto: Little, Brown and Company, 1961, p. 451.
[6] *Ibid.*, p. 456.

submission to the dominant social lie, the evil that Strindberg traces has its roots not in the social matrix but in the heart of man. Though largely asocial in its treatment of the theme of evil and in its despairing conclusion – sin and suffering are universal; life is a curse – *The Ghost Sonata* constitutes a severe attack on the immoralities of modern civilization.

Expressionist theater was obviously not suited to the needs of the Marxist or "committed" theater. It was too subjective in content to be effectively utilized for doctrinaire or propagandistic purposes. Brecht in one passage sums up the reasons why the Expressionism of the postwar period was found lacking and had to be rejected. Based as it was on Schopenhauer's philosophy of the world as Will and Idea, it led

to a special kind of solipsism. It was the theatre's answer to the great crisis of society, just as the doctrines of Marx were philosophy's. It represented art's revolt against the world: here the world existed purely as a vision, strangely distorted, a monster conjured up by perturbed souls. Expressionism vastly enriched the theatre's means of expression and brought aesthetic gains that still have to be fully exploited, but it proved quite incapable of shedding light on the world as an object of human activity.[7]

Though Brecht recognizes the rich contribution made by Expressionism to the modern theater, he overlooks the fact that the chief aim of the Expressionists was to break out of their isolation and, in some cases, to usher in a better world. What they voiced was the central theme of loneliness and estrangement; they felt alienated from the society of their time. Against the collectivizing tendencies of their land they directed their battle-cry of individualism. If they assailed the regnant values of German society, it was because they dreamed of overthrowing the ruling authority so as to clear the way for an ideal form of life. Though some of them, like Strindberg, espoused "negative" views, the majority fought against things as they were in the hope of building a new world closer to the heart's desire. Hence some of them became politically active, like Ernst Toller. Members of another group based their hopes not on the reconstruction of the social order but on a spiritual revolution. They preached the gospel of mankind united in a spirit of universal love.[8] That is why they violently attacked the *status quo* or else focused their

[7] *Brecht on Theatre.* Edited and translated by John Willett. New York: Hill and Wang, 1964, p. 132.

[8] In his monograph, *Style and Society in German Literary Expressionism,* Egbert Krispyn stresses the social origins of the Expressionist movement. "The expressionists wanted to break through their isolation and establish contact with their fellows; they were driven by the desire to affect them and their outlook on the world." Egbert Krispyn, *Style and Society in German Literary Expressionism.* University of Florida Monographs, Humanities No. 15, Winter 1964. Gainesville: University of Florida, 1964, p. 27.

gaze on their conception of the more attractive world that could be brought into being. Here, as in the aesthetic of the absurd, we observe the underlying connection between asocial literature and the literature of social criticism.

3. The Asocial Aesthetic of the Absurd

Brecht, as we have said, is wide of the mark in his contention that Expressionism sheds no light on the world as an object of human activity; it sheds plenty of light in that direction, though it is certainly not the kind of light Brecht wanted or happened to admire. However much the asocial writer may avoid the social conditions of his age and concern himself with the timeless metaphysical vision or crimes of conscience or the battles that take place within the closed arena of the self, he cannot possibly sustain the aesthetic purity of his position. Something of the unsought and perhaps undesired social element inevitably creeps into his picture of human life. The Expressionist nightmares of Strindberg and Proust's remembrance of things past are invested, in however shadowy and "unrealistic" a form, with a local habitation and a name. Surrealism, the epiphany of the numinous, the symbolic apprehension of the absurd, the terrifying vision of the Apocalypse, all this is brought out by contrast with the illusory world of material, mundane reality.

For that matter, the absurdity that much of modern literature deals with is not nonsensical. Actually it is an imaginative protest against the absence of ultimate meaning in the world. By comparing the activities of socially defined man in the realm of the finite with the lack of a confirmatory purpose, secular or sacred, in the cosmos, by delineating the demoralization of the questing self as it confronts the always present menace of death, it underscores the futility, however heroic, of human striving. Like the mystic, the creative absurdist beholds the unreality of all that men foolishly mistake for reality, but this mystical sense is essentially negative in character; there is no fitful revelation of the light that shines beyond the outermost limits of darkness, no hint of redemption beyond the portals of death. It culminates in no triumph of affirmation, no ecstasy of union with something Wholly Other.

Despite the negative note it consistently sounds, asocial literature of this type is as much absorbed by the social theme as it is obsessed by the theme of alienation. The metaphysical vision of the absurd in *The Trial* is fundamentally a scathing indictment of the dehumanization of life. The Kafkaesque hero, identified only by an initial, is lost in a bureaucratic, hierarchical maze where the source of supreme authority, the highest court of justice – presumably it must exist, because trials are held and sentences meted out – cannot be reached, and the reason for the victim's conviction – he is always judged guilty – is never made clear. The surveyor in *The Castle* fails to gain access to the lord of the castle. The Kafka protagonist seeks to belong but is, alas, never sure of his identity. He must question all things in an effort to obey orders that emanate from remote and nameless powers, but he receives no unequivocal answer. Since he has no assigned role in the social order, he cannot fulfill himself.

As an artist, Kafka was penetrating in his social criticism precisely because he transcended the game of temporal politics. His was the creative mind, alienated, apolitical, but incorruptible, that cannot be drawn to any party loyalty. Heinz Politzer correctly defines his temperament as anarchic. Kafka's vision revealed the tragicomic disparity between the ideal and the real, ideology and truth; he would allow nothing to hold him back from releasing the full force of his vision. "In his books he criticized the invisible authorities of the universe by taking the secular powers to task. He would have suffered under any regime and would have rebelled against it." [9] He discerned, prophetically, the danger posed by the Socialist as well as Fascist State. Kafka is thus a paradigmatic example of an asocial writer whose work is nevertheless charged with social significance.

Another gifted and influential exponent of asocial literature is Ionesco. His apolitical dramas of the absurd project universal motifs of anguish and estrangement at the same time that they speak out on the crucially important issues of his age. *Rhinoceros* is an anti-Nazi play as well as a plea for preserving our humanity in a period of destructive fanaticism, though this animal fantasy contains no topical references and indulges in no rhetoric of righteous indignation. *The Chairs*, like *The Bald Soprano*, suggests, as one of its multifaceted meanings, the difficulty of achieving communication in a world of mechanically conditioned selves.

Another difficult case is presented by the work of Samuel Beckett who, like Jean Genet, is not interested in the passion of politics, and yet his vision of an absurd universe is rendered more tragic by its implicit contrast with the world of business, work, religion, and government. It is this suggested contrast with the social sphere of getting and begetting, saving, spending, and emulative striving for success that intolerably heightens the sense of the absurd. In *Murphy*, this is brought out with hallucinatory power as the anti-hero, stubbornly refusing to participate in the meaningless round of "normal" social existence, retreats within the fastness of his mind, which

[9] Heinz Politzer, *Franz Kafka*. Ithaca: Cornell University Press, 1962, p. 119.

"pictured itself as a large hollow sphere, hermetically closed to the universe without." [10] In *Watt*, as in the trilogy of novels, *Malone Dies, Molloy,* and *The Unnamable,* the symbolic allusions, however ambiguously couched, to religious rituals, master-servant relationships, travels in search of a home or a person, wounds, accidents, and infirmities, imply the existence of a social macrocosm. In Beckett's as in Ionesco's writings, the characters, though generalized as types, still retain some of their socially defined roles: they appear as servants, homeless tramps, policemen, demagogues, officials.

The writer who, like Beckett and Ionesco, views the world through an absurdist perspective is perfectly aware of the charges leveled against him by those who demand a socially "committed" literature. Why, he questions himself again and again, must he dwell so insistently on his own anxieties and obsessions, seizing on and grotesquely magnifying the theme of human impotence, instead of devoting himself to some cause or ideal that will help lessen the sum total of evil and suffering on earth? Why does he not, like Camus, transcend the myth of the absurd and take upon himself the humanistic responsibility of revolting against "the plague"?

If the asocial writer of the absurd persists in his metaphysical "madness," it is because he is impelled by a creative urge that is stronger than the dictates of his social conscience. He writes as he must, faithful to his conception of the imaginative "truth," which cannot be limited by the formal disjunction between good and evil, optimism and pessimism, social and anti-social. He is literally obsessed by his vision of the universe of the absurd. The imagination cannot lie and he is not willing, for whatever reason, to falsify it or betray it. If he seeks to justify his singular preoccupation with themes that others, the healthy-minded, regard as morbid, decadent, nihilistic, fantastically out of touch with social reality, it is on the ground that their notion of reality is too time-bound, narrow, and constricting. To tell the truth about the human condition is in itself a socially liberating force.

Alfred Jarry, who enjoys the perhaps dubious distinction of being the founding father and patron saint of the absurdist aesthetic, demonstrates the nature of the impulse that motivated his suicidal gesture of defiance, his rabid repudiation of all that his society stood for. *Ubu Roi,* produced in 1896, was a scandalous provocation, a scatological insult flung in the face of complacent bourgeois society. The writer, identified with his outrageous hero, was in full revolt against the established moral conventions of his age. Jarry became a fighting symbol, a *cause célèbre.* He set about living according to his anarchistic, self-destructive principles. Drink was his refuge

[10] Samuel Beckett, *Murphy.* New York: Grove Press, 1938, p. 107.

against despair, a form of violent protest against the cult of middle-class respectability and mediocrity. He cultivated his eccentricities to a point where his life became a manic myth, a deranged poem. He had only contempt for the useful or even the intelligible. Gabriel Brunet describes this prophet of pataphysics as follows:

He offered himself as a victim to the derision and to the absurdity of the world. His life is a sort of humorous and ironic epic which is carried to the point of the voluntary, farcical and thorough destruction of the self. Jarry's teachings could be summarized thus: every man is capable of showing his contempt for the cruelty and stupidity of the universe by making his own life a poem of incoherence and stupidity.[11]

Jarry has had his posthumous revenge on time. Posterity has redeemed his name and vindicated the seriousness and importance of his work. There is a magnificent irony in the history of his reputation. He is remembered now as the founder of pataphysics; a Collège de Pataphysique has been established to continue his discoveries. Here is the poseur, the dandy, the alcoholic, revered in the present as a secular saint; here is a comedian whose nihilistic visions were grimly prophetic of the age of nuclear fission. His creation of the science of pataphysics is designed to exalt and intensify the life of the imagination. Jarry himself defines pataphysics as the science which goes beyond metaphysics. As the science of the particular it is the apotheosis of art rather than science. Instead of striving for universal laws, it postulates the uniqueness of the individual. "Pataphysics will examine the laws governing exceptions and will examine the universe supplementary to this one . . . ." [12]

The literary absurdist is, in effect, saying to his readers: "Look up, gaze around you, probe within yourself: the world is a strange and haunted place. The reality you take so much for granted is an inexplicable and therefore absurd phantasmagoria of shapes and shadows in the time-space continuum. This you must perceive if only occasionally in the depths of your mind, but you brush the perception aside as nonsense, the will-o'-the-wisp of illusion. It cannot be true because it is too painful to believe. On with the dance, you cry, let joy be unconfined. Life is real, life is earnest, and the grave is not its goal. But despite all the psychic defenses you build up against the invasion of the demonic, the obsession of the absurd repeatedly takes hold of you, as it took hold of Tolstoy in the middle of his life's journey so that he could find no peace until he could solve to his satisfaction the obscene mystery of

[11] *Four Modern French Comedies.* New York: Capricorn Books, 1960, p. 23.
[12] Alfred Jarry, *Selected Works of Alfred Jarry.* Edited by Roger Shattuck and Simon Watson Taylor. New York: Grove Press, Inc., 1965, p. 192.

death." It is this vision of the void that throws a spiritually disturbing light on all that men call life. In revealing the tragicomic predicament of the human condition, the creative absurdist endeavors to restore man to a state of authenticity. He shows that the individual is not summed up by his social security number, his occupation, his place in the huge economic apparatus. It is not, to be sure, the only kind of revelation that literature affords; indeed, asocial literature as a whole makes it clear that no one perspective can exhaust the infinite variety of the mystery that is man.

It is no paradox to point out that the literary absurdist, for all his frantic rituals of repudiation, does not secede from the social compact; he does not reject society. He simply refuses to be taken in by the current social myths and political ideologies. If he portrays the absurdity of this our life, he pictures it in relation to the social world, deploying objects, gestures, movements, and language to convey the ubiquitous presence of the absurd in the seemingly well-ordered and purposeful activity of society. Like the mystic, he performs a valuable service in calling our unwilling attention to things between heaven and earth not included in our social philosophy. Asocial literature, by virtue of achieving the order of art, negates its own being. It expands and enriches the definition of what is embraced by the term "social."

CHAPTER II

A TRINITY OF THE ABSURD

1. Ionesco's Dramaturgy of the Absurd

Perfectly consistent in his "absurdist" metaphysic, Ionesco is resolved to retain his integrity as an artist and exercise his freedom of thought and expression as an apolitical writer. According to him, dreams and desires, not the tendentious stuff out of which socialist realism is compounded, are the generative and authentic medium of truth in art. What Ionesco wishes to release is the pure play of his imagination, without the intrusion of alien "realistic" elements. Consequently he is not as a dramatist drawn to problems that can be solved; what drives him to create is only the challenge of the insoluble. If the theater of his time has fallen on evil days, it is, he maintains, because it is too topical in its concerns. Predominantly political in aim and content, it echoes too faithfully the ideological slogans of the hour. In Ionesco's critical judgment, thesis plays, problem plays, propaganda plays present only a thin doctrinaire slice of life and therefore falsify the total truth of reality. "Drama is not the idiom for ideas. When it tries to become a vehicle for ideologies, all it can do is vulgarize them. It dangerously oversimplifies . . . . All ideological drama runs the risk of being parochial." [1] Far from apologizing for his neglect of the social theme, Ionesco cogently defends the asocial aesthetic that governs the construction of his work. Why be forced to listen to political demagogy on the stage when such speeches can be read in the local newspaper or be heard daily on the radio or television?

Instead of dealing with the conflicts raised by the contemporary social world he explores the mysteries of the metaphysical realm, exaggerating feelings to a point beyond which the outlines of familiar reality are disrupted. In order to do that effectively, he also dislocates, as in *The Bald Soprano*, the traditional structure of the spoken language, most of which consists of mean-

[1] Eugène Ionesco, *Notes and Counter Notes*. Translated by Donald Watson. New York: Grove Press, Inc., 1964, p. 24.

ingless chatter. He tears aside the iron veils of habit so as to reveal the incredible strangeness of the world that man inhabits and thus to produce an
image that is startling in its surrealist context. Hence the technique of counterpoint he so deftly employs, the device of treating the most solemn and
affecting situations in a calculated spirit of buffoonery and farce. By these
means and others in his armamentarium of techniques he aims to abolish
the time-honored distinction between the comic and the tragic.

As the "comic" is an intuitive perception of the absurd, it seems to me more
hopeless than the "tragic." The "comic" offers no escape. I say "hopeless," but
in reality it lies outside the boundaries of hope or despair.[2]

Ionesco therefore calls his comedies "anti-plays" and his dramas "pseudo-
dramas" or "tragic farces." [3]

Polarity (a better term than counterpoint) is the dynamic principle that
animates his dramaturgy: the blending of the familiar and the uncanny, the
ordinary and the surprising, the farcical and the pathetic, the commonplace
and the numinous, the prosaic and the poetic. It is by the clash and co-exis-
tence of these contradictory elements that he achieves the tension of conflict, but this dramatic conflict is never harnessed to a social message. He
is not unaware that plays of the imagination induced by the vision of the
absurd may be profoundly social in their implication and effect, but he draws
a basic distinction between being "social" and being politically partisan
in the Marxist or Fascist sense. He has no patience with Brecht's type of
propagandistic play or with the kind of positive hero he presents. Brechtian
man, he says, "is shorn of one dimension, the writer's sense of period is
actually falsified by his ideology, which narrows his field of vision; this is
a fault common to ideologists and people stunted by fanaticism." [4] Strong
language, but it explains why Ionesco correctly identifies Brecht as his chief
opponent, the enemy who is guilty of deliberately perverting the nature of
the dramatic art.

Though man, as Ionesco repeatedly acknowledges, is social in spite of
himself, since he is involved willy-nilly in the historical vicissitudes of his
age, this does not represent his fundamental character. Granted the limi-
tation that man is closely linked to his society and that this inevitably affects
every work of the imagination, there is no reason why the writer must yield
to the temptation of confining himself to the pressing problems of his social environment; he can subordinate the contemporary social theme to his
vision of the universal and the timeless: those intuitions of the ineffable

[2] *Ibid.,* p. 27.
[3] *Ibid.,* p. 27.
[4] *Ibid.,* p. 29.

strangeness of the world that are in essence non-historical, the frightening perception, expressed in the great tragedies of the past, that in the midst of life we are surrounded by death. It is this revelation of the fact that man is mortal that is hard to bear and yet it is the perennial source of the tragic emotion. Philosophical systems are in time discredited, thesis plays are soon forgotten, empires perish, ideologies are superseded, but the experience of death in art never fails to stir man to his depths.

If Ionesco is determined to experiment freely and not obey the arbitrary laws of the theater of the past, it is because he distrusts all *systems* of thought. That is why he inveighs against the pernicious practice of using the stage as a medium for edification or conversion. For him art must owe nothing to external interests. Instead of proclaiming this or that redemptive ideology, Ionesco plumbs the depths of his own secret, ever-changing self. In thus projecting his own private obsessions, he is not cutting himself off from humanity but is speaking for all men, regardless of class. In line with his asocial dramaturgy, he makes it clear that his plays are meant to show "that man is not simply a social animal, a prisoner of his time, but also and above all, at all times, different in his historical context, identical in his essence." [5] Imagination, which is essentially a form of revelation, is instinct with complexities that go far beyond the frontiers of social realism. Ionesco dismisses as deluded those who think they can write plays which will not only enlighten mankind but also save the world. Only in solitude, Ionesco holds, can the visionary playwright establish authentic communion with others, while as a member of organized society he is reduced to a functional role and feels himself alienated from his fellow men.

Such heretical views were bound to invite attack. A number of critics blamed Ionesco harshly for his alleged irresponsibility, his lack of social awareness and concern, his inexcusable espousal of the aesthetic of the absurd. Kenneth Tynan provoked a stormy controversy with his article on Ionesco published in *The Observer* (London) in 1958. In originally reviewing the production of *Amédée* in 1957, he had hailed its mastery of the technique of farce, its ability to call forth the catharsis of laughter, but he then hastened to add that it offered convincing proof that Ionesco's

philosophy of despair is pure humbug. A man who triumphantly succeeds in communicating his belief that it is impossible to communicate anything is in the grip, I cannot help thinking, of a considerable logical error.[6]

The following year Tynan scented danger in the growing Ionesco cult, with its anti-realist program for the theater and its mystagogical nonsense that

---

[5] *Ibid.,* p. 78.
[6] Kenneth Tynan, *Curtains.* New York: Atheneum, 1961, pp. 168-69.

communication is unattainable. "Here was a writer ready to declare that words were meaningless and that all communication between human beings was impossible." [7] Ionesco's attempt to break out of the confines of realism was but an escape into a blind alley or "a self-imposed vacuum, wherein the author bids us observe the absence of air." [8]

With self-controlled irony Ionesco replied by categorically denying that he ever aspired to the title of messiah. Neither a religious prophet nor dedicated politician, he has no evangel of salvation to deliver. As a playwright he is simply bearing witness to the truth of life, and that cannot be summed up in neat logical or ideological formulas. An exercise in tautology, the ideological play competes in vain with the more efficient mode of discursive statement. Opposed to socially slanted plays, Ionesco declares that he will carry out no political directives, from whatever source they emanate. His talent is not for sale or open to conscription. The anxieties and obsessions which go into the making of his plays transcend the plane of ideology and go deeper than political slogans or utopian schemes. "No society has been able to abolish human sadness, no political system can deliver us from the pain of living, from our fear of death, our thirst for the absolute; it is the human condition that directs the social condition, not vice versa." [9]

Ionesco's dignified defense did not, of course, succeed in convincing the liberal-minded critic, Kenneth Tynan, who misinterpreted the label "absurd" in an invidious sense and overlooked the socially meaningful content of the theater of the absurd. The motive behind Ionesco's plays is manifestly social, without ever being political or propagandist in theme. *The Bald Soprano* seems to despair of the possibility of communication, despite the babble of inane talk, but this display of disturbing the air waves with zany platitudes that finally take on a maddening quality because they are unrelieved by any real human contact or genuine dialogue, reveals the depth of our alienation and, in revealing it, protests against it, without making any explicit statement to that effect. But the state of violent, hate-charged frustration to which the participants in this round of dehumanized chatter are reduced is enough to make Ionesco's point. The satiric sting and thrust is in the dramatic experience, not in the preachment of any kind. To take still another example: in *The Tenant*, the situation presented would seem to be essentially "absurd." A man moves into an apartment and the objects he possesses pile up steadily; the moving men come in carrying load after load of his furnishings until he is walled-in as if in a prison. What better "lesson" of the danger of

---

[7] *Ibid.*, p. 408.

[8] Eugène Ionesco, *Notes and Counter Notes*, p. 89.

[9] *Ibid.*, p. 91.

the endless acquisition and proliferation of things could there be? And again it is done quietly, by indirection. Marriage, the bearing of children, love, death, the irrational but coercive pressure of public opinion: each of these themes is elaborated according to the aesthetic of the absurd, and yet the social meaning is manifestly there. The social meaning is invariably shown by contrasting it with the metaphysical dimension. Against the absurdity of death the bureaucratic inefficiency of the police, the routine of work, the gabble of demagogic appeals, are ludicrously out of place. In the kingdom of death, Ionesco is saying, all discourse is in vain. But *The Rhinoceros* is a forceful and moving indictment of the instinct of the herd which leads to a collective wallowing in bestial conformity.

Ionesco's contribution exemplifies the creative ideal to which asocial drama is committed. The drama of the absurd is asocial in content because it sees life as irremediably tragic; it is absurd because instead of crying it laughs at the human condition. To be human is to be absurd. Comedy for Ionesco has, therefore, no direct relation to satire, though a great deal of potent satire enters by indirection into the substance of his work. His "anti-plays" are not intended to reform human nature or reform the structure of society; they convey but a grotesquely heightened image of the tragic sense of life. Like *The Killer*, they provide no guide to salvation; they give voice to nostalgias and oppressions of the spirit that are universal, unaffected by time-bound ideologies. It would never occur to Ionesco to ask, as Sartre does in "Situation of the Writer in 1947," if a writer can become a Communist and still remain "free." [10] Ionesco categorically rejects the casuistry involved in the ethic of political commitment.

We are told that to belong to our own times we ought to join some party or other. This limits us and falsifies our essential truth. "Commitment," as it is now understood, is a catastrophe. Perhaps it is good to choose and be militant about something in practical life. But it is all the more necessary, if we are not to suffocate, to have complete freedom in creation . . . it is indispensable to be able to dream. When one tries to belong to one's own period, it usually happens that one belongs to no period at all. Any uniform, unilateral or partisan view is an expression of bad faith. There are many signposts in history. Naturally we carry within us the anxieties of our own epoch. An artist should allow them expression quite freely and naturally: when they contain their own lively contradictions they will reveal to us a complex and astonishing truth that is far more instructive than any lesson. . . .[11]

[10] Jean-Paul Sartre, *What Is Literature?* Translated by Bernard Frechtman. New York: Philosophical Library, 1949, p. 253. Sartre later adds: "If it should be asked whether the writer, in order to reach the masses, should offer his services to the Communist Party, I answer no." *Ibid.,* p. 256.

[11] Eugene Ionesco, *Notes and Counter Notes,* pp. 126-27.

Thus the opposing forces are joined in battle: freedom versus commitment, creative independence as contrasted with the spirit of political partisanship. Ionesco repays Sartre in his own coin by accusing the politically "engaged" writer of bad faith. The writer who has not mortgaged his mind does not, before he begins work, pledge allegiance to a fixed body of ideas. He begins, like Ionesco, with an image, an emotional state, not an abstract system of thought. By being thoroughly subjective, Ionesco declares, he achieves, like Dostoevski, the drama of the objective. This is no superficial play on words. As he says in a mood of ironic raillery: "Perhaps I am socially minded in spite of myself." [12]

Yet if he is socially minded he is so in a way that Brecht would find utterly reprehensible. Brecht and Ionesco: they constitute for our purpose a perfect study in contrasts. The former is frankly didactic, ideological, and propagandistic in his conception of the epic theater; the latter is, as we have seen, asocial in outlook, committed to no political doctrine. The object of the Brechtian dialectical drama is to fill the spectator with confidence that the world of social reality can be made subject to his control; it can be changed. The epic theater can help in this process by exposing the mechanism at work behind the social scene. Brecht's theater is meant to be more than a forum, a discussion center, a parliament of the people; it is used to proclaim a militant political program, a messianic but at the same time eminently practical and attainable ideal. Instead of evading the social problems of the age by probing the interior of the mind or indulging in solipsistic introspections, the new activist or agitational drama comes to close grips with these problems. There is nothing sacred or esoteric about art, declares Brecht, for

mankind's highest decisions are in fact fought out on earth, not in the heavens; in the "external" world, not inside people's heads. Nobody can stand above the warring classes, for nobody can stand above the human race. Society cannot share a common communication system so long as it is split into warring classes. Thus for art to be "unpolitical" means only to ally itself with the "ruling" group.[13]

For Ionesco all this is anathema. Brecht, Ionesco charges, is but the mouthpiece of a Marxist ideology, repeating what is already known. Because he is portrayed only in his social role, Brechtian man represents a "flat," one-dimensional character. Ionesco believes there is a metaphysical dimension in man which constitutes his deepest inner reality and which transcends the social sphere, whereas Brecht deprives man of this dimension. Ionesco con-

[12] *Ibid.,* p. 132.
[13] *Brecht on Theatre.* Translated and edited by John Willett. New York: Hill and Wang, 1964, p. 196.

trasts Brecht with a truly tragic dramatist like Samuel Beckett, who interprets the ultimate fate of man without reference to any particular social or political organization. Ionesco concedes that the theater, whatever it sets out to do, cannot function without being social in content. "As man is not alone, everything is naturally social." [14] Ionesco insists, however, that the struggle of the classes is only one aspect of the social world. Though everything is social, he holds that man cannot be explained simply as the product of his social machinery. Sociologize man and he ceases to be himself. His individuality, his uniqueness, is destroyed.

Ionesco is no shut-in fantasist, a wild-eyed dreamer who creates a type of schizophrenic or paranoid art in order to throw off the burden of intolerable reality. He knows what he is about. Like Samuel Beckett, he writes about the human condition as a whole, those situations which are asocial as well as those which are social. He specifies those situations – death, for example – which are essentially non-social in character. He tries to picture the unaccountable strangeness of the world, the numinous sense of wonder that one exists at all, the feeling that everything in the universe makes up the pageant of a dream or a comic phantasmagoria. He is not being perverse or irresponsible in cultivating an art of the drama that goes beyond the limits of the social. As he points out: "A work or art may or may not fulfill a social function, but it is not equivalent to this social function; its essence is supra-social." [15] In short, though a play springs from the soil of society, it does not have to be conditioned by that society. Ionesco endeavors to embody his vision of the world as frightening, mysterious, and absurd even when it seems most familiar. He explores a reality that is insubstantial and yet material, recognizable and yet uncanny. Ionesco confesses that he really does feel

that life is nightmarish, painful and unbearable, like a bad dream. Look around you: wars, catastrophes and disasters, hatred and persecution, confusion, death lying in wait for all of us, we talk without understanding one another, we struggle as best we may in a world that appears to be in the grip of some terrible fever. . . .[16]

What then is real? What is the true nature of the world?

Some of Ionesco's subjective confessions (and these are voiced in a number of superb scenes in *The Killer*) reveal that he is a mystic who can never quite get used to existence. He can make no sense of this apparitional universe: these phantoms that he identifies as people, those gleaming lights and

[14] Eugène Ionesco, *Notes and Counter Notes*, p. 135.
[15] *Ibid.*, p. 148.
[16] *Ibid.*, p. 110.

shadows all around him. The vision of the absurd he glimpses is at times glorious and exhilarating but at most times darkly oppressive. Looking within himself, he finds that he is driven by a host of disparate and conflicting emotions; here, too, he can make no sense of the battle raging within him. He has no unitary self. It becomes clear to him that just as he cannot comprehend the meaning of the universe around him, so he cannot hope to understand himself, who he is or why he exists. If he writes for the theater, he does so as a means of releasing the obsessions that haunt his inner world.

In his efforts to push back the frontiers of reality and oppose the doctrinaire method of naturalism, Ionesco reminds one of the Surrealists, but actually he goes beyond Surrealism. He makes no attempt to justify his art of the absurd. If everything in the universe, including the theater, is absurd, then the boundary line between probability and improbability, the real and the unreal, the fantastic and the factual, vanishes. Thus Ionesco's metaphysical vision governs his dramatic technique. He safeguards himself against the temptation of "commitment" by regarding his work with astringent irony. As for art being this or that, it is what it is, "and what is the point of the existence of the universe? Simply that it should exist." [17] Art has no other purpose but to be. Never mind trying to make it solve the troublesome problems of the world. We have had enough of fanaticism.

It is the meaninglessness of existence that Ionesco seeks to convey. There is no evolutionary purpose to be achieved, no goal of perfection to be reached. It is the artist who, by penetrating to the root of things, by exposing the false premises on which society is based, is the true revolutionary. As a dramatist of the absurd, Ionesco holds all mass movements in contempt. The metaphysical problem, Ionesco maintains, is not to be confused with the social problem. Whatever improvements man may make in his social existence, the ultimate mystery – the fact of death as annihilation – remains. There are no political nostrums which can satisfy man's hunger for the infinite. Even if the utopian commonwealth were finally established on earth, man would still be confronted by the problem of ultimate meaning. As Ionesco says: "no political programme can ever deliver us from the malaise of existence, from our fear of death, from our thirst for the absolute." [18]

To sum up: Ionesco's plays, born of inner necessity, are not void of social content. His theater of the absurd protests against the tyranny of the machine, the abuse of power, the dehumanization of life in a regimented world. His work, however, aims not to prove anything but to communicate the experience of the absurd. Instead of propagandizing in behalf of any

[17] *Ibid.*, p. 103.
[18] Richard N. Coe, *Ionesco*. Edinburgh and London: Oliver and Boyd, 1961, p. 100.

social or political solution, he attempts to communicate the elusive nature of the reality in which man lives. The most daring innovations in the theater were undertaken by those dramatists (Beckett, Genet, and Harold Pinter) who looked upon man not as a creature shaped by his society but as a metaphysical being who must needs relate himself to the universe around him as well as the universe within himself and discover their meaning or total lack of meaning. The absurdist revolt called forth a rich variety of asocial literary forms.

2. Beckett's Universe of the Absurd

Beckett is never really concerned with politics or the social theme, but as soon as one states the fact and reviews the evidence that confirms it some doubts begin to arise. As happened in the case of Ionesco, one is compelled to redefine the leading terms in the argument and then to qualify judgment. Beckett conjures up heroes who are aged, infirm, their body decrepit, their memory still active but failing, the outcasts of the world of men, the personification of impotence, struggling hard to keep alive as they crawl, wounded and lost, on the surface of the earth, longing for the final peace of death. These battered wrecks, their voices forever questioning the meaning of their faith, are objects of ridicule and detestation. Neither society nor God can save these useless, submerged creatures, but the point is that the social and religious background is postulated, included as an integral and ironic part of the human condition. The religious references in Beckett's novels and plays, the concentration on the agony of the Crucifixion, the inconsistencies that appear in the report of the four Evangelists, the hope of Heaven that is rejected as a false dream, all this is borrowed from the culture of the West. Then, too, Beckett portrays the master-slave relationship. For example, Pozzo appears in *Waiting for Godot*, symbol of wealth and power in the world of time, cruelly exploiting his servant and beast of burden, Lucky. Beckett takes his revenge upon this arrogant plutocrat, or rather he is shown as the victim of time and fortune, for in the second act he returns blind, helpless, led by his servant. No one is spared in Beckett's universe of the absurd, but the metaphysical vision he brings is so frightening because it is placed in stark contrast with the world of time and work.

In *Waiting for Godot*, the two protagonists, though they still cling out of habit to the illusion of waiting for Godot, have actually gone beyond illusion. The only social identification Beckett gives Vladimir and Estragon is that they are homosexual tramps, sharing no common body of faith, devoid of hope, committed to nothing except the unavoidable tedium of waiting. The same effect of dark, unrelieved futility is communicated by *Endgame*. Beckett strikes variations on a single theme of doom. In his quest for ultimate meaning, he examines the nature of the self in its ambiguous relationship to others. Time is a fugitive phantom. Nothing endures except a ghostly memory of the vanished past. In *Happy Days* (the title is characteristically ironic in its inflection of meaning), the two characters are portrayed, as trapped in a situation of appalling misery. Winnie, who is about fifty, is partly buried in earth, though she can still use her arms. In the second act she is buried still further, and the hopelessness of her situation grows upon her. Willie, the husband, a man about sixty, propels himself like an animal on all fours. Occasionally he responds to Winnie's doleful monologue. She talks to him even though there are days when he hears nothing. Talking is all in vain, but the talk must go on, the protracted monologue that relives the days of the past. Like *Waiting for Godot*, the play accentuates the depressing mood of futile waiting, the impression rendered of time as a burden not to be borne, and yet it must be endured till the very end. "There is little one can say, one says it all." [19]

Beckett presents the paradoxical spectacle of a writer who keeps on writing books that elaborate the obsessive theme that there is nothing to say. He spares us none of our illusions. He has gone to the end of the line, but if his work expresses the absence of meaning and laughs at the tragic absurdity of the human condition, he does not like Swift hate mankind. There is no touch of misanthropy in his delineation of life. His pessimism is ironic rather than cruel. He depicts the misery of being human, the sheer suffering that is the lot of every man. But there is no promise of God in his creation and no longing for His presence.

In his first novel, *Murphy*, as in his latest, *How It Is*, Beckett discloses the aimlessness and uselessness of human striving. *Murphy* highlights the incredible mania of people working steadily at a job. The anti-hero Murphy passes dire judgment on his society, its queer conception of what is sane and worthy of effort. It is the social order that represents a repressive mental institution, a hierarchical bedlam. Murphy challenges the established values, refusing to conform to standards that are absurd. His experience "as a physical and rational being obliged him to call sanctuary what the psychiatrist called exile and to think of the patients not as banished from a system of benefits but as escaped from a colossal fiasco." [20] Not the clicking cash-register is the measure of mental health; the mind is its own heaven and hell.

[19] Samuel Beckett, *Happy Days*. New York: Grove Press, Inc., 1961, p. 51.
[20] Samuel Beckett, *Murphy*. New York: Grove Press, 1938, pp. 177-78.

In the conflict between the confined inner world of freedom and the big world of work and business as usual, the psychiatric patient unhesitatingly chooses the former while the doctors prefer the latter. Once Murphy discovers the blessedness of dwelling within his own mind, he rejects society with all its petty ambitions and paltry rewards, renouncing everything that lies outside the feeling of consciousness. "How should he tolerate, let alone cultivate, the occasions of fiasco, having once beheld the beatific idols of his cave?" [21]

In *How It is*, the paradigmatic example of the asocial novel, Beckett is using the resources of fiction for a metaphysical enterprise designed to expose the utter ineffectuality of metaphysics and the bankruptcy of meaning. *How It Is* marks the disintegration of the novel as a traditional form. Not only is there no plot, no sustaining pattern of motivation, and no identifiable characters; the language itself has undergone a drastic change. The words are still meaningful, but there are no marks of punctuation, no commas or periods, only a muddied, interminable stream of consciousness, the almost inarticulate cry of a mind baffled and in pain, lost in the night of being. The anti-hero is a character who is nameless, crawling somewhere in the mud, preoccupied with his body and its needs but also reaching out for human contact, vaguely remembering the past. He suffers the unremitting torment of existence, too overwhelmed by inner and outer confusion to say yes or no to life, knowing that the torment will soon cease and that he must report what he has experienced. He has no social interests or responsibilities; he is concerned with recording what the voices within tell him as he creeps along in the mud. His quivering consciousness, all that remains of him, that is still restlessly alive dissolves the last outlines of reality.

in the familiar form of questions I am said to ask myself and answers I am said to give myself however unlikely that may appear last scraps very last when the panting stops last murmurs very last however unlikely that may appear
if all that all that yes if all that is not how shall I say no answer if all that is not false yes
    all these calculations yes explanations yes the whole story from beginning to end yes completely false yes
    that wasn't how it was no not at all no how then no answer how was it then no answer HOW WAS IT screams good [22]

Here we have an isolated consciousness hurling its questions at the silence of the night and receiving no answer. This anti-hero can be sure of nothing; there is something, but perhaps it is only his voice muttering, waiting until

[21] *Ibid.*, p. 178.
[22] Samuel Beckett, *How It Is*. Translated by the author. New York: Grove Press, 1964, p. 144.

the panting stops. The struggle for breath, the murmurs in the dark, the movements in the mud, all this apparently went on, but even this is hard to believe:

hard to believe too yes that I have a voice yes when the panting stops yes not at other times no end that I murmur yes I yes in the dark yes in the mud yes for nothing yes I yes but it must be believed yes [23]

The Cartesian ego has altogether broken down; it moves in circles of perpetual doubt, incapable of saying yes, no longer in communion with the world of men, no longer even certain of the problematical I am. Only the darkness is true and real. If consciousness is a dream, whose dream is it? The whole past seems like a surrealist scenario, a nightmare that is all sound and fury signifying nothing. There is no self, no identity, not even a name to go by; there is only this vain delusive epiphenomenon of a brooding consciousness whose light will soon be spent. Beckett is alone with his voice, his agonized search, but there is "no answer YES OR NO." [24]

If Beckett provides characters and the semblance of a story, they are but strategic devices to demonstrate the impossibility of saying anything at all. Literature is declared to be absurd in the very act of being created, and that, too, is part of the overriding mystery of being. Cognition is an exercise in uncertainty, the exploration of the unknowable and the unnamable. Life is terrorized by cruel powers but the mind cannot make out who or what they are or why they punish human beings for the crime of having been born. Beckett, like Ionesco, is not wedded to any ideological system. As the poet laureate of the spiritually maimed, the defeated, the hopeless, he reveals the depths of human impotence, thus specializing in a theme that is in conformity with his asocial outlook. As he himself declares:

I don't think impotence has been exploited in the past. There seems to be a kind of aesthetic axiom that expression is achievement – must be an achievement. My little exploration is that whole zone of being that has always been set aside by artists as something unusable – as something by definition incompatible with art.[25]

It is this whole hitherto tabooed zone of being, the universe of the absurd, that Beckett employs creatively as the basis for his asocial aesthetic.

[23] *Ibid.*, p. 145.

[24] *Ibid.*, p. 146.

[25] John Fletcher, *The Novels of Samuel Beckett*. New York: Barnes & Noble, Inc., 1964, pp. 232-33.

3. Genet and the World of Fantasy

Genet provides an image, however violently distorted, of the life of society of his time, but it is not society that constitutes the center and substance of his theme. Like Ionesco, he portrays with hallucinatory intensity the various obsessions which cast men into the social roles they play with such deadly seriousness. Genet is the high priest of the world of fantasy. In his plays as in those of Ionesco, the division between reality and illusion is obliterated; the difference between them entirely breaks down; the constituent terms no longer mean what we thought they meant; they defy exact definition. Dream is reality and reality – so-called – is spun of the gossamer thread of dreams.

An outcast, a homosexual, and a professional thief who has spent many years in prison, Genet inverts the moral values of his society and strips off its hypocritical mask of righteousness. Like Marx and Engels in the *Communist Manifesto* but with a different motive in mind, he tears aside the pretence of virtue, debunks the official cult of altruism, as so many cunning "ideologies" contrived to conceal the pressure of vested interests. Though he is, of course, no revolutionary, no Marxist, in his debunking of hidden "interests," he does picture a world that is governed by the symbols of power. His object is to expose the ugly lies of civilization by yoking together, in grotesque conjunction, the sacred and the profane, the holy and the obscene, the normal and the perverse. Thus Genet's asocial dramatic vision results, paradoxically, in a shocking critique of the social order.

In *The Balcony* (1960), the demolition of established values takes place right at the start. The opening scene shows us a Bishop, with his sacerdotal vestments, robe and mitre, discoursing loftily, but he is only impersonating a bishop in a French brothel. In real life he is a gasman. It is by putting on this disguise that he can gratify his private fantasies. The brothel, the Grand Balcony, is a house of illusions. Madame Irma furnishes studios with mirrors conveniently situated, where the patrons can act out their most secret and exorbitant wishes. And what an astonishing variety of roles they assume, what wild perversions and fetishistic practices they indulge in! One man desires to be a general, another a judge. Madame Irma makes all this possible, for a price: the fulfillment of each grandiose wish, however peculiar, and no questions asked. This is not only a house of prostitution but a theater which stages plays in which the client is allowed to be the dramatist, the director, the actor, and the protagonist, all in one.

This emporium conducts its flourishing business in the midst of a revolution. (There are no social revolutions in Beckett. Ionesco does introduce a scene of demagogic incitement in *The Killer* but treats it characteristically as pure farce.) Machine-guns keep firing and serve to remind the illusionists as well as the audience of "the reality" of politics outside, the ferocity of the struggle for power. But this external social reality is also, in effect, a staged illusion; the revolutionaries practise their own magic rituals and canonize their own saints. Chantal, one of the girls in Madame Irma's establishment, becomes their chief symbolic figure of worship. The only one who is capable of defeating the revolutionary forces is the Chief of Police, who exercises his power by appealing to the fantasies cherished by the minds of the people.

When the old rulers are overthrown, new symbols of power instantly move in to replace them. Madame Irma is to play the role of Queen and her clients will enact the roles of bishop, judge, and general. That is how the revolution is brought to naught. Complications, however, enter in: power achieved is sweet, but the life of fantasy is sweeter still. The Chief of Police wishes to have a mausoleum built in his honor, with a huge phallus as his identifying symbol. Roger, the leader of the revolutionary movement, visits the brothel and masochistically acts out his own fantasy of power.

What, then, is this 'absurd" play about? Esslin sums it up incisively by saying that it

represents a world of fantasy about a world of fantasy; Genet's dream about the essential nature of power and sex, which, to him, have the same roots; his wish-fantasy about the true nature of judges, policemen, and bishops.[26]

That is how Genet defies the ruling images of power in the modern world and vengefully debunks the motives that prompt men to play their curious roles in the hierarchy set up by society and the State. What they crave inordinately is the power to dominate others, but the outcasts, the deviant, the deprived can revenge themselves upon a power-structured society by living out their fantasies in a ritual of their own choosing. By mobilizing their will to dream, by nourishing their need for illusion, they can overcome the threat of the massive, impersonal aggregate of forces that society brings to bear on the individual. Fantasy is, after all, the supreme power.

As Madame Irma says, who is not in the least disturbed by reports of the advance of the rebel forces: "Everyone is free, and I'm not concerned with politics." [27] It is true: she need not be concerned with politics. She performs a more useful and important function by catering to the universal, all-too-human hunger for illusion. She is justly proud of her place, its professional atmosphere and world-wide reputation. She satisfies the cravings of

---

[26] Martin Esslin, *The Theatre of the Absurd*. Garden City: Doubleday & Company, Inc., 1961, p. 156.

[27] Jean Genet, *The Balcony*. Translated by Bernard Frechtman. New York: Grove Press, Inc., 1958, p. 17.

her clients, releasing them as if from the bondage of a spell, so that they return happily resigned for the time being to their humdrum reality. The brothel, according to Madame Irma, offers an ideal solution: "Here, Comedy and Appearance remain pure, and the Revels intact." [28]

The modern asocial writer is drawn temperamentally to the depiction of lonely, frustrated souls, the dreamers and rebels, the victims of society. Genet presents the criminal as hero, who denounces the nightmarish cruelties of society, its destructive mania for wielding power. Like Madame Irma, he is not interested in political issues. Genet, says Sartre, "does not want to change anything at all. Do not count on him to criticize institutions." [29] But he does criticize institutions. True, he is no radical, no reformer, but he does hold up for our contemplation the vicious injustices and evil contradictions of our civilization.

We have seen that the asocial literature Ionesco, Beckett, and Genet produce does not preclude an astringent consideration of the social theme, but it does so obliquely and by implication. Ionesco protests against the dehumanization of man by authority and the machine. Beckett explores the subject of human impotence. Genet reveals the degree to which all men are dominated by their fantasies, and in doing so he creates plays which reflect the degeneracy and corruption of our society. He could therefore be regarded as a social dramatist.[30]

---

[28] *Ibid.,* p. 32.

[29] Jean-Paul Sartre, *Saint Genet.* Translated by Bernard Frechtman. New York: George Braziller, 1963, p. 55.

[30] In "The Revenge of Jean Genet," Charles Marowitz defines a social dramatist as "anyone who sheds light on the nature of the struggle which people have been waging with people since the beginning of time. On this basis, Genet is a thoroughgoing social dramatist." *The Encore Reader.* Edited by Charles Marowitz, Tom Milne, and Owen Hale. London: Methuen & Co., Ltd., 1965, p. 176.

B. THE REVOLT AGAINST SOCIETY: ANARCHISM, ALIENATION, THE BEAT ETHIC AND MADNESS

CHAPTER III

THE INDIVIDUAL VERSUS SOCIETY

As a reaction to the former exaggerated individualistic trend, *a compensatory regression to the collective man* has set in. Collective man has become paramount, and his authority simply consists of the weight of the masses. No wonder that we have a feeling of impending disaster ... Collective man is threatening to suffocate the individual. . . .[1]

Individual independence is an illusion; and the independent individual, the isolated self, is a nonentity. In ourselves we are nothing; and when we turn our eyes inward in search of ourselves we find a vacuum. . . . It is only in relation to others that we exist as persons. . . .[2]

No human life, not even the life of the hermit in nature's wilderness, is possible without a world which directly or indirectly testifies to the presence of other human beings.[3]

Where there is no sharing there is no reality. Where there is self-appropriation there is no reality. The more direct the contact with the *Thou*, the fuller the sharing.[4]

Society everywhere is in conspiracy against the manhood of every one of its members. Society is a joint-stock company, in which the members agree, for the better securing of his bread to each shareholder, to surrender the liberty and culture of the eater. The virtue in most request is conformity. Self-reliance is its aversion. It loves not realities and creators, but names and customs.[5]

1. The Protest Against Collectivization

"Whoso would be a man, must be a nonconformist." Emerson's battlecry of self-reliance must sound strangely offbeat to a generation brought up to res-

---

[1] C. G. Jung, *Essays on Contemporary Events*. Translated by Elizabeth Walsh, Barbara Hannah, and Mary Briner. London: K. Paul, 1947, p. 76.

[2] John Macmurray, *Persons in Relation*. London: Faber and Faber, Limited, 1961, p. 211.

[3] Hannah Arendt, *The Human Condition*. Chicago: The University of Chicago Press, 1958, p. 22.

[4] Martin Buber, *I and Thou*. Edinburgh: T. & T. Clark, 1950, p. 149.

[5] *Selections from Ralph Waldo Emerson*. Edited by Stephen E. Whicher. Boston: Houghton Mifflin Company, 1957, p. 149.

pect the prevailing ethic of "adjustment." Society in our time seems to have reached such a pitch of efficiency that the individual, a unit of mobilized energy in the productive process, is the victim, passive or resisting, of external collective pressures. His relationship with others is impersonal, purely functional. Fragmented by its occupational role, the human self is denied the possibility of achieving authentic community. All this, the exploitation of labor for the purpose of a higher rate of productivity, the fetishism of commodities, the stupendous growth of science and technology, the increasing specialization of life, seems to rob man of his autonomy. The development of modern civilization is characterized by a movement away from individual autonomy toward some form of corporate existence. Utopia incorporated lies tantalizingly within reach, and yet the specter of disaster looms darkly on the horizon. Collectivism, as Jung says, threatens to stifle the individual.

This development could not go on indefinitely without calling forth a spirited reaction. The protest against collectivism took a variety of forms. On the literary front the fight was waged not only against the coercive demands for conformity on the part of mass-society but against the mechanization of industry, the domination of practically all aspects of life by the imperialism of technology and the supremacy of scientism. What the nineteenth century had hailed optimistically as the dawn of the millennium, the scientific advance that would make possible the full realization of the utopian dream, turned into an air-conditioned nightmare. It was not Soviet Russia alone that gloried in the triumph of the machine. Collectivism transcends political differences and is international in its appeal. Growing out of applied science and technology, it ignores ideological considerations and sweeps everything before it. As Eric Kahler points out: *"The roots of collectivism are to be found in rationalism and technology and not in any specific social or economic doctrine."* [6]

The result of all this is that the individual as such is sacrificed, compelled of necessity to become the slave of the machine his own ingenuity has created. The aim of technological coordination is not to cultivate self-reliant individuals but an army of labor that can be trained to exploit the world of things. Specialization of function inevitably entails the maximum of standardization. The individual is henceforth identified as a social security number, a statistic in the highly complex, interdependent task of production. Absorbed in the mass, depersonalized in his contact with others, he lives in and for his job, which nevertheless affords him neither joy nor fulfillment. Writers like Ernst Toller, Georg Kaiser, and Ionesco cried out, but cried

[6] Eric Kahler, *The Tower and the Abyss*. New York: George Braziller, Inc., 1957, p. 17.

out in vain, against the dangerous acceleration of the tempo of alienation in the modern world. Other writers stressed the irony of the situation: how through the agency of science man has been the author of his own calamity. As the French critic, Paul Ginestier, remarks:

> We may say that from the human point of view the poetry of industrial progress is the saga of a gigantic failure and of the relentless growing disparity between the creator and his creation. Man cannot seek to become God with impunity. The more he understands nature and dominates matter, the greater becomes the gap between his knowledge and his moral evolution.[7]

Much of modern literature represents a rebellion against the Moloch of the machine, especially against the technological coordination of society. The major novelists of the nineteenth century, Stendhal, Dickens, Thackeray, Dostoevski, Tolstoy, however much they may criticize specific evils in the society of their age – its corruption, the snobbery of rank and caste, the miserable condition of the poor – never assail the idea of society itself. Taking its existence and continuity for granted, they assume that the individual knows his place in it. Hence the social theme in their work is of paramount importance.[8] But in the twentieth century the relationship between the individual and society as well as that between the writer and his audience becomes increasingly equivocal. The protagonist we encounter in the fiction of Richard Wright, Ralph Ellison, Camus, Faulkner, Beckett, and Alexander Trocchi is generally embittered, rebellious, or withdrawn; the modern novelist faithfully reflects the spirit of his age by exploring the theme of alienation or impotence or anomie. In a number of cases, the traumatic loss of identity, the syndrome of depersonalization, is symbolized, as in Expressionist drama, by the fact that the hero becomes a cipher, an abstraction, an initial, a man without a name.

The literary culture of the West is infected with the widespread feeling of alienation in our time. After the holocaust of the First World War, the drama, like the novel, presented heroes who are decidedly not at home in their world, unable to fit into the established scheme of things. They are isolatoes, absorbed in themselves, at odds with their society or withdrawn from it. Virtually all the heroes of major French dramatists in the twentieth century (Anouilh, Montherlant, Giraudoux, Lenormand, Sartre, Camus, among

---

[7] Paul Ginestier, *The Poet and the Machine*. Translated by Martin B. Friedman. Chapel Hill: The University of North Carolina Press, 1961, p. 38. See the chapter on "Love and Hatred of the Machine," in Jacques Barzun, *Science: The Glorious Entertainment*. New York, Evanston, and London: Harper & Row, 1964, pp. 31-58.

[8] For the social background of such novels as *Pride and Prejudice, Great Expectations,* and *Vanity Fair,* see Dorothy Van Ghent, *The English Novel.* New York: Rinehart & Company, Inc., 1953.

others) bear the burden of their loneliness: "they vociferously reiterate at all possible moments their sense of solitude by being distinctly anti-social." [9] If we translate this into our terminology, we would say that they adopt a characteristic asocial attitude.

If the mechanical or collective man finally takes over, as he bids fair to do, then the Proustian exploration of the intimacies of the heart will become a futile occupation; there will be only emptiness inside; auscultation will make clear not the systole and diastole of the heart-beat of sensibility in its indivi-dualized response to memory, dreams, nostalgias, and desires, but the whir-ring of wheels, the meshing of the gears of conditioned reflexes, the intro-jected rhythm of the all-powerful social apparatus. The modern hero is often but a stereotyped echo of the voice of the crowd, like Mr. Zero in Elmer Rice's play, *The Adding Machine*. Well worth quoting in this connection are Nathalie Sarraute's remarks on the loss of identity that is so depressing a feature of many anti-heroes of modern fiction:

Today, a constantly rising tide had been flooding us with literary works that still claim to be novels and in which a being devoid of outline, indefinable, in-tangible, an anonymous "I," who is at once all and nothing, and who as often as not is but the reflection of the author himself, has usurped the role of the hero, occupying the place of honor. The other characters, being deprived of their own existence, are reduced to the status of visions, dreams, nightmares, illusions, re-flections, quiddities or dependents of this all-powerful "I." [10]

All this, as it happens, neatly defines the character of asocial literature or at least one significant aspect of it: the flight into subjectivity. This is what Sarraute means by saying that what we are now witnessing is the age of suspicion. The mechanical organization of society leads gradually but relent-lessly to an attempt on a mass scale to control the feelings that are private. For the sake of attaining the ideal of corporate efficiency the disturbing and refractory element of individuality must be sacrificed. This can be done, as Orwell suggests in *Nineteen Eighty-Four*, by the use of thought-condition-ing and the mass media of communication. An image of the collective "ideal" is officially proclaimed as sacred and the internalized pressure to conform on the part of the individual is so strong that the collectivistic image triumphs. There is, in short, a dialectical relationship between the concep-tion a man has of himself and the position he occupies in the social struc-ture. In capitalist society managed by technological means and geared

---

[9] Robert Emmet Jones, *The Alienated Hero in Modern French Drama*. University of Georgia Monographs, No. 8. Athens, Georgia: University of Georgia Press, 1962, p. 6.
[10] Nathalie Sarraute, *The Age of Suspicion*. Translated by Maria Jolas. New York: George Braziller, 1963, pp. 55-56.

to the profit-motive, man is reduced to a thing in a world of mechanical and manipulable things, and authority becomes at once anonymous and despotic. Since people are looked upon as commodities to be bought and sold in the open market, no one trusts the other. More than a century ago, Emerson saw society as everywhere in conspiracy against the manhood and liberty of everyone of its members. Society has not changed for the better since then. As Bertolt Brecht reveals with forceful comic satire in *The Threepenny Opera,* modern life is a jungle. No one really feels he belongs to a community or possesses a deep sense of social responsibility. Each one is concerned more or less with furthering his own advantage. The cash-nexus, to use Carlyle's pejorative term, is the only bond that unites mankind.

2. *The Literary Anarchists in Action*

The pendulum was bound sooner or later to swing to the other extreme. The denunciatory voice of a band of aroused literary Jeremiahs was heard. The Apocalyptic writers emphasized the importance of the inner life, the sacredness of the individual self, and hence were principally asocial (in our sense of the term) in their orientation. Neither Leviathan nor politics, they preached, could save man, who must work out his salvation alone.[11] In "Considerations on Revolt," Henry Treece states the reasons for his disillusionment with politics and sets forth what the literary movement known as the Apocalypse is trying to do. The members of the Apocalypse revolted against the existing social order in the name of individual wholeness, but they differed sharply from the beat generation on the other side of the Atlantic in the fifties in that their revolt sought to usher in a new, healthy, responsible society. Distrusting the efficient but inhuman way in which the huge social machine operated, they envisaged the possibility of establishing organic local groups, thus safeguarding themselves against the danger of being swallowed up by the State. Fundamentally what they wished to restore was the means of achieving personal contact, a form of genuine communion in shared work. In defining Apocalypse, Treece says it means

apprehending the multiplicity of both Inner and Outer worlds, anarchic, prophetic, whole and balanced in the way a man becomes whole and balanced when he has known black as well as white, death as well as life, kindness as well as cruelty, madness as well as sanity, and all the other paradoxes and opposites, in his own nature as well as in the world around him.[12]

[11] See Henry Treece, *How I See Apocalypse.* London: Lindsay Drummond Ltd., 1946.

[12] *New Road.* Edited by Alex Comfort and John Batliss. London: Gray Walls Press Ltd., 1943, p. 146.

The significance of the Apocalypse is that, in reacting against the Surrealist obsession with psychic automatism and the dreamworld of the unconscious, it broke away from all political directives or party domination and embraced anarchism as the only desirable solution: the anarchism of small, local collectives worked by individuals.

Though the Apocalypse had little or no impact upon the social structure of England during the forties, the philosophy of anarchism it advocated found strong support in other quarters. Alex Comfort published *Art and Social Responsibility*, a manifesto denouncing as criminal the waging of warfare and proclaiming his intention of defying the irrational power wielded by the state. Man, as Herbert Read argued in *Existentialism, Marxism and Anarchism*, must regain his vital freedom by liberating himself from the authority of the State. The poet, Read maintained, is an anarchist at heart because anarchism is the one doctrine which does not violate his sense of justice and fulfills his basic need for freedom. The dedicated agent of destruction in society, the poet

must oppose all organized conceptions of the State, not only those which we inherit from the past, but equally those which are imposed on people in the name of the future.[13]

This declaration, which is primarily a personal confession of faith, marks the intensified resistance of writers from the forties to the sixties to the monolithic rule of politics, especially the ideological absolutism imposed by Stalinism. Though he deplores the unkind fate which made him a poet in a technological age, Read would not, like the writers of the Apocalypse, reject the fruits of industrialism and revert to an idealized medievalism. He accepts industrialism in the hope that its enormous potentialities will make for an economy of abundance and make it possible for man to re-establish life-nourishing contact with the soil. Like Alex Comfort, he is not concerned with expediency or the practicability of a program. He will affirm his individuality and speak out freely even if this means prison "rather than submit to the indignities of war and collectivism." [14]

If the arts have suffered both in Communist Russia and Nazi Germany, it is because these countries deliberately stifled the spirit of freedom essential for the flowering of the creative mind. Both the Fascist and the Marxist States exploited the poet for overt political ends, whereas the poet, possessed of a heightened sensibility and clairvoyant power of vision, must stand apart from the masses and their leaders and throw off the mephitic abstractions of the intellect. The true poet can neither be coerced into accepting political

[13] Herbert Read, *Anarchy and Order*. London: Faber and Faber, 1954, p. 58.
[14] *Ibid.*, p. 59.

doctrines nor be made to subscribe to a static, externally formulated version of reality.

> Disfranchized by his lack of residence in any fixed constituency, wandering faithlessly in the no-man's-land of his imagination, the poet cannot, without renouncing his essential function, come to rest in the bleak conventicles of a political party. It is not his pride that keeps him outside; it is really his humility, his devotion to the complex wholeness of humanity....[15]

Imaginative truth thus supersedes and nullifies the claims of political loyalty.

Herbert Read is, of course, perfectly aware that economic realities cannot be ignored. Nevertheless, art as a discipline cannot without disastrous consequences be fitted within the framework of the Marxian dialectic. As we shall see in the section on literature as social commitment, what the Communist critics utterly fail to recognize or refuse to acknowledge is, paradoxically, the revolutionary nature of art. Herbert Read recognizes that the relation of the individual to society raises a formidably complex issue in art as well as in politics, but he is determined to work out and abide by his own conception of what that relation should be. His chief passion both as a poet and critic is for the maximum degree of liberty in life and literature. To be sure, liberty is relative, not absolute, but the complete sacrifice of the individual to the interests of the State is not to be borne. Based on the principles of anarcho-syndicalism, the cooperative commonwealth, Read declares, must supplant all authoritarian systems of government. [16]

3. Alienation and the Search for Integrity

What the literature of the forties, especially in the United States, bore witness to was a pronounced and almost penitential shift in emphasis from the social to the private realm. It inaugurated a movement away from Marxism and the dialectics of the class war. The struggle to recover the integrity of the self seemed more important to writers than laboring for the triumph of the revolution. They came to perceive that political Marxism entailed the subordination, if not total extinction, of selfhood; the myth of the State, the immortal collectivity, was supposed to override the needs of the individual. The battle they fought two decades ago is still being waged today on an even wider front. What they were desperately concerned about was to insure the survival of the self in a mass society. The new fiction that sprang up in

[15] *Ibid.*, p. 74.
[16] See Charles I. Glicksberg, "Herbert Read: Reason and Romanticism," *University of Toronto Quarterly*, XVI (October, 1946), pp. 60-67.

America after the depression was by and large anti-utopian, unpolitical, and asocial in temper. It was not supported by a clear-cut idea of society or an urgent and sustaining sense of social responsibility. As Eisinger says in his perceptive analysis of the literary situation at the time:

> Its writers want to create a pure fiction, apolitical and asocial. In this desire lies one aspect of its separateness. Since, in my judgment, no fiction is without some connection with the society in which it is created, the safe generalization about the new fiction is that it is without loyalties to any order of society and without hope for a different or better order than the one it sees. . . . It has no allegiance to a particular social structure. Yet in regarding society as a subject for satire or a reason for nihilistic despair, it reveals its dependence upon a social order, or disorder – the given social situation which it tends to view with contempt, or horror, or indifference.[17]

This is a cogent summing up of the dilemma faced by the modern writer of asocial fiction: his inability to get away from his dependence on the very social order he repudiates or flees from in despair. This dilemma further confirms the truth of the paradox that the alienated and asocial writer, by virtue of producing books that point out the intolerable defects and deficiencies of the social order, is nevertheless performing a social service. But where does the writer of this persuasion turn for material when he virtually excludes the social and political theme from consideration? He explores, as Henry Miller does in the *Tropic of Cancer*, the underworld of the mind, the vagaries of desire, the compulsions of sex, the illuminations of the visionary self. Writing in a period when Fascism was on the march and the Nazis were busy building concentration camps for their host of "enemies," Henry Miller accepts the oppressions and insanities of his age; he had to struggle to survive creatively at a time when the autonomous individual, as Orwell feared, was "going to be stamped out of existence." [18] Henry Miller decided to enter the belly of the whale. Since the world for him had lost its meaning, he had to get rid of it before he could be restored to life. Like a number of his contemporaries, he had died within and was making a desperate effort to be reborn. This was, he knew, no political or economic or social solution. It was, as his friend, Michael Fraenkel, declares,

> really no solution at all. But what was there to solve? We were at the end of an age, a whole culture; a way of life, an historical past, was coming to a close: we were caught up in a process, a cyclical or organic process. . . .[19]

[17] Charles E. Eisinger, *Fiction of the Forties*. Chicago and London: The University of Chicago Press, 1963, p. 232.

[18] George Orwell, "Inside the Whale," *New Directions in Prose & Poetry*. Norfolk, Conn.: New Directions, 1946, p. 244.

[19] Michael Fraenkel, *The Genesis of the Tropic of Cancer*. Berkeley, California: Ben Porter, 1946, p. 5.

In short, during this period of totalitarian dictatorship and world war, there were no more corporate allegiances, only individuals. The gospel of Emerson, Thoreau, and Whitman was re-discovered and revindicated. The most asocial writer is, of course, fully aware that he derives or can under optimum conditions derive positive benefits from his association with society, but in a time of barbarism he is forced to retreat into the sanctuary of the self. The creative intellectual, Alex Comfort insists, has not seceded from society. It has ejected the intellectuals, he charges, "by its refusal to grant the fundamental conditions which we are entitled to lay down in the capacity of artists." [20]

Henry Miller hurled his yawp of defiance at a civilization that he condemned as corrupt and decadent and diagnosed as dying. He detested Communism, technological America, industrialization, big business, and the shabby ethics of conformity. The unreconstructed anarchist in life as in literature, all he seems to care about is the freedom he needs in order to fulfill himself as a writer. Like Max Stirner in *The Ego and His Own*,[21] what he pleads for is the absolute of individualism. By renouncing all formal social ties and obligations, he can launch forth on a voyage of self-liberation. The individualist *par excellence*, he appeals strongly to the beat writers. Both Miller and Kerouac profess to be more interested in promoting the cause of self-liberation than in literature *per se*. The latter revolts against all that society and its moral tradition represent; his picaresque heroes violently oppose practically everything their social order stands for.[22] It is not surprising that the beat writers, in their bid for untrammeled originality, reject the critical discipline and rely on the spontaneous and uncensored revelations of the personal self; they would fain give expression to the incommunicable.[23]

[20] Stefan Schimanski and Henry Treece (eds.). *A New Romantic Anthology.* London: Grey Walls Press Ltd., 1949, pp. 36-37.

[21] Though Miller, who is a far-ranging and omnivorous reader, never mentions Max Stirner, the latter's exaltation of the ego as the sole measure of value, defines Miller's own position as a writer. "My concern," writes Stirner, "is neither the divine nor the human, not the true, good, just, free, etc., but solely what is mine, and it is not a general one, but is – unique, as I am unique." Max Stirner, *The Ego and His Own.* Translated by Steven T. Byington. Edited by James J. Martin. New York: Libertarian Book Club, 1963, p. 5.

[22] Like Miller's characters, they are "absolutely cut off from all normal pursuits of those affiliated with the social order." David L. Stevenson, "James Jones and Jack Kerouac: Novelists of Disjunction," in Nona Balakian and Charles Simmons (eds.), *The Creative Present.* Garden City, New York: Doubleday & Company, Inc., 1963, p. 207.

[23] See Cyril Connolly's essay, "The Beats," in his book, *Previous Convictions.* New York, Evanston, and London: Harper & Row, 1963, p. 352.

Disoriented and disaffiliated as the beat writers are, they are committed to the belief that the modern artist cannot be nourished by the values of the society he lives in.[24] The beat spokesmen are right in contending that every true work of art has its origin in a unique personal vision, but their cardinal mistake lay in assuming, and in acting on the assumption, that the individual artist can function in isolation from the life of his own time. Writing can never be wholly asocial, but their work is of distinct value in that it reveals so vividly the alienated state of the American artist during the fifties.

The artist revolted against the social order because he felt – and rightly so – that it had no room for men like him. It accorded him no special honor or respect or did so only posthumously after he had become famous and therefore respectable. Hence the avant-garde artist is forced to join the ranks of the opposition. A dedicated nay-sayer, he fiercely assails the values of the dominant mass culture. He feels like a pariah, though he has himself taken the radical step of cutting himself off from the life of his time. Nonetheless, he is full of resentment as well as anguish at having been rejected, for he has lost, it seems to him, his audience and therefore his professional role. He must function henceforth as an outsider, as the spokesman of a dissident and despised minority. The conditions which make for his alienation turn him into a rebel, a member of the beat generation, or a hipster who makes common cause with the Negro, the criminal, and the psychopath.[25]

But he could not long sustain this state of alienation. He found himself isolated, excluded, ignored. He was shut up in a prison of his own making. His rebellious gesture impressed no one and least of all did it deceive himself. He viewed himself ironically as a parasite, a clown. In one recent English novel, the hero, a would-be writer, debunks the myth of writing for fame or for posterity. Why assume that the worship of art will last. "It's already respectable. It hasn't a chance." [26] Or else the writer saw himself tragically as a victim, a scapegoat of society, but in this version he could picture himself as a martyr. But it is the factor of economic alienation that

[24] D. S. Savage, like Alex Comfort, states the issue squarely: "The modern artist cannot take his values from contemporary society, because that society lacks all coherent standards and values." D. S. Savage, *The Personal Principle*. London: Routledge, 1964, p. 5.

[25] For many of the ideas included in the section dealing with the alienation of the artist, I am indebted to the essay, "The Artist in the Modern World," in Renato Poggioli, *The Spirit of the Letter*. Cambridge, Mass.: Harvard University Press, 1965, pp. 323-342.

[26] Thomas Hinde, *Happy as Larry*. London: Macgibbon & Kee, 1957, p. 110.

accounts in large measure for the emergence of social and cultural alienation. Art has no cash value in capitalist society.

For this reason it happens that so much of art in bourgeois society is
militantly anti-bourgeois. Creative rebels arise who refuse to conform to the
pressing demands of the majority culture; they will not commit themselves
to that in which they do not believe. The public may stigmatize them as
neurotic or mad because of their persistence in the strategy of alienation,
but they are proud of the courage that prompts them to secede from a war-
ridden, profit-minded, and therefore pathological society. Instead of glorifying the *status quo* or celebrating the march of progress, they are angry voices
of protest. Particularly in the United States is this true. As one critic remarks: "Our best writers are alienated men writing about alienated heroes
in an alienating society." [27]

[27] Kenneth Keniston, *The Uncommitted.* New York: Harcourt, Brace & World,
Inc., 1965, p. 412.

CHAPTER IV

REVOLT AND MADNESS

1. The Beat Generation

The fifties in the United States marked the emergence of a small group of writers who proudly called themselves "beat," as if the name were a badge of distinction, a banner of revolt unfurled in the face of a hostile and benighted world of "squares." They attracted a considerable following among the discontented, the frustrated, the maladjusted, the neurotic who, in the name of creative freedom, embraced a life of poverty and alienation. Unlike the literati in England at the time who desired on the whole little more than their equitable share of the benefits conferred by the Establishment, the prophetic spokesmen of this group were in violent opposition to their society; they rejected both the specious lure of the Communist program and the promise of the American Dream in an age of affluence. Reacting bitterly against the dominant native myth of success, what they sarcastically dubbed the religion of "Moneytheism," they sought to keep spiritually alive by experimenting with drugs and sex and art.

The members of the beat generation voice their rebelliousness by flouting the conventions and debunking the ideals of middle-class society.

This attack upon conventional ideals is not merely an intellectual and critical analysis but has hot emotional overtones which stem from the deep-rooted anger and hostility that govern their behavior.[1]

Professed individualists, they are full of unresolved conflicts and contradictions. Their revolt frequently takes the paradoxical form of passivity, of mutely accepting whatever fate befalls them. Despite the erotic adventures they engage in without thought of contracting a permanent union, they remain lonely, unattached, given to tormenting bouts of introspection. Beaten down, chronically depressed, vulnerable, many of them cannot bear up under social pressure.

[1] Francis J. Rigney and L. Douglas Smith, *The Real Bohemia*. New York: Basic Books, Inc., 1961, p. 71.

Nevertheless, they chose this way of life, for all its dangers and deprivations, because they hoped it would make it possible for them to write, compose music, paint, but most of them can work at their art only fitfully. The creative life is ostensibly the goal toward which they wish to strive, but they tend to practice their art chiefly as a mode of therapeutic self-expression. Their attempts to write are brief, spasmodic, undisciplined, arrested often by a change of mood or a sudden irresistible desire to wander from place to place. Craving intensely to achieve fulfillment in their art and wholeness in their living, they turn intemperately against a society that they feel is dull, artificial, and repressive. Instead of actively participating in the competitive game of striving for status and wealth, they withdraw from the social arena and decide to live their own life as they see fit. Their gesture of "civil disobedience" is motivated by an underlying need to live fully in the present, without bearing the onerous, externally imposed burden of social duty. Society, as they view it, is engaged in a conspiracy to exploit the individual for its own utilitarian, profit-making ends. Hence their adamant refusal to commit themselves to the bogus ideals of bourgeois culture. Jealously they safeguard their threatened individuality by avoiding the trap of intimate friendship, love, marriage, or too close personal relationships. The only thing that binds them together as a group is their rage of repudiation. Determined to retain their precious charter of freedom, they resist all attempts at regimentation, but their non-conformity frequently manifests itself in a nihilism that believes it is useless to make any effort. The majority actually do not believe in anything. Some exalt "madness" as a way of attaining the highest degree of illumination. Some have spent time in a mental hospital. Still others develop an interest in Zen Buddhism.

Thus the lives the beat lead and the work they produce present a striking case study in the history of alienation in the United States. The beat who are attracted to the communal haven in West Venice, California – the misfits, the botched and broken, the deviants, the despairing – are fleeing from the meaningless round of existence in conventional society. In throwing off the moral and economic responsibilities imposed by the social order, they feel free to cultivate their private garden of feeling and to drift with the tide of time. By hook or crook, they live off the fruits of the established scheme of things while revolting against it. Though they accept the libertarian values of their own group, they make no contribution to the larger social whole, with the exception of course of the few talented and productive writers who succeed in getting their work published. They offer a paradigmatic illustration of the phenomenon of self-induced alienation. Aesthetic parasites, they worship a cult of negative freedom.

> To them, the entire structure of conventional society is: (1) a prison or work-house, whose obligations are to be shunned and whose rules are to be gotten round as best one can; and (2) a scene, whose kicks are to be taken (dug) where found. . . .[2]

They have no desire to reform the social structure, much less overthrow it; they simply wish to be left entirely to their own devices.

But their literary productions – and that is what chiefly concerns us here – offer a good example of what we mean by asocial literature. Febrile, confused, ejaculatory, they consist of outbursts of delirious subjectivity, exercises in drug- or alcohol-induced states of "madness." The beat writers canonize those in their group who have gone through the experience of insanity, those who, like Carl Solomon, have been institutionalized. Some beat prophets profess to be searching for God, and it is this quest for the beatific vision, for satori, for sainthood, that accentuates their sense of separateness. In their pads in West Venice, living among their own kind in a freemasonry of the outcasts (nymphomaniacs, homosexuals, Lesbians, drug addicts, alcoholics), they do not have to feel that they are, in fact, standing alone against the world:

> it is *we* against *they*. We against the Others. No attempt is made to define *we* or *they*. No definition is necessary. *We* is what this generation is all about, whether you call it beat or disaffiliated or anything else.[3]

The inimical ones comprised under the invidious rubric of "they" are the squares, the censors, the money-grubbers, the persecutors who invoke the unholy name of the law, the beasts of prey in the jungle of cities, those who are deaf to the rhythms of jazz, their sensibility deadened, and who condemn a book because it is "immoral" in content.

The creative representatives of the beat movement emulate the example of Henry Miller in seeking to forge a style that is spontaneous, earthy, un-affected, unliterary. Jack Kerouac, in his picaresque novel, *On the Road,* celebrates characters who are perpetually on the go, using up their vital energy to the last ounce in a determined effort to live life to the full. The beat hero in this novel is Dean Moriarty, who is obsessed not only with sex but with jazz and the smoking of the weed. That is how he struggles to ward off the creeping paralysis of death, to defeat the implacable enmity of time, and continue the search for the truth of reality. Kerouac is de-

---

[2] Orrin E. Klapp, *Heroes, Villains, and Fools.* Englewood Cliffs, New Jersey: Prentice-Hall, Inc., 1962, p. 129.

[3] Lawrence Lipton, *The Holy Barbarians.* New York: Julian Messner, 1959, p. 48.

scribing the cult of sensation for its own sake. It is his pseudo-religious devotion to this cult that drives Dean to keep constantly on the move. Every source of experience is to be explored. That is how the beat generation endeavor to make the most of their madness. Like Pater in *The Renaissance,* they believe that to burn always with a hard, gemlike flame, to maintain a high pitch of ecstasy, is success in life. That is why they indulge in "the sacred" ritual of jabbing a needle in their veins. Heroin inspires them to compose poetry and calls forth in them the numinous feeling that everything is right. Blowing off steam, releasing pent-up energies in sex orgies, smoking marijuana, listening to the primitive incantation of jazz, which is the language of the orgasm – this is the way and the life, the road to the transcendence that annuls the fatality of time and neutralizes the pressure that makes for social accommodation.

The blurb in the paper-bound edition of *On the Road* mentions marijuana, jazz, and Zen as the boosters of the beat generation. Struggling to fulfill themselves personally, the two main characters, Sal Paradise and Dean Moriarty, have no thought of undermining the foundations of society. The novel relates the odyssey of their wild travels across the continent, it chronicles the adventures of a group that feels defeated, inwardly dead, and therefore resorts to the neurotic expedient of being forever on the move, never stopping long enough in one place to sink roots in the soil of social life. Every moment must furnish a new thrill, but since the moment vanishes as soon as it is savored these characters must be committed to a hectic and endless race against time. Dean, the beat saint, has seen everything and experienced everything. He has been in jail. Impelled by an insatiable hunger for more and more of life, a hunger that brooks no moral or legal restraints, he steals cars and drives the length and breadth of the land, ignoring speed limits and traffic lights. Sal Paradise is drawn to him because he represents an admirable type:

because the only people for me are the mad ones, the ones who are mad to live, mad to talk, mad to be saved, desirous of everything at the same time, the ones who never yawn or say a commonplace thing, but burn, burn, burn like a fabulous yellow roman candle exploding like spiders across the stars. . . .[4]

Those who, like the beat, adhere to an ethic that is both hedonistic and asocial must find "the normal" pattern of life stale and stultifying. They must devote their nights and days to a religion of "Natural Joy," the uninhibited pursuit of pleasure, desirous in their romantic excess of enjoying everything at the same time, regardless of the opposition of the society of

---

[4] Jack Kerouac, *On the Road.* New York: The New American Library, 1960, p. 9.

squares. Dean cares not for wealth or power, only for the sensation of sex. If he has enough to eat and drink today, why worry about the economics of the morrow? He will do anything to get out of the rat-race of modern civilization. And Kerouac romanticizes these nomads and outlaws, without disclosing the sorry limitations and miseries of their Ishmaelite existence.

And yet what does this seemingly gay, irresponsible gypsy life consist of? Sleeping out in the open air or in railroad stations, stealing gas, stealing cars, stealing food and cigarettes. In his refusal to "sell out," to mortgage his future, the beat hero runs a futile race against time, shutting his eyes to the reckless wastefulness of his life. Since the aspirations and activities of society have no meaning for him, he is inevitably brought face to face with his own confusions and conflicts. When he feels spiritually disoriented or lost, he gets drunk or consumes powerful doses of marijuana – and then the splendid visions come. What if he has to pay the price later? Nothing will stop him from attempting to gratify his desires of the moment. Committed fundamentally to nothing in the world, all he knows is that everything is there to be enjoyed, and he is resolved to enjoy it come what may. That is "the mystical" way Dean has of saying yes to life. In the name of "digging" experience to the limit, he feels justified in casting aside all social restraints.

The asocial writing of the beat generation fails not because it is asocial but because, in its contempt for tradition and discipline, it neglects the problem of communication, the problem of art. To them, in their alienation from the society of their time, the problem of communication is a matter of indifference; their main object is to pour out their feelings, to "swing" freely, to discharge their inner state of tension. Anarchistic in their rejection of the coercive machinery of the State, they make the mistake of trying to compose anarchically, like the method of psychic automatism the Surrealists practiced.

The most extreme manifestation of alienation in the asocial literature of our day takes the form of madness. We shall examine this phenomenon briefly as it appears on the international scene. The metaphysical madman not only refuses to play the game of life according to the prescribed rules; in a manic rage he hurls the pieces of chess across the room, breaks up the chess board, and then retires within the fortress of his own mind. He will allow no one entrance, shutting off all means of communication with the outside world. He harbors paranoiac suspicions of the malevolent intentions of the enemy, the anonymous and accursed "they." The whole world of men, he comes to believe, is leagued against him.

2. *Metaphysical Madness*

The metaphysical madman is not easy to define, either clinically or semantically; he is ruled by his manias but he is not literally mad, though there
are some (Strindberg, Antonin Artaud) who may at times cross over the
border of sanity. He beholds visions, often of that which he cannot as yet
name or identify, which reduce to absurdity the activities and preoccu-
pations of the temporal sphere. By giving in to his mythomanias, in ways
characteristic of his particular temperament, he achieves, even if only for
a brief spell, the absolute of alienation from the idolatrous worship of the
social gods. Nineteenth-century literature provides memorable examples
of writers who in their life or work, or both, betray in some measure this
type of madness: Kierkegaard, Lautréamont, Nietzsche, Rimbaud, and
Alfred Jarry. More recent names that might be cited are those of Kafka
and William S. Burroughs. The writer need not, of course, be himself mad
in order to paint a psychologically convincing portrait of the metaphysical
madman. In fact, the achieved work of art is a triumph over madness. As
Michel Foucault concludes in his study, *Madness and Civilization: "where
there is a work of art, there is no madness. . . ."* [5]

As we have already indicated, a particularly fine example in modern
fiction of a metaphysically mad anti-hero is to be found in Beckett's
Murphy. The protagonist not only works in a mental institution but identifies himself with the psychiatric patients in the ward. What Murphy yearns
for all along is "The freedom of indifference, the indifference of freedom,
the will that is dust in the dust of the object, the act a handful of sand let
fall. . . ." [6] He is an eccentric who saves himself from the perdition of social
conformity by refusing to become involved. Why, he asks himself, should
adjustment to "reality" be the touchstone of mental health? What earthly
good, then, did therapy provide?

The function of treatment was to bridge the gulf, translate the sufferer from his
own pernicious little private dungheap to the glorious world of discrete particles,
where it could be his inestimable prerogative once again to wonder, love, hate,
despise, rejoice and howl in a reasonable balanced manner, and comfort himself
with the society of others in the same predicament. [7]

Thus the tables are neatly turned. What is reason? Beckett asks. The mad-

[5] Michel Foucault, *Madness and Civilization*. Translated by Richard Howard. New
York: Random House, 1965, pp. 288-89.
[6] Samuel Beckett, *Murphy*. New York: Grove Press, 1938, p. 105.
[7] *Ibid.*, p. 177.

ness of all, he answers. And what is madness? The reason of one.[8] For Murphy, the singular madman, it is the social order that is reprehensibly insane. He is revolted by its demands for adherence to a collective system that is ridiculous in the extreme; his experience as

a physical and rational being obliged him to call sanctuary what the psychiatrists call exile and to think of the patients not as banished from a system of benefits but as escaped from a colossal fiasco.[9]

Cut off from his immediate surroundings, Murphy reaches a point of total indifference; his greatest pleasure – consummate, ineffable bliss – is to lie in a mystical state of immobility, contemplating the infinite nothingness of space.

Beckett's novel communicates a desolating message of existential dread. Existential madness, whether it is characterized by a sense of emptiness or estrangement or nausea or suicidal despair, is caused not by social or economic alienation but by a traumatic vision of the void. Existence seems to crawl like a worm or snake; life is permanently arrested or it consists, as in Beckett's fiction, of movements in a circle of mud. There is no meaningful space to breathe in; everything is dark, viscous, confined. The heights which the spirit once aspired to reach are seen as vain illusions; there is no goal toward which to strive. The suicide takes the plunge by disposing of existence itself, while the metaphysical madman, rebelling against the loss of his inner freedom, shuts out the trivial distractions of the social world, which for him is not only Vanity Fair but the kingdom of the absurd. In his alienated condition, the latter knows that truth is an illusion, consciousness a disease, language a lie.[10]

Metaphysical madness, in its literary embodiment, may best be defined by applying the principle of polarity: by considering what it is not. Don Quixote is plainly mad, a monomaniac, but his madness is definitely of a social order: the mania of an idealist drunk on tales of chivalry who endeavors, single-handed, to redress wrongs and bring the sorry world nearer to the heart's desire. He is God's emissary, a true Christian, in that he takes seriously the injunctions of Christianity, but the world judges him a downright fool for giving in to his obsessions. Kierkegaard, the cripple, the religious "madman," was also laughed at by his contempora-

---

[8] Gironella, the Spanish novelist, attributes these remarks to Rensi. " 'What is reason?' he asks. 'The madness of all. And what is madness. The reason of one.' " José Maria Gironella, *Phantoms and Fugitives*. Translated by Terry Broch Fontseré. New York: Sheed and Ward, 1964, pp. 6-7.

[9] Samuel Beckett, *Murphy*, pp. 177-78.

[10] See Rollo May, Ernest Angel, and Henri F. Ellenberger (eds.), *Existence*. New York: Basic Books, 1958, p. 306.

ries because of his prophetic writing. On May 12, 1839 he records in his journal:

The whole of existence frightens me, from the smallest fly to the mystery of the Incarnation; everything is unintelligible to me, most of all myself; the whole of existence is poisoned in my sight, particularly myself.[11]

Before his morbidly introspective gaze the social and historical scene with all its vicissitudes faded to insignificance. Kierkegaard, however, accepted the absolute paradox that God should have existed in human form, while freely acknowledging that it cannot be understood.

But the metaphysical madman, precisely because he suffers from the absence or death of God, is faced with the tormenting problem of discovering some ultimate meaning in the universe. A negative, if not nihilistic, seeker, he cannot, like the beat saint, accept a hedonistic solution to his problem. Like Malraux's heroes he may dedicate himself to a political cause, though he knows he cannot logically justify his choice. Malraux's protagonists in *The Conquerors* and *Man's Fate* do not secede from society, whereas the usual fate of the metaphysical madman is to fall into suicidal despair, like Stavrogin in *The Possessed* or Quentin in *The Sound and the Fury*. The symptoms of metaphysical madness form a complex but often fairly recognizable syndrome: they spring chiefly from the loss of God and the disappearance of the horizons of the absolute; they are heightened by the oppressive feeling that man is governed by mechanical forces beyond his control. Georg Büchner dramatizes this condition in his tragedy, *Wozzeck,* a remarkable study of mental alienation. Büchner shows how society and the individual, both, are at the mercy of forces that follow no moral design and thus projects, long before Kafka, a world that is a nihilistic chaos.

In the literature of the twentieth century, this process of alienation becomes sharply intensified. Isolated, socially uprooted, incurably introspective, the metaphysical hero dwells in the dark depths of his own mind. Lenormand's alienated heroes are incapable of relating to the world around them or of taking upon themselves the social responsibilities which life imposes on them. Spiritually sick, decadent, they are always alone and in conflict with themselves. The world they live in seems to them not only chaotic but malignantly hostile. It is a world in which they can find fulfillment only by committing suicide. A more representative example of metaphysical madness is afforded by the ambiguous character of Caligula in Camus's play. The death of his sister, Drusilla, who was also his mistress, has

---

[11] Sören Kierkegaard, *The Journals of Sören Kierkegaard.* Edited and translated by Alexander Dru. London and New York: Oxford University Press, 1951, pp. 72-73.

plunged him into inconsolable grief. Now that he has encountered the reality of death and finds life insupportable, he reaches out desperately for that which is impossible. Though this seems like an outbreak of pure madness, there is a method in it, a perversely lucid logic that will not be gainsaid. He has discovered the shocking truth – namely, that death exists – which renders all of human existence meaningless. In his logical madness he decides to reject the world and teach his subjects the utter unimportance of mankind.

The outburst of what in France is loosely called "aliterature" is characterized not only by a profound distrust of language as a means of communication but by a suspension of belief in the truth of reality. The writers whom Claude Mauriac includes under this heading are bound together by their awareness of their depersonalized condition. Antonin Artaud describes with anguish the loss of his sense of identity, his acute attacks of anxiety neurosis. Like Rimbaud, he is not himself. Madness, he feels, is the source of literature that negates literature. Try as he will to overcome his mental disorder, he cannot establish communion with the world of men. According to Claude Mauriac, Artaud's dementia "reveals the dementia of all living men who think. . . . It is not so much insanity as the impossibility of being, the horror of essential solitude." [12] It is not surprising that these asocial and aliterary writers say they feel nothing but contempt for what they produce. But the writer of our time, however "mad," will not consent to abdicate his creative function.

The beatification of the madman is coupled with the vindication of the criminal and junkie as hero. The madman, because he breaks out of the straitjacket of rationalism, is the holy man, the inspired visionary. Extremism, excess in all its rebellious forms, is the road to happiness. If the beat saint resorts to violence it is because he believes that this is the only way in which he can resist the pressure of a mechanized society which menaces his freedom, undermines his very manhood. If he joins the underworld of the Negro, it is because there he can let himself go, release his primitive instincts, give in without shame or guilt to his sexual cravings. His adventure in madness and crime represents his efforts to awaken from the nightmare of death-in-life that his society holds up as the ideal. In "Report from the Asylum," Carl Solomon, the culture hero of the beat generation, describes the fight he waged against the horror of becoming enslaved by the modern mechanized world. For him insanity

[12] Claude Mauriac, *The New Literature*. Translated by Samuel I. Stone. New York: George Braziller, 1959, p. 40.

is the ultimate retreat, more insulating than heroin, weed or bop. In a world where the "upward and onward" assurance of positivism always rings false, madness is the most sure way (next to death) of breaking the clock, stopping time, and splintering life into a stream of acutely felt sensations that impose no demands and bring no consciousness of guilt.[13]

There we behold the recurrent motif in much of contemporary asocial literature: the metaphysical madman's escape from the trap of chronological time and the rat-race of technologized life by withdrawing completely into his own hallucinated world. Though he identifies himself with K. in Kafka's fiction, he goes far beyond his prototype in mental and spiritual disorientation. The insulin treatment to which he is subjected marks a radical departure from the Kafka script, for in the wards of the mental hospital the authorities are not malign but benevolent.[14] Solomon records the visions he beholds, the coma induced in him and how the coma brought on inexplicable psychic transformations. Solomon's confession sounds no spirited call to revolt; the enemy is too powerful to be openly attacked. He quotes Artaud as saying that a lunatic "is a man who has preferred to become what is socially understood as mad rather than forfeit a certain superior idea of human honor. . . ."[15] Allen Ginsberg, who dedicates *Howl* to Carl Solomon, begins his poem with the line: "I saw the best minds of my generation destroyed by madness." [16]

Even more extraordinary in its revelation of a series of drug-induced fantasies is *Naked Lunch*, by William S. Burroughs. In its violent explosion of imagery and metaphor and in its unmitigated hatred of society it reminds one of Lautréamont's *Maldoror*. It is an Inferno Burroughs pictures for us, a hell shaped by the creative moods of drug addiction. In testifying in court in behalf of this book, Norman Mailer declares: "To me, this is a simple portrayal of Hell. It is Hell precisely." [17] Precisely because it is the testament of one burning in Hell, it holds nothing back, none of the asocial bitterness or black humor or obscenities or physical degradation. But if

---

[13] Gene Feldman and Max Gartenberg (eds.), *The Beat Generation and the Angry Young Men*. New York: Dell Publishing Co., 1958, p. 171.

[14] The theme of madness is handled differently by Ken Kesey in *One Flew Over the Cuckoo's Nest* (1962). It is a bitter protest against the bureaucratic despotism of mental hospitals and the inhumanity of the treatment forced upon the patients. It is all part of a vicious conspiracy to make the weak conform by robbing them of their initiative. Any show of resistance is summarily punished: by shock therapy, straitjackets, and solitary confinement.

[15] Gene Feldman and Max Gartenberg (eds.), *The Beat Generation and the Angry Young Men*, p. 180.

[16] *Ibid.*, p. 182.

[17] William S. Burroughs, *Naked Lunch*. New York: Grove Press, Inc., 1966, p. xvi.

Burroughs is in hell, he at least knows why he is there. If he is a drug addict and homosexual, he is, like Genet, not unmindful of the fact that others who pass as "normal" are afflicted with their own insidious forms of addiction: the acquisitive mania, the passion for conformity, the ravening lust for power. Burroughs protests fiercely against "the perverts" who seek to use their authority as leaders to brainwash the masses and keep them abjectly under control.

It is therefore not at all strange that this dervish dance of fantasy is, like Genets' plays, instinct with damning social implications. With fearless honesty Burroughs exposes the ghastly social sadism involved in capital punishment, but he reserves his choicest passages of satiric abuse for those who derive pleasure from gaining dominance over others socially, sexually, and politically. He pillories the high-minded bureaucrat and cries out against the fiendish techniques (as Allen Ginsberg states in his testimony) "of mass brainwash and mass control, and theories of modern dictatorship, theories of modern police states. . . ." [18] Burroughs indicts a whole civilization, denouncing the machinations of those who would homogenize the entire population, reducing everyone to uniformity of thought and behavior. That is the worst of the deadly sins, the crime of crimes: the attempt to establish totalitarian control over people.

In the wild fantasies of *Naked Lunch* the supreme terror is evoked by the idea of thought control. Electronics can make possible control of bodily movement, sensory impressions, and emotional reactions. Bioelectric signals can be injected into the nervous system. Each subject can thus be properly conditioned by State-managed transmitters or by telepathic means. The object in every case is to achieve social uniformity. Burroughs' horror of brainwashing comes out in his diatribe against the Liquefactionists:

We must reject the facile solution of flooding the planet with "desirable replicas." It is highly doubtful if there are any desirable replicas, such creatures constituting an attempt to circumvent process and change.[19]

He calls for maximum diversity and opposes "any form of organized coercion or tyranny on the part of pressure groups or individual control addicts." [20] The vision of a single bureaucrat determining what the populace is to think and how it is to respond – that vision fills him with horror and indignation. Absolute power over people is the absolute evil.

William S. Burroughs' metaphysical madness is evident in his drugged withdrawal from reality, his flight from a competive and computerized

[18] *Ibid.*, p. xxiii.
[19] *Ibid.*, p. 167.
[20] *Ibid.*, p. 167.

world. Another writer who suffers from similar symptoms of metaphysical madness is Alexander Trocchi, whose *Cain's Book* is only superficially a novel about drug-addiction. It is a defense of the peace that drugs make possible and a metaphysical diatribe against a society that demands conformity and crucifies the rebel. It is about a writer and his struggle, in lucid moments, to discover himself, finish his book, and make sense of his life. Significantly enough, he quotes Sade and Beckett, his favorite preceptors, one in the field of morality and the other in that of fiction. Essentially it is a spiritual autobiography he is composing. The hero writing this book makes clear that, in his case as in that of the other addicts, the motive for taking drugs is to throw off the intolerable burden of time. The present moment is all in all, though he does not, under the influence of heroin, seriously occupy himself with the question of the "here-and-now." "That is one of the virtues of the drug, that it empties such questions of all anguish, transports them to another region, a painless theoretical region, a play region, surprising, fertile, and unmoral. One is no longer grotesquely involved in becoming. One simply is." [21]

For against the paranoia of living in a persecutory world the man under heroin feels adequate, secure, inviolable. This is no illusion, the hero-author insists, but a fact of experience, utterly unlike the gross facts of Freud and Marx. He repudiates the facts of science, sociology, and psychoanalysis; he preferred to exist "simply in abeyance, to give up (if you will), and come naked to apprehension." [22] But this state of being cannot be attained without heroin or marijuana. He sought the sensation the drug brought him, the incandescent feeling of the present moment, and then the sense of being alone overcame him; he desired nothing more than to remain thus suspended, never to go back to the frenzies of the city and its sinister power of alienation. The only fact that stood out in these drug-nurtured visions was that America never stood still; it was forever strenuously on the move, and anyone who failed to join in the mad race was automatically accused of high treason.

The heroin addict retreats but his retreat is at the same time an act of defiance, a rejection of society and its values. The world is the enemy to be locked out or circumvented. These underground rebels refuse to be brainwashed. Drugs are a means enabling the user to dig deep into himself, to discover who he is, Cain or Abel. It is important to retain one's identity in all the labyrinths of distraction that the mechanical city provides. The hero is the Kafkaesque ghost in search of identity, longing for those mo-

---

[21] Alexander Trocchi, *Cain's Book*. New York: Grove Press, Inc., 1960, p. 11.
[22] *Ibid.*, p. 12.

ments when awareness comes to a luminous focus. He is alone, always alone, even in company. The main thing to avoid is to become a hired part of the industrial treadmill. He will not accommodate himself to this absurd world that made work a sacred obligation and which presumed to reward a man in terms of effort or to punish him if he did not wish to measure up to its standards. He would sign no loyalty oath to the State or support a socioeconomic system that thrived on inequity. He is what he is, and the self he is rejects America, rejects the world, and turns to heroin and writing as a means of entering reality. "Sometimes," he confesses, "at low moments, I felt my thoughts were the ravings of a man mad out of his mind to have been placed in history at all, having to act, to consider. . . ." [23] The difficulty lies in trying to achieve timelessness, to jump out of the polluted context of history, while rejecting the kingdom of eternity.

A more clear-cut case of metaphysical madness, with its accompanying asocial bias, is given in the story Seymour Krim tells of his breakdown and commitment to a mental institution. He assails the cruel and confused attitude society adopts toward the insane. Anything abnormal or "mad" or "neurotic" poses a threat to our established standards of conduct. Neither metaphysical nor existential madness is defined in any of the medical dictionaries. When Seymour Krim could no longer control his frustrations and burst out in a manic rage, he was brought to Bellevue Hospital and then transferred to a private institution, which subjected him to shock therapy. His case, he contends, was wrongly diagnosed. He denies that he ever suffered from hallucinations. He had merely come to believe that God had given him "the right and the duty to do everything openly that I had secretly fantasied for years." [24] He was later tempted to commit suicide but then thought better of it. When he confessed the whole story to his psychologist, he was committed, under drugs, to another institution. Krim insists that he was not psychotic. "I was simply a tormented man-kind who had never steeled himself to face the facts of life. . . ." [25]

He fought for his freedom from the shut-in world of the insane and finally managed to gain it. Insanity, he holds, is largely a matter of definition. Madness, he declares, has today become a literary word. The intellectuals of our time are harrowed by fear that, as measured by the norms of their community, they may possibly not be sane. Krim, who admires the beat movement, argues that the writer, by virtue of his calling, must chal-

[23] *Ibid.*, p. 237.
[24] Seymour Krim, *Views of a Shortsighted Cannoneer*. New York: Excelsior Press, 1961, p. 61.
[25] *Ibid.*, p. 62.

lenge the truth of what is collectively regarded as right and normal and
real. Since he is by temperament different from the majority of his fellow
men, the artist is bound to be considered dangerous and be penalized for
his "mad" heresies. Anyone who dares flout the conventions of his land
must expect to be condemned as psychotic by his society. Krim believes

that the fear and even the actual living through of much that used to be called
"insanity" is almost an emotional necessity for every truly feeling, reacting, to-
tally human person in America at this time. . . .[26]

This is not the isolated judgment of a literary eccentric. Norman Mailer, a
novelist of achieved stature, subscribes to this transvaluation of values.
As the self-appointed philosopher of Hip, he asserts that it is the psycho-
pathic element in the hipster which differentiates him from the alienated
Bohemian. The hipster draws no arbitrary distinction between good and
evil. Responsive only to the call of desire, however illicit, he lives in an
eternal, flowing present. Hence he rebels of necessity against the formal
code of conduct prescribed by his society. What the hipster suffers from
– much more so than the Existentialist or beat hero – is the paranoiac
suspicion that the world is leagued against him and that, in order to fulfill
himself, he must be prepared to take what he needs, even if this means
breaking the law. He will live dangerously from moment to moment. As
Norman Mailer acknowledges in "The White Negro":

the nihilism of Hip proposes as its final tendency that every social restraint and
category be removed, and the affirmation implicit in the proposal is that man
would then prove to be more creative than murderous and so would not destroy
himself.[27]

If the hipster in the present state of society occasionally resorts to lawless-
ness and violence, this, according to Mailer, is not only justifiable but
admirable, since the collective violence unleashed by the State is infinitely
worse.

We have analyzed the revolt of the beat and the hipster, the alienation
of the metaphysical madman and the hero as drug addict, in order to show
that asocial literature, whatever its aesthetic rationale, cannot sustain the
logic of its position. The literature of the absurd is at least consistent in
giving expression to a metaphysical vision which, by a process of ironic
reduction, exposes the grotesque comedy of the social enterprise. The
farces and anti-dramas of Ionesco, like the fiction of Beckett, stress the
truth, however irrational, of the inner life of consciousness and the force

[26] *Ibid.*, p. 74.
[27] Gene Feldman and Max Gartenberg (eds.), *The Beat Generation and the Angry
Young Men*, p. 390.

of dreams, just as the illusionistic plays of Genet, by unmasking the hypocrisy of social and political life, emphasize the necessary and important role of fantasy in human affairs. The anarchistic protest shades off imperceptibly into the literature of social criticism, for it holds up the image of a free, communal life that will safeguard the autonomy of the individuals who compose it. Beat literature also moves tentatively in this direction, but it fails to take the decisive step of revolt. In its exaltation of the rebel without a cause, it forgets, like the prophets of Hip, the Buberian wisdom that without self-transcendence there can be no genuine relationship to reality. Basically the beat, like the hipsters, reject all values, and in particular those promulgated by a society that is acquisitive, mechanized, and repressive.

By way of summing up, we can say that in the asocial aesthetic man is pictured as thrust back upon himself. The only reality is that of the self, and in a world of technological coordination that is hard to keep alive. The asocial writer accepts no binding source of moral authority. He looks upon the mysterious universe of matter that is energy in motion and finds there no order that constitutes an answer to his ultimate question. If he turns to art it is because he realizes it provides no truth, only illusion. Bereft of faith in the redemption of man to be achieved through the dynamics of the social process, he creates the anti-hero who is alienated from society and at odds with the universe. As the result of his withdrawal from the troubled and tumultuous life of his time, he suffers from solitude, from periods of dementia, and the temptations of suicide.

One thing remains clear: literature, like painting, is not a direct instigation to social action, though both arts deeply affect the consciousness and sensibility of those who lay themselves open to their beneficent influence. The literature of power settles none of life's embroiled issues. Though it may deal with any subject under the sun, it enunciates no definitive social evangel and supports no political cause. It may run counter to its nature and labor to arouse men to go ahead and change their world, but it is so much wasted effort. And yet, as one critic points out, there is a significant sense in which art at its best acts as an awakener, a summons to full awareness. In questioning all that is, art "is revolutionary and rebellious in character." [28]

[28] Paul B. Fallico, *Art & Existentialism*. Englewood Cliffs, New Jersey: Prentice-Hall, Inc., 1962, p. 124.

PART II

THE LITERATURE OF SOCIAL CRITICISM

A. THE VOICE OF SOCIAL CRITICISM

CHAPTER V

THE PROBLEM OF DEFINITION

The literature of social criticism is vast indeed – so vast, in fact, that even a brief consideration of all the writing that falls within this category in the period of time we have chosen for this study, would require a book of encyclopedic length. Better than asking what constitutes the literature of social criticism is the question of what is not comprised under that all-embracing rubric. Even those productions which we have classified under asocial literature and which seems to be remote from the life of social institutions or the play of politics prove, on closer examination, to be instinct with damaging social implications. As a matter of fact, politics encompasses all of life and is therefore inescapable. It is accordingly impossible as well as irresponsible, in the judgment of some critics, to stand apart from or above the battle. To remain non-political in a world that is full of conflict is to accept the world as it is; it is to renounce the idea that one is an active member of his society, who must bear the guilt for failure to do his part in shaping the world. Looked at in this light, all literature, however fantastic or mystical in content, is animated by a profound social concern, and this is true of even the most flagrant nihilistic work.

For every novel – and this applies to the drama as well – creates an image, however distorted or idealized, of the society in which its characters move and have their being. Every novelist is concerned, but in strategically different ways, with the task of picturing the life of society as the background against which his *dramatis personae* act out their destiny, but it is these differences in the presentation – differences in tone, emphasis, mood, attitude, and belief – that are for our purpose of fundamental importance. Otherwise, social fiction, like social realism, becomes a blanket term that accommodates itself readily to a multitude of meanings. Once it is granted that all literature is social in content, it is possible to introduce a number of needful social distinctions. In asocial literature the social theme, though present by indirection, is blurred by the writer's repudiation of society and by his overriding

interest in the liberation of the self. The hero, often an introspective individual, is shown to be primarily in quest of himself or in search of ultimate
meaning. Even with the literary anarchists as with the Dadaists, their relation to society is reflected in the very violence of their attack on its evils. On
the other hand, what we designate as the literature of social criticism does not
reject society. It holds up a magnifying mirror to the abuses and abominations of the age; it is a spirited cry of protest against specific miscarriages of
justice; it is an attempt to expose by imaginative means and, by exposing,
denounce the inhumanity of man to man. Literature of this type – polemical,
satiric, allegorical, homiletic, prophetic, and visionary in character – has
a long and fruitful tradition behind it, from *Piers the Plowman* and Voltaire's
Candide to such modern plays as *The Crucible* and *The Deputy*. Our third
division deals with the more familiar branch of politically "committed" or
"revolutionary" literature.

We are using the phrase, "the literature of social criticism," in a eulogistic
rather than pejorative sense. Perhaps a better term for it would be the literature of social protest, as referring to those novels or plays that are dedicated
to a humanitarian cause, without being revolutionary in aim or propagandistic in content. It pictures, for example, the wretched plight of the small farmers in the thirties evicted from their land by the erosion of the soil and
their desperate search for work; it appeals to the aroused conscience of mankind to put an end to the abominations perpetrated in Nazi Germany where
"the enemies" of the State were incarcerated in concentration camps and
millions of them put to death in crematoria; it cries out against the horror of
warfare and warns prophetically of the apocalyptic disaster that the use of
the atomic bomb will inflict on the human race.

The problem the modern writer faces in registering his protest against the
destructive forces let loose in his age, is, as we have seen, complicated by his
anomalous position in the community. He feels himself alienated from and
therefore hostile to mass society. Glorying in his temperamental difference,
he exaggerates the uniqueness of his talent (Salvador Dali publishes his
Diary of a Genius and Norman Mailer his *Advertisements for Myself*) and
makes a cult of art in order to stress his opposition to those forces in collective life that he finds abhorrent. Gradually, as the effects of the industrial
revolution made themselves felt on a massive scale and technology increasingly took over the control of life, he tended in a number of cases to rebel
by withdrawing more and more from the mechanized world around him.
He stood apart in order the more freely and fully to cultivate his art. In
particular, he resisted the rapid growth of collectivism by defiantly affirming
his individuality.

In proportion, as society grew more collectivistic, the artist, the intellectual, became more and more individualistic: his very isolation turned him into a hypertrophical individual, into an outpost of individual man. This worked like a vicious circle in the relation between artist and society.[1]

In devoting himself exclusively to his art, the writer, willingly or not, deepened his already unhappy state of alienation. He cut himself off from the possibility of communication with his mass audience, since his restless search for new technical modes of expression would appeal only to a select few, the literary elite. As a result he frequently felt shut in. He struggled to redefine his function and to reappraise the true value of his contribution to the world. His social conscience smarted as he wondered at times if he were not sacrificing the precious stuff of life itself for the sake of producing inutile works of art.

Hence he labored under the painful necessity of reexamining his relation to the world of man as organized at present. In order to preserve his creative freedom and individuality, he must perforce revolt against a mechanical civilization that would exploit him for ends which he has not chosen and which he rejects as essentially anti-human. As we have indicated in the first part of this book, modern life bears witness to the progressive breakdown of the individual. The corporate group steadily extends its influence over larger areas of life until a point is reached where the individual is invested with significance only by virtue of his participation in the collectivity. It is the collectivity, as represented by political parties, economic organizations, and governmental power, which has little regard for the integrity of the individual. Even the State functions as a huge and efficient bureaucratic system. In this world of proliferating anonymous collectives, as Alex Comfort reveals in his Kafka-like novel, *The Power House*, the self is annulled, the freedom of the individual abrogated.

Not that freedom for the artist or anyone else is ever absolute. Freedom cannot be implemented in society unless order is first established. Otherwise we get anarchy. From the dawn of civilized time man has been under the rule of customs and conventions. "Neither ontogenetically nor phylogenetically," says Malinowski, "is 'man born free'." [2] Growing-up implies a process of cultural conditioning, and culture means, even in the Freudian lexicon, that some degree of instinctual renunciation must be exercised. Nothing that man does takes place outside the context of culture. Even the thoughts and dreams

[1] Eric Kahler, *The Tower and the Abyss*. New York: George Braziller, Inc., 1957, p. 149.

[2] Bronislaw Malinowski, *Freedom and Civilization*. New York: Roy Publishers, 1944, p. 33.

that rise up in the privacy of the conscious or unconscious mind must find their expression "in overt behavior, hence also in institutionalized, social reaction." [3] Not even the anti-heroes of Samuel Beckett, in their solipsistic exploration of the benighted universe of the absurd, can entirely shut out, except by retreating into madness, the intrusion of the social world. What the writer does for those who feel too heavily oppressed by the pressure of the modern world is to spell out imaginatively, to disclose symbolically, the threat posed by the rigid ethic of conformity, the danger of men being reduced to mere functions, robots in a mechanical nightmare. He upholds the sanctity of the self, whether or not he explicitly recognizes that the struggle to achieve identity is inevitably tied up with the character of the social world in which he lives.[4]

The relationship of the individual to society is, then, a dialectical one. Without the vital nourishment and support he derives from society the individual is greatly impoverished, if not helpless, but if he worships idolatrously the image of the collectivity and slavishly obeys its behests he suffers an even worse impoverishment of spirit. Nor can the writer afford to dwell in proud isolation exclusively within himself. He must first satisfy the exacting demands of his art, but fundamentally he writes for others. He cannot function apart from his membership in society.

At bottom, the writer as social critic does not wish to destroy society but to purify it or redeem it. He cannot remain silent or indifferent while injustice reigns on earth. He can, of course, adopt the stoical stance of A. E. Housman in "Be Still, My Soul, Be Still," in which the poet, resigned to the human condition, cries out in accents of anguish:

> Ay, look: high heaven and earth ail from the prime foundation;
>   All thoughts to rive the heart are here, and all are vain:
> Horror and scorn and hate and fear and indignation:
>   Oh, why did I awake? When shall I sleep again?

Most writers refuse to call out pessimistically, "Let us endure an hour and see injustice done." Instead they are resolved to voice their full-throated indignation, but the effectiveness of their protest is measured not by ideological criteria nor by the rightness, whatever that may be, of the cause they support nor by the amount of influence their writing is supposed to

---

[3] *Ibid.,* p. 85.

[4] According to Helen Merrell Lynd, the search for identity is a social as well as individual problem. "The kind of answer one gives to the question Who am I? depends in part upon how one answers the question What is this society – and the world – in which I live?" Helen Merrell Lynd, *On Shame and the Search for Identity.* New York: Harcourt, Brace and Company, 1958, p. 15.

wield in a time of crisis. It is determined, basically, by the degree to which the topical controversy that called forth their protest has been integrated organically into their works so that it achieves universality of appeal.

The lasting works of the imagination are not committed to any formal ideology or social movement. *The Adventures of Don Quixote, Hamlet, Faust* point no moral and promote no social cause. Most novels and plays of our troubled time, however, have their roots planted deep in the soil of social conflict. Today society has grown so vast, so complex, so interdependent, that the social theme not only looms large but seems like a colossus to dominate the literary landscape. Since the writer cannot possibly produce (though some have tried) a *roman-fleuve* that will comprehend the totality of the life of mankind in the present, even within the confines of a single nation or city, he restricts his passion for all-inclusiveness by singling out some urgent social problem for treatment: racial antagonism, neo-colonialism, strife on the labor front, prostitution, the corruption of politics, the threat of nuclear warfare, the dehumanization wrought by the machine.

What does the writer as social critic hope to achieve by his efforts? He must know that literature alone is impotent to cure the social disorders of his age. He is not a social engineer. Nor is he an expert in the field of economics, though he may, like Dreiser in *The Titan* and *The Financier*, study the operations of a traction magnate or, like Frank Norris in *The Pit*, familiarize himself with the technical workings of the Stock Exchange. Nor, whatever he may think or say, is his role as artist that of a reformer or moral crusader. If he endeavors to moralize his fiction, he turns out allegories that simplify and thus falsify human reality. As we shall see later, the demands of Socialist realism in Russia transformed the writer into a partisan who was required, if his work was to be published at all, to promulgate views in accordance with the official decrees of the Communist Party. Those Soviet writers during the Stalinist regime who conformed – and they had no choice in the matter unless they were willing to keep silent or go into exile or like Mayakovsky commit suicide – composed manifestoes, slogans, tracts for the times, politically slanted fables. The tenets of realism were perverted in order to afford the reader an optimistic picture of the new collective order and the new Soviet man in the making. Bertolt Brecht, the most eminent and talented practitioner of propagandist drama, though his imagination wrought better than he had planned, made no secret of his intention of converting the people in the audience to the truth of the class struggle and the imperative need for changing the world in line with the Marxist image of social redemption.

Yet even those writers in the West who are not bitten by the Marxist mania, often conceive of themselves as the articulate conscience of their race. No matter how aberrant a form their revolt assumes, they are taking up arms, in one way or another, against a sea of troubles. For example, Dada, which is anarchy personified, the apotheosis of the unintelligible, triggered a violent reaction against the moral decadence of the world at the time of the First World War. The Dadaists issued manifestoes, composed poetry and prose, that rejected all that their civilization professed to hold sacred, but they did so in order to expose the vicious lies on which this civilization was based. They believed in nothing and had nothing to affirm, but that was far better than condemning millions of men to slaughter in the name of toplofty humanitarian principles. As Leonard Forster says:

All were revolted by a self-satisfied, profiteering bourgeois world which had brought the war about, and were anxious to demonstrate against it in the sphere of art, the only sphere in which action seemed possible.[5]

They were rebels against an intolerable social order but their rebellion was conducted in the name of society, in behalf of a cultural ideal which they felt was being subverted. Driven by the need to save art from bourgeois contamination, they fulminated against a world that had run amok in its celebration of the myth of progress and its deadly exploitation of the machine. War was the dance of death of the West, the apocalyptic culmination of its headlong will to die.

  For the magnetic chain that unites mankind and gives it a common psychic base had been broken. As Tristan Tzara wrote: " 'love thy neighbor' is a hypocrisy. . . . After the carnage we still retain the hope of a purified mankind." [6] In short, the Dadaists were engaged in a negative but indispensable work of decontamination. They were aware that they could accomplish nothing by means of direct political action. The only hideout to which they could retire, while they found refuge in neutral Switzerland, was the realm of art.

But supposing life to be a poor farce, without aim or initial parturition, and because we think it our duty to extricate ourselves as fresh and clean as washed chrysanthemums, we have proclaimed as the sole basis for agreement: art.[7]

Though they dedicated themselves to the task of symbolic destruction, they produced work for themselves alone, regarding art as a purely private affair,

[5] Leonard Forster, *Poetry of Significant Nonsense.* Cambridge: At the University Press, 1962, p. 27.

[6] Robert Motherwell, *The Dada Painters and Poets.* New York: Wittenborn, Schultz, 1951, p. 77.

[7] *Ibid.,* p. 80.

but their disillusionment with the society of their time leaps forth in almost every utterance they make. Their negative revolt contains its implicit countermotif of affirmation; they affirm "the cleanliness of the individual after the state of madness, aggressive complete madness of a world abandoned to the hands of bandits, who rend one another and destroy the centuries." [8]

The Dadaists could not long continue in their state of strenuous but futile negation. When the movement petered out, some joined the newly organized band of Surrealists. Surrealism later completed the cycle of development by throwing in its lot with revolutionary Marxism, though the misalliance lasted but a short time.[9]

No, the horrors of the social world are not to be blinked – the recurrent cold and hot wars, the blight of poverty, the inhumanity of racial persecution, the purges of alleged counter-revolutionary elements in Soviet Russia, the genocidal policies carried out by the Nazi leaders. What is the writer's bounded duty in such a world? As a citizen he is free to make his opinions known, as some intellectuals are doing in voicing their protest against the war in Vietnam, and to participate actively in some libertarian or radical cause. Thoreau, an arch-individualist, preached the doctrine of civil disobedience and refused to pay the poll tax on the ground that he would not support a State that upheld the institution of slavery. Zola faced the aroused hostility of the people of his land by courageously defending Captain Dreyfus. Anatole France, toward the end of his life, became an active Socialist. Gide opposed Fascism. Later, after his trip to Soviet Russia, he printed his criticism of conditions in that country, though warning writers against "all forms of doctrinaire contagion." [10] During the thirties in the United States a number of prominent writers displayed their sympathy for labor by joining the picket line. There are many other examples, particularly in Europe, of writers taking an active part in the social conflict of their time.

All this, however, while providing important data for the biography of these writers, throws little light on the complex problem whether imaginative literature can be legitimately used as an instrument of social protest and reform. For the writer, knowing that the topical is soon consigned to the limbo of the ephemeral, is fearful of debasing his art by making it serve ends which are alien to its nature. The controversies of the day are soon forgotten and superseded on the morrow, when a new social battle looms on the hori-

---

[8] *Ibid.*, p. 81.

[9] For the social and historical background of the Surrealist movement, see Maurice Nadeau, *The History of Surrealism*. Translated by Richard Howard. New York: The Macmillan Company, 1965.

[10] Germaine Brée, *Gide*. New Brunswick, New Jersey: Rutgers University Press, 1963, p. 2.

zon. Nevertheless, whatever the risk they run, a number of writers heed the call and take their stand. We have chosen to consider the work of such representative figures as Shaw, John Dos Passos, John Steinbeck, and the group in England known as the Angry Young Men. This will be followed by a section devoted to an analysis of the literature of social protest.

CHAPTER VI

SHAW THE SOCIAL PROPHET

1. Socialism and the Drama

What constructive effect, if any, do problem plays or literary works of impassioned propaganda have on the life of society at a given time? Specifically, what changes for the better do they help to bring about? The problem of social causation is so complex, the variables in the equation so numerous, that the answer to questions of this type is hard to arrive at objectively. On the one hand, as measured in terms of the social changes literature directly or indirectly initiates, its impact would seem to be of negligible importance. On the other hand, the literature of power, as distinguished from ephemeral journalism or discursive writings of topical interest, does serve to enlarge the horizons of the mind, does provoke discussion and debate, and thereby in the long run works its subtle alchemy in transforming the attitudes of men open to its beneficent influence. It stirs the imagination and makes the audience or readers aware of evils to which hitherto they had been blind or which they could grasp only in abstract intellectual terms.

Concretely, how much did Bernard Shaw, one of the most articulate and aggressive exponents of the drama of ideas, accomplish by those of his plays that fiercely criticize the inequities of his society? How much agitational effectiveness do the dramatic parables of Bertolt Brecht possess? Both men, one an outspoken Socialist and the other a believer in Communism, utilized the theater as a means to provoke controversy, to condemn abuses, and to point out salutary ways of reform or revolutionary action. Shaw, a matchless satirist, exposed the flagrant contradictions in social reality between precept and practice, the ideal and the real. But if Shaw was the dedicated master of moral criticism, he was also a poet at heart.

Shaw the artist was as a result often in conflict with Shaw the playwright of ideas and impatient reformer. He attempted to resolve the conflict by reserving his lengthy formal argument, brilliantly polemical in style, for his prefaces, which had only a loose connection with the plays themselves. A

Fabian Socialist, Shaw did not fool himself into believing that by urgently setting forth idealistic programs he could transform the social order. Though he retained to the end his faith in the power of reason and in the cult of progress, he was no diehard rationalist. There was much of the dreamer and mystic in his make-up. He knew the reality of evil as well as the reality of power in the world, and realized the utter ineffectuality of proposing spiritual solutions to the problem of poverty and human exploitation. He was not deceived by his own earnestly proffered Socialist remedies. Then, too, he was held back from indulging in simplistic propaganda by his artistic conscience. Hence he brings in the comic note and the ironic touch to balance his Socialist evangel. Though he had, in the course of a long productive lifetime, dealt in various ways with the major issues of his age – marriage, prostitution, war, poverty, religion, vivisection, love – he nevertheless insisted that he did not thereby sacrifice his function as an artist. Though on a superficial reading the dominant impression his plays leave is that of preachment, the estimate of Shaw as a crusading Socialist will have to be revised, as Edmund Wilson contends, so as to recognize the importance of his contribution as an artist.[1] His ideas are, after all, not the essential mark of his achievement. It is the cunning power of his art, not his defense of "the new" social morality, that has made him a living force in the theater.

Though Shaw never seriously contemplated creating "art for art's sake" (whatever that much abused phrase means), he nevertheless considered himself an artist. He tried to combine the functions of poet and moralist, to achieve a synthesis of beauty and dynamic social purpose. When his reformist impulse clashed with his aesthetic vision, he invariably allowed the former to triumph. Dudebat, for all of his genuine endowment of talent as a painter, is shown in *The Doctor's Dilemma* to be a scoundrel, and Shaw has no hesitation in sacrificing him for the sake of the mediocre but conscientious servant of society, Doctor Blenkinsop. In Shaw's book of values, the welfare of society took precedence over the claims of art.

As for the jester's cap and bells Shaw put on, that was but a superficial disguise which could not hide the face of the angry and embattled social prophet. He adopted satire as the most suitable method for his attack on the vested interests of his day for two reasons: one, it suited his taste and temperament, and second and more important, it assured him of a wide hearing he might not have gained in the theater if he had turned to more direct forms of denunciation. Whereas forthright exhortation would only serve to arouse psychic resistance, if not resentment, on the part of his audience,

[1] Edmund Wilson, *The Triple Thinkers*. New York: Oxford University Press, 1948, pp. 165-196.

people would gladly pay for the privilege of being entertained. Laughter, he discovered, could be used as a potent weapon to break down their defenses. Beneath his irrepressible outbursts of humor and wit and the diverting display he put on of high jinks burned the authentic fire of social passion, the zeal of a reformer who was both mystic and artist. In practically every one of his plays, the spirit of reform plays a supporting or central role. Looking upon himself as the inspired evangelist of the stage, he attempted to do for his contemporaries what Bunyan sought to do for his sinful readers – wean them away from the pit of damnation, lead them to a critical state of repentance, and finally guide them to the Delectable Mountain, the Heavenly City of Socialism. The only difference between the two men – and Shaw admired Bunyan extravagantly, quoting him frequently – is in their approach to literature: one using the frontal assault of religious allegory, the other exploiting expertly the more subtle and deadly resources of comedy.

It is Ibsen rather than Bunyan who showed him the way to accomplish his ends. Ibsen taught him not to be swayed by majority opinion or the ideological truth enshrined by tradition. Ibsen, together with Karl Marx, familiarized him with the major issues that were convulsing the intellectual life of Europe: the woman question, the dangers of abstract idealism, the need for a revolution in the drama to be engineered by the realistic treatment of social problems, the fraudulence and corruption of politics, the life-negating lies sanctioned by society. Shaw's loyalty to the memory of Ibsen never wavered. Whatever doubts and qualifications he might have about Nietzsche, the mention of Ibsen's name always called forth from him a burst of adoring praise. Had Ibsen's message been heeded, he declared in his preface to the third edition of *The Quintessence of Ibsenism* (1922), the wanton slaughter of the First World War, a conflict fought ostensibly in the name of high ideals, might have been averted. It is these very high-minded ideals that were converted into engines of wholesale destruction.

What matters in Ibsen, Shaw insists, is not simply his greatness as a dramatist but the challenging and redemptive force of his message. A fearless social critic, he attacked the hydra-headed evils of his time. Though Ibsen is now acclaimed on all sides as a genius, his original ideas have not been comprehended and have made no breach in the fortress of institutional conservatism. (Here Shaw seems to be acknowledging the limited efficacy – in Ibsen's case at least – of literary ideas on the course of social evolution.) The political journalists, in particular, have been obtuse in their mad-hatter defense of outmoded ideals.

The credit of our domestic ideals having been shaken to their foundations, as through a couple of earthquake shocks, by Ibsen and Strindberg (the Arch Individualist of the nineteenth century) whilst the Socialists have been idealizing, sentimentalizing, denouncing Capitalists for sacrificing Love and Home and Domestic Happiness and Children and Duty to money greed and ambition, yet it remains a commonplace of political journalism that Socialism is the deadliest enemy of domestic ideals and Unsocialism their only hope and refuge.[2]

But if Shaw vigorously administered a verbal drubbing to others for the illogic of their position, he was himself a curious study in contradictions. He was a Socialist who believed staunchly in the virtue of individualism. Though individualism is also Ibsen's gospel, Shaw argued that it must not be confused with narrow egotism. For Ibsen, as Shaw is careful to point out, "the way to Communism lies through the most resolute and uncompromising individualism." [3] As a pioneer in the realm of ideas, Shaw departed from the model set by his master. He realized that in order to gain the attention of his contemporaries, he must disguise his iconoclastic proposals as born of the comic spirit. However, in all the varied roles he played so well, Fabian Socialist, novelist, musical and dramatic critic, playwright, journalist, amateur philosopher and lay preacher, he remained a mordant critic of society.

In writing to his future biographer, Archibald Henderson, Shaw declared that his plays assumed the character they did because of his conversion to the economic doctrines of Karl Marx. His early plays, *Widowers' Houses* and *Mrs. Warren's Profession*, he asserted, could only have been written by "a Socialist economist." [4] What Shaw, unlike Brecht, rejected in Marxism was its doctrine of inevitableness, its surrender to a philosophy of absolute determinism. Though he agreed that the present conflicts in society were rending it in half, he had no faith in the potentialities of the proletariat who would struggle in militant unity for the seizure of power. Such a mystique is guilty of romanticizing the character of the proletariat. He was at one with the Fabians in denying the cataclysmic nature of social change. He saw no sense in the expectation that revolutions could be consummated over night.

Shaw was given the opportunity to disseminate his Socialist ideas on the stage. The Independent Theater, which had brought out *Ghosts*, accepted *Widowers' Houses*, a vigorous exposé of the exploitation of the slums for profits. *Mrs. Warren's Profession* elaborates the shocking theme that prostitution is the inevitable offshoot of capitalist society. And *Major Barbara*,

[2] Bernard Shaw, *The Quintessence of Ibsenism.* The Ayot St. Lawrence Edition of *The Collected Works of Bernard Shaw.* Vol. IX (New York: William H. Wise and Company, 1930), p. 10.

[3] *Ibid.*, p. 109.

[4] Archibald Henderson, *Bernard Shaw, Playboy and Prophet.* New York: Appleton & Co., 1932, p. 7.

a problem play, boldly examines the root-causes of the evil of poverty, vehemently refuting the idea that it can be abolished by an appeal to men's spirituality. In these three plays and indeed in most of his dramatic work, Shaw strives to be a reformer as well as artist, impelled by a profound moral passion to enlist as far as he could his creative gifts in the cause of social justice. Anyone who failed to leave the earth better than when he found it – such was his unfaltering faith – was a loss to society. Life had a purpose, and Shaw the optimist never tired of holding up a shining vision of what individual and collective life at its best might become. Though he witnessed two world wars, revolutions, the temporary triumph of Fascism, he did not, like H. G. Wells, come to feel that the mind was at the end of its tether. His belief in progress and in the limitless potentialities of the human spirit never wavered. To what degree his creative contribution helped to bring about the progress he desiderated as an ideal must remain a matter of conjecture. His first play, however, set the tone of social criticism that was to characterize his work for the rest of his enormously productive career.

2. Three Plays

It is easy to ask a woman to be virtuous; but it is not reasonable if the penalty of virtue be starvation, and the reward of vice immediate relief. If you offer a pretty girl twopence half-penny an hour in a match factory, with a chance of contracting necrosis of the jawbone from phosphorus poisoning on the one hand, and on the other a jolly and pampered time under the protection of a wealthy bachelor, which was what the Victorian employers did and what employers still do all over the world when they are not stopped by resolutely socialistic laws, you are loading the dice in favor of the devil so monstrously as not only to make it certain that he will win, but raising the question whether the girl does not owe it to her own self-respect and desire for wider knowledge and experience, more cultivated society, and greater grace and elegance of life, to sell herself to a gentleman for pleasure rather than to an employer for profit.[5]

In *Widowers' Houses*, a fine example of a play that is outspokenly critical of society, Shaw lashes out at those who batten on the rents extracted from the poor dwelling in ugly, unsanitary, and malodorous slums. What had originally started out as a romantic play in collaboration with William Archer, Shaw transformed into a realistic satire exposing the evil of slum landlordism. The play created an immediate sensation. The English theater had found a new voice. Though *Widowers' Houses* was enthusiastically supported by the Socialists, the regular theatergoers damned it as an outrageous af-

[5] Bernard Shaw, *The Intelligent Woman's Guide to Socialism and Capitalism.* New York: Brentano's, 1928, p. 199.

front. The newspapers raged with the storm of controversy. The battle for social realism on the stage was begun in earnest.

The cure for the existence of slums is not to be found, Shaw argues, in preaching moral sermons nor is the fault to be attributed to a single individual. Not even those who accumulate wealth in this shameless fashion are to blame. If they were moved by moral scruples not to engage in this sordid business, others would quickly take over this lucrative source of income. If, on the other hand, they attempted to salve their conscience by improving the property and then raising the rent, the poor would simply be thrown out on the street. No, spiritual panaceas are of no avail. The solution must be achieved by a radical reconstruction of society. Shaw hits out right and left, sparing none of the susceptibilities of his audience. Everyone, he charges, who lives off an unearned income is implicated in this collective guilt.

Shaw was immensely delighted by the reaction his first play provoked; he had done what he set out to do. In *Widowers' Houses* he has shown "middle class respectability and younger son gentility fattening on the poverty of the slums as flies fatten on filth." [6] *Mrs. Warren's Profession* deals with an ancient, if not entirely honorable, profession, monopolized by females but patronized by males. The attack, again, is directed not against individuals. Shaw maintains that the sin of bodily prostitution is venial compared to the daily prostitution of mind and spirit committed by journalists, lawyers, teachers, and politicians. It is not the prostitutes who are responsible for the persistent growth of this institution but the fundamental defects of society. "Society," Shaw cries out, "and not any individual, is the villain of the piece...".[7] Shaw, in short, is condemning not the rampant evil of prostitution but the wicked organization of society which makes prostitution not only possible but profitable. Basically it is the cruel pressure of poverty which drives young girls into prostitution. Faced with a choice between economic slavery and polyandry, they are scarcely to be blamed if they choose the latter, the more attractive, if conventionally immoral, alternative.

The scene in the second act in which Vivie confronts her mother, Mrs. Warren, and threatens to leave the next morning for good unless she learns the secret of her mother's past, is one of the high moments in the play and one which conveys the burden of the central theme. Vivie naively insists that though economic conditions may be hard, the individual still has a choice between one means of livelihood and another. It is then Mrs. Warren proceeds to tell her the grim truth about the price a miserably poor girl has to

[6] Bernard Shaw, *Plays: Pleasant and Unpleasant*. New York: Dodd, Mead & Company, 1905, II, p. xxvi.

[7] Bernard Shaw, *Nine Plays*. New York: Dodd, Mead & Company, 1947, p. 31.

pay for remaining respectable. The mother had found herself trapped in poverty. First as scullery maid and then as waitress in the bar at Waterloo station she toiled like a slave for a bare pittance. It was Liz, her sister, who revealed to her the type of profession open to a smart, attractive young woman. That is how she went into "business" and prospered. What, she asks her daughter, was wrong with her decision? Then, as in *The Intelligent Woman's Guide to Socialism and Capitalism*, using Mrs. Warren as his mouthpiece, Shaw spells out the economic lesson:

The house in Brussels was real high class – a much better place for a woman to be in than the factory where Anne Jane got poisoned. None of our girls were ever treated as I was treated in the scullery, or at the Waterloo bar, or at home.[8]

She chose this particular business because it was the only one in which a woman could save money. Mrs. Warren considers herself to be completely justified in having done what she did. Prostitution is a career like any other; it involves work. Whether or not it is morally wrong, the condition exists and must be realistically faced. As the result of her investment in this profession, Mrs. Warren was able to give her daughter the benefits of a decent education and bring her up as a lady.

Vivie is thoroughly disillusioned when she learns that not only her mother but a large part of so-called respectable society lives off the profits derived from this traffic in female flesh. She has caught hold of the unpalatable but liberating truth that everyone is responsible for her mother's degradation, a condition which is imposed on economically underprivileged women the world over. She sees now that she has no reason for condemning her mother. Had she been caught in the same iron net of economic circumstances, she would have been forced to act in the same way. "I know very well that fashionable morality is all a pretence . . .".[9]

Shaw does not paint a picture all in black and white. A writer with an intuitive sense of dramatic values as well as a fervent Socialist reformer, he stood ready, when it came to a pinch, to sacrifice the overt preachment of doctrine to the complex requirements of character portrayal, but he never tampered with the truth of the message of social redemption he was proclaiming to a benighted world. He fought energetically in behalf of social realism, but he sought to communicate his "message" convincingly within the framework of drama, relying chiefly on his prefaces, when the play was published,

[8] *Ibid.*, p. 67.
[9] *Ibid.*, p. 102.

as a sounding board for his "revolutionary" ideas.[10] If he warred against idealists (though he was himself one in opposition to current false ideals), it was because they espoused a fictitious morality that condoned starvation, economic injustice, disease, war, selfishness, and crime.

I see plenty of good in the world working itself out as fast as the idealists will allow it; and if they would only let it alone and learn to respect reality . . . we should all get along much better and faster. At all events, I do not see moral chaos and anarchy as the alternative to romantic convention; and I am not going to pretend I do merely to please the people who are convinced that the world is held together only by the force of unanimous, strenuous, eloquent, trumpet-tongued lying. To me the tragedy and comedy of life lie in the consequences, sometimes terrible, sometimes ludicrous, of our persistent attempts to found our institutions on the ideas suggested to our imaginations by our half-satisfied passions, instead of on a genuinely scientific natural history.[11]

In retrospect, it is difficult to say what effect Shaw's plays had in bringing about needed social reforms in his day, but they certainly served, by the controversies they sparked, as agents of social and moral enlightenment.

Major Barbara is a puzzling problem play. In "The Problem Play – A Symposium," Shaw deals frankly with the question whether the drama should concern itself with the embattled social issues of the time. Does art categorically forbid the writer for the stage from handling such controversial problems as the conflict between social institutions and human beings? These conflicts inevitably arise and therefore afford a rich quarry for the dramatist sensitive to the temper of his age. Shaw recognizes, however, that the drama may take up conflicts which are not social in origin but constitute an inescapable part of human destiny. As Shaw says: ". . . age, like love, death, accident, and personal character, lies outside all institutions . . .".[12] Dramas that embody such themes achieve a universality that reaches beyond the accidents of time and place. That is why such dramas outlive their period. "Whereas a drama with a social question for the motive cannot outlive the solution of that question." [13] Once the wrongs perpetrated by an existing institution have been permanently righted or the institution responsible for these abuses has been abolished, the plays that grappled with such matters are rendered obsolete.

---

[10] "The full-dress Shavian preface, written after the play is produced, is not an introduction but a series of after-thoughts on the play or – more often – a treatise on the subject out of which the play arose." Eric Bentley, *Bernard Shaw*. New York: New Directions, 1947, p. 215.

[11] Bernard Shaw, *Nine Plays,* p. 121.

[12] Robert W. Corrigan (ed.), *The Modern Theatre.* New York: The Macmillan Company, 1964, pp. 972-973.

[13] *Ibid.,* p. 973.

And it is true, Shaw concedes, that the greatest dramatists are drawn to non-political motifs, whereas the average dramatist steers clear of topical problems because of his ignorance in the field of politics and economics. But the amazing growth of the population in the latter half of the nineteenth and the beginning of the twentieth century witnessed the increasing impact of social questions on the creative imagination. "When we succeed in adjusting our social structure in such a way as to enable us to solve social questions as fast as they become really pressing, they will no longer force their way into the theatre." [14] So long, however, as poverty and unemployment and starvation exist, it is the imperative duty of the dramatist to speak out, since no one else is doing anything to remedy the situation. Thus Shaw, opting for social realism, stresses the timely value of the problem play.

In *Major Barbara*, he sums up for us the gospel of Andrew Undershaft, the millionaire who personifies the redeeming truth "that the greatest of our evils, and the worst of our crimes is poverty, and that our first duty, to which every other consideration should be sacrificed, is not to be poor." [15] Shaw deliberately made him the hero who grasped the saving knowledge that it is a crime to be poor. Undershaft is cast in the role of a redeemer, a liberating force, a mystic whose religion hails money as the highest virtue. In his preface to *Major Barbara*, Shaw informs his readers exactly what he had in mind when he built up the character of the dynamic, domineering Undershaft, the Machiavelli of the play, the spokesman of uncomfortable home truths.

A kind of contest takes place between Barbara's Salvation Army Christianity and her father's morality, which depends on the manufacture of armaments. Undershaft is, paradoxically, presented as a "religious" or Dionysian figure, an instrument in the service of the Life Force. The Salvation Army, he argues, is thoroughly justified in taking his money as a contribution, for all money, regardless of its source, is tainted. No one can hope to escape complicity in the collective guilt through an evangel of personal righteousness. It is the anarchy of the competitive economic system that is the cause of widespread social misery. [16]

If Shaw diligently preached the gospel of Socialism, it was because he believed that the principles of Socialism applied to all of life – love, marriage, prostitution, poverty, war, politics, even religion and art. He held that God

[14] *Ibid.*, p. 974.

[15] Bernard Shaw, *Collected* Plays. New York: Dodd, Mead & Company, 1963, I, 305.

[16] For a close analysis of the social implications of the play, see Louis Crompton, "*Major Barbara*: Shaw's Challenge to Liberalism," in *Literature and Society*. Edited by Bernice Slote. Lincoln: University of Nebraska Press, 1964, pp. 121-141.

dwells in man and that each life represents an experiment in reaching out to achieve other than selfish ends. Though he skilfully adapted the drama to his socio-economic creed, he never wrote "Socialist" – that is, narrowly doctrinaire or didactic – plays. In his best work he remains the incorruptible artist, the poet triumphing over the preacher, though without ever abandoning his devotion to the cause of social reform. Shaw wrote many plays which shocked, delighted, and edified the audience of his day, but it is doubtful if they had any appreciable influence in improving socioeconomic conditions in England. This does not mean that his work was without its measure of "usefulness." It pointed to conditions of chronic illness in the body politic; it identified the symptoms and named the malady and directly or by implication drew an image of social life that was healthy and whole. It did more: it helped to create a climate of opinion which was favorable to social change.

If literature fails to achieve much as a reformist or revolutionary force, it is because it serves a different and perhaps higher function. By opening wide the gates of vision, by questioning and thereby transforming the nature of reality, it actually revolutionizes the consciousness of man. By exposing the character of suffering which all men must endure it creates a bond of sympathy and makes the reader or spectator aware of the indisseverable ties of solidarity that unite him to his kind. By deepening his sensibility and enlarging his imaginative horizon, it makes him more receptive to human projects for curing those evils and afflictions which are remediable. In these subtle and devious ways it acts upon those who open their mind and heart to its influence.

CHAPTER VII

THE SOCIAL CONSCIENCE OF THE THIRTIES

1. The Decade of Causes and Ideologies

If Shaw's problem plays and dialectical drama of ideas have thus far survived the test of time, it is because, as we noted in the previous chapter, he is preeminently the artist: a special kind of artist, it is true, one who sought to reform society by writing witty, high-spirited satire. He is a trenchant realist who, without ever abandoning his role as social prophet, composed sparkling comedies that underscored the relativity of moral values. If his plays are largely talking plays he deliberately set out to make them so, but then Shavian dialogue is unlike any other talk that had been heard on the stage in his time; intensely dynamic, it exploits all the available resources of irony, paradox, and epigrammatic wit to achieve its intended effect. It is evident, however, that Shaw, despite the urgency, as he conceived it, of the task he imposed on himself, did not expect that his plays alone, when produced and then published, would be instrumental in initiating immediate reforms or eventually bring about the realization of the devoutly wished-for social ideal. The writer with a social message designed to combat and perhaps eradicate the social evils of his age generally knows what he is doing; though he is surely aware of the limitations of the medium he is using, his aim is to enlighten and thus convert the mind of his public. That is the least he can hope to accomplish through the ministry of his art, and it is a great deal. Like his predecessors from the time of the Greeks, he strives to effect a revolution in consciousness, a change of heart as well as mind. (Who can predict the explosive impact of a book – the New Testament, the *Pensées*, *Walden*, the essays of Emerson – on the mind of a man prepared to receive its message?) The "committed" playwright, however, attempts to go further than this. Like Brecht, he believes that by providing critical insight into the basic causes of the multiple ills that afflict society, he can lead men and women to perceive that the power to change the world rests entirely in their hands, and to act on that rationally arrived-at understanding. A new idea that once takes root is charged with an incalculable potential. Thus a new thought, a new vision, communicated from the stage represents a blow struck in the cause of social justice.

Serious difficulties arise, however, when the writer makes the effort to use art as a species of magic, particularly as a weapon in prosecuting the class war. He cannot, for all his earnest endeavors, overcome the ingrained resistance of the medium he works in. Art abhors the strategy of propaganda, which belongs of right in an entirely different world of discourse. Ideology imposes a procrustean framework that limits the horizon of vision. The writer, when he is not hemmed in by a restrictive social or political philosophy, is able to include within his work many elements that may be in diametrical opposition to his underlying theme or conscious intention. In short, literature at its best transcends any formal profession of a creed or doctrine, and that holds true of writers as diverse as Cervantes, Balzac, Flaubert, Dostoevski, Gide, and Proust.

Even in its imaginative embodiment, however, the literary work reflects the strains and stresses of the contemporary social order: what forces are locked in battle, what symbols of acceptance or rejection are utilized.[1] But the implicit relationship between the socioeconomic structure and the work of art is highly complex; the play or novel that handles a social theme is not a direct reflection of conditions as they exist.[2] Moreover, the writer, though he is necessarily a part of his culture, can stand apart from it and even be in opposition to it when it fails to nourish the self in its quest for identity and to develop what he considers the ideal of community. In any event, he is no mere echo of abstract, anonymous social forces. The spokesman of an aesthetic that is critical of society may, and frequently does, use his creative gifts to affirm the need for sustaining the integrity of the individual as opposed to a culture that crushes the self in the name of conformity.

For another test case of dramatists essaying the role of social critic we turn to the American literary scene during the embattled thirties. That de-

[1] See "Literature as Equipment for Living," in Kenneth Burke, *The Philosophy of Literary Form*. New York: Vintage Books, 1957, pp. 253-62.

[2] Diana Spearman, in examining the complex relationship of literature to society in the eighteenth century, questions the truth of the assumption that a writer voices the spirit of his age. Certainly the version of eighteenth-century life that Defoe, Richardson, and Fielding provide is not actually a good "reflection." Genius introduces a disturbing variable. This affects the theory of social causation as applied to the creative process. If we concentrate on the literary work itself and not on its background, we can see how the element of the unpredictable that is the sign of genius enters in. "The greater the work the more it seems to belong to the writer and less to the society in which it was written." Diana Spearman, *The Novel and Society*. New York: Basic Books, Inc., 1966, p. 240.

cade is of compelling interest for our purpose because it demonstrates so vividly the confused process of transition, confused in its very intensity of ideological passion, from an aesthetic that sharply criticized the inhumanity of capitalism to an aesthetic of commitment. Capitalism stood condemned because of its failure to provide work; the millions of unemployed in the nation bore eloquent witness against it. Added to this grievance was the growing menace of Fascism, the rise of Hitler to power in Germany, the outbreak of civil war in Spain. The Communists, hoping to enlist the services of writers and intellectuals in the battle against the forces of reaction, organized the United Front. A number of fellow travelers, as they were then called, joined in the common struggle against barbarism. Republican Spain in danger became the symbol of all that the liberals believed in at the time. Many felt it was their moral duty to commit themselves to the cause of democracy; "most writers and artists seemed to turn to the Spanish Civil War ... as a way of saving the world and, with the world, themselves." [3] The temper of the times generated and kept alive the faith that literature could be used as a weapon against the advance of Fascism.

It is not surprising that Shaw attracted some creative followers in the United States during this troubled period, but those on the extreme left felt that he did not go far enough and turned to other masters for guidance. Inspired by the innovations introduced abroad by Erwin Piscator and Bertolt Brecht, they wished to use the theater for purposes of agitation and propaganda – technically called agit-prop – so as to awaken the social consciousness of the members of the audience and win them over to the revolutionary cause. The idea gained ground that the arts could be effectively utilized to help usher in the reign of Communism. Hence the emergence of proletarian drama, proletarian fiction, and proletarian poetry, none of it satisfactorily defined or embodied as a genre, in which the one constant factor was that the economic motif, in the guise of the class war, loomed so large as to dominate the landscape of vision.

Despite the strenuous organizational efforts of its adherents, Communism failed in the thirties to gain control of the American theater. This was their basic, if not always avowed, aim: to capture the stage and use it as a medium of intensive propaganda for the triumph of the social revolution. In this they were supported by a group of liberals who believed that the theater could be legitimately required to do its share in the fight for social justice. Though the Communists failed in their attempt, the debate they provoked brought sharply into focus a number of important controversial issues: the function

[3] Allen Guttmann, *The Wound in the Heart*. New York: The Free Press of Glencoe, 1962, p. 126.

of propaganda in the drama, the role of politics in relation to art, the strategy of commitment and how it was to be given embodiment in dramatic terms. The committed writers on the left played their role of social responsibility with prophetic earnestness. The ivory tower was demolished once and for all. No one was henceforth to consider himself exempt from the class struggle. As John Gassner says: "Engagement to a cause became a guilt-enforced virtue that was to lead to some kind of activism as signing a petition or a protest, marching in a parade, and writing a story, poem, or play of so-called social consciousness." [4] Thus the thirties, a contentious decade, witnessed the transition from the drama of social criticism to one of radical commitment.

There is still a distinction to be drawn, however thin the line, between plays of social criticism and those written by the politically committed playwrights of the left. Though both categories overlap, since the Marxist dramatist is also a critic of capitalist society, there is a marked difference in practice between the militant propagandistic plays by John Howard Lawson and the work of a liberal playwright like Elmer Rice. It is fairly easy, looking back over the past with a critical eye, to see the nature of the mistakes the "committed" writer made: his excessive ideological zeal, the dogmatic intemperateness with which he lent himself to the revolutionary cause, the fury of fanaticism that infected his work and charged it with a melodramatic message it was ill adapted to carry. In bidding farewell to the thirties, Harold Clurman in *The Fervent Years* recalls with a mixture of nostalgic affection and compassion the spirit that characterized that turbulent decade. These playwrights of the left, whatever their outstanding faults, were not, he insists, politically enlightened. He furnishes a charitable assessment of their contribution.

The truth is that none of them had anything but the most rudimentary, naive understanding of politics: they were all essentially apolitical no matter what they may have once argued, or clamored about – no matter what cards, documents, statements they may have signed. They were *yearners* seeking a home – a home in the theatre, a home in the world of thought and action, something that would call forth their most selfless efforts in behalf of some concrete cause.[5]

The fact remains that whatever the motivation that impelled these "yearners" to write, the drama of social criticism they produced during the thirties treated capitalism as the enemy to be defeated. But first let us take up the career of Elmer Rice.

[4] Morgan Y. Himelstein, *Drama Was a Weapon*. New Brunswick, N. J.: Rutgers University Press, 1963, p. xi.
[5] Harold Clurman, *The Fervent Years*. New York: Hill and Wang, 1957, p. 286.

2. Elmer Rice: Critic of Society

Of the writers who helped shape Elmer Rice's thinking during the formative and rebellious years of his youth, the most influential was Bernard Shaw. The reading of Shaw's books not only deeply affected his way of thinking but altered the direction of his life. He became a convert to Socialism. "There was opened to me a whole new world and a whole new orientation in politics, in religion, in education, science, art and sex. . . ." [6] Interestingly enough, it was through the study of literature rather than economics that he came to perceive the evils of capitalism. Not Marx, Engels, Lenin but Ibsen, Shaw, Hauptmann, Gorky, Galsworthy, Zola, and Upton Sinclair were his teachers. Though he believed in Socialism, he never became a member of the Socialist Party nor a simon-pure Marxist. He exhibited the characteristic virtues of the liberal, the tolerance of different points of view, the open mind, the habit of suspended judgment, but also the feeling of sympathy for the underdog. He preferred to call himself a utopian Socialist. As he declares in his auto-biography: "The concept of a human community based upon principles of truth and justice interested me more than the establishment of any rigid system." [7] His consistent espousal of liberalism or utopian Socialism explains why he never became a Marxist spokesman. Unlike the Marxist brethren, he distrusted government control and balked at obeying political directives. Though he joined the radical playwrights in attacking the dehumanizing system of capitalist exploitation, he refused to become the mouthpiece of leftist ideology or to recommend a revolutionary solution.

The Adding Machine (1923) is an Expressionist play that depicts the hopeless case of a soul enslaved by a mechanized society. In it Rice voices his horror and indignation at a civilization that is capable of producing such an abject and degraded creature as Mr. Zero. From this the next logical step for him to take was to cry out against the evils of capitalism. *We, the People* (1933), which pictures the chaotic condition of American society during the depression, is intended to serve a social purpose; it dwells on the heartlessness of big business, the curse of mass unemployment, the indifference of capitalism to the legitimate grievances of the unemployed workers; but the play, far from preaching revolutionary Marxism, invokes the traditional American ideal of freedom and justice. *We, the People*, which consist of twenty scenes and introduces fifty-six characters in the course of the action, is Rice's most ambitious play of social criticism.

It manages to capture the hectic spirit, both despairing and desperate, of

---

[6] Elmer Rice, *Minority Report*. New York: Simon and Schuster, 1963, p. 86.
[7] *Ibid.,* p. 138.

the time. It exposes for our contemplation the worst malignancies of American capitalism: the displacement of skilled workers by the machine, the repression of labor by the bosses, the use of armed force against workers and ex-soldiers who petition for jobs and bread, the clamping down on the freedom of thought and expression of students and liberal-minded professors, the closing down of banks thus forcing many families to lose their homes and the savings of a lifetime, the insidious and unconscionable corruption of politics, the use of the courts and the police to keep the poor and the underprivileged resigned to their fate. Unfortunately Elmer Rice is so carried away by a sense of outrage that he paints everything in black and white. There is no redeeming color of hope in his composition, not even a touch of gray. He focuses attention obsessively on the terrible conditions that exist: the joblessness, people without homes or enough to eat, the frustrations of the young who are in love but cannot afford to get married, the close connection between war and the profits of industry, the ineffectuality of religion to provide an adequate solution to the economic problem. In scene after scene Rice harps on the difference between the rich, who can enjoy cruises in their yachts and purchase costly paintings abroad, and the poor, who can barely manage to survive.

Allen, the son of the Davis family, is intellectually gifted but has to leave college because of the financial reverses his father suffered. It is he who questions the justice of the established order: "Is it common sense to let people starve?" [8] In the meantime, the powers that be are urging preparedness for the war that is bound to come and insisting that the government put a stop to agitators who are sowing the seeds of discontent. At a mass meeting held to protest a flagrant miscarriage of justice, of which Allen is the victim (he is convicted on perjured testimony of having killed a policeman and is sentenced to die), Rice sounds his message of denunciation. Helen, Allen's sister, wonders why things are as they are. What was her brother's crime? Why is he being punished? "Because he is not willing to submit to being poor. That is the crime. In America, you must not cry out." [9] And the professor at the University, a descendant of the Mayflower, reminds his listeners (the stage is so arranged that the spectators are supposed to constitute his audience at the mass meeting) of the promise of democracy, the principles on which the Declaration of Independence and the Constitution are based. He protests vehemently against the deeds of those in power that violate the American ideal. All that these workers and Allen Davis ask for is the right to live.

[8] Elmer Rice, We, the People. New York: Coward-MacCann, Inc., 1933, p. 152.
[9] Ibid., p. 249.

And no social system that denies them that right has a claim to a continuance of its existence. . . . We are the people, ladies and gentlemen, we – you and I and everyone of us. It is our house: this America. Let us cleanse it and put it in order and make it a decent place for decent people to live in! [10]

The contents and the tone of *We, the People* make this a dated play. Though it makes its appeal at the end in the name of the American Dream, it depends on an overt didactic device to achieve its intended effect of swaying the mind of the audience. To be sure, Elmer Rice did not employ his art as a weapon nor would he allow any political party to dictate the content of his work. As he says, "wherever art is subject to political control it is stunted and distorted. . . ." [11] But in *We, the People* the spirit of righteous indignation led him astray and caused him to write a topical, tendentious drama that now possesses only historical or sociological interest. It was a financial failure on Broadway. No one goes to the theater to be politically edified. Literature that is utilitarian in design, i.e., that is propagandistic or narrowly didactic, defeats its own ends. But the truly committed dramatist is not halted by such considerations; for him the aim of consummating the revolutionary ideal transcends in importance the purely aesthetic factor. For John Howard Lawson, drama was decidedly a weapon to be wielded with quasi-religious fervor.

3. John Howard Lawson and the Marxist Commitment

In the work of John Howard Lawson, a militant left-wing dramatist, radicalism wars against his artistic conscience. His early experimental plays, written before he became a convert to Communism, showed authentic promise, gifts of a high order, but after his conversion he dutifully devoted his talent to the preachment of Marxist ideology. In an article, " 'Inner Conflict' and Proletarian Art," replying to a hard-hitting attack by Michael Gold calling him a bourgeois Hamlet, John Howard Lawson humbly admits that Gold is right in seventy percent of his strictures. He declares that Marxist criticism is "the only criticism with which I am in the least concerned." [12] In answer to Gold's challenging question, "Where do I belong in the warring world of two classes?," he announces his intention of taking his stand "with as much clarity and vigor as I possess." [13]

His career illustrates perfectly the harmful consequences of following too

[10] *Ibid.,* p. 253.
[11] Elmer Rice, *The Living Theatre.* New York: Harper & Brothers, 1959, p. 54.
[12] *New Masses,* April 17, 1934, p. 30.
[13] *Ibid.*

literally an ethic of commitment. Now that he belonged to a sacred cause, now that he was wholly on the side of the workers, he labored diligently to make his contribution to the emerging revolutionary theater in America. He wrote *Marching Song* (1937), a play that is "orthodox" in its deployment of Communist ideology as it unfolds the theme of class warfare. As in *We, the People*, only more so, the characters are depicted in black and white contrasts. The proletarians are the personification of virtue whereas those who oppose and oppress them are assigned the role of villains.

A year before this play appeared, Lawson had published *Theory and Technique of Playwriting* (1936), which endeavors to formulate the ideological justification for proletarian drama. Though art is emotional in its appeal, Lawson argues, it is thoroughly social in content. The dialectical philosophy which governs the revolutionary playwright in his work is predicated on the assumption that change is fundamental both in nature and society and that the rate of change can be not only charted but even controlled. Lawson affirms his belief that problems of aesthetics can be solved by the application of dialectical materialism. Socialist realism, as distinguished from subjectivism or naturalism, is the method which traces the way events are causally related in reality, the connection between conscious will and social necessity. The drama of "escapism," he declares, is growing increasingly impossible. He frankly points out, however, the salient defect of many leftwing plays: namely, that they use ideas as a substitute for dramatically effective action. Then, too, many plays of this type suffer from the tendency to schematic contrasts of good and bad, virtue and vice. But the most pernicious and widespread fault of proletarian drama is "the substitution of a sentimental appeal for sympathy for the logical development of the action." [14] Alas, Lawson is himself guilty of indulging in this kind of appeal in *Marching Song*.

Marching Song represents a brave attempt to produce a proletarian play based on strictly Marxist principles. There is no question now as to where Lawson belongs in the warring world of two classes. The woes caused by the depression – joblessness, hunger, eviction, vigilant ruthlessness practiced against those workers who dare to organize a strike – are exaggerated to the point of melodramatic pathos. The forces of law and order are shown to be venal, mercenary, corrupt, vicious. The union leaders, on the other hand, the suffering workers and their wives and sweethearts, are portrayed as self-sacrificing martyrs in a cause which, if they succeed in closing ranks,

---

[14] John Howard Lawson. *Theory and Technique of Playwriting*. New York: G. P. Putnam's Sons, 1936, p. 285.

they are bound to win. Thus the battle lines are arrayed: capitalist greed and unconscionable cunning pitted against the United Front.

The lesson of the class war is relentlessly driven home. On this issue there can be no compromise. A man without work is not a man but an economic cripple, a victim of the class war. Pete Russell, married, the father of a child, is thrown out of his home. Jobless, desperate, he drinks to drown his sorrow. Slowly, however, the light of redemptive truth dawns upon him. Bill Anderson, the leader, plans to hold a meeting to protest the eviction of Pete Russell. The workers must be taught how to fight for their rights. Bill tries to convince Pete and his distraught wife that the only way out of their misery is not by provoking a bloody riot; "it's organizing and telling people and getting a solid union." [15]

The first heartening sign of unity among the workers is the report that those employed in the Brimmer plant are conducting a sitdown strike. What they demand is the reinstatement of the blacklisted workers; the right to belong to a union which must be recognized for purposes of collective bargaining; the reduction of the speed-up; the thirty-hour week; and equal opportunities and equal pay for Negroes. Bill and his men plan to picket the plant to prevent scabs from entering. As they march they sing the inspiriting song of worker unity. Then the women, too, gather their forces for militant action; they must join in the struggle with their men. The authorities and their armed henchmen are on the alert; they torture the fearless Bill Anderson until he dies and they use tear gas against the demonstrators. But the workers in the power plant come providentially to the rescue: they turn off the electricity and plunge the city in darkness. Despair is transformed to euphoric hope as Lucky, a Negro militant, cries out exultantly: "power is people!" [16]

Marching Song is typical of the proletarian plays produced during the thirties. It not only dealt with the pressing social and economic problems of the time but provided a solution: an urgent appeal to the worker to achieve unity or to join the Communist Party in the common, world-wide war against oppression. But the results were thoroughly disappointing. The anticipated conversions were not forthcoming. What did a Marxist melodrama like *Marching Song*, marshalling its ideology of the class war, hope to gain by its propagandistic assault? For if art is to be at all effective as propaganda it must first satisfy the requirements of art. Is a play to be judged in terms of its doctrinal purity, by the number of converts it wins to the cause of Com-

---

[15] John Howard Lawson, *Marching Song*. New York: Dramatists Play Service, Inc., 1937, p. 76.
[16] *Ibid.*, p. 158.

munism? Even *Waiting for Lefty*, by Clifford Odets, the most genuinely talented of the left-wing dramatists, is vitiated by the inclusion in it of doctrinaire elements; the urge to preach and propagandize is barely kept under control.

4. Clifford Odets: the White Hope of the Proletarian Theater

Son of a middle-class Jewish family, Clifford Odets became obsessed at the beginning of the depression with the plight of the poor and the jobless. He joined the Communist Party but left after eight months, unwilling to submit to its demand for ideological conformity. He turned to the drama as a means of presenting his indictment of capitalism. Though he was convinced that all literature, from the highest to the lowest, constituted a form of propaganda, he also felt that the revelation of the truth on the stage is in itself a revolutionary act. What lends vitality to his "social" plays is that he wrote about people he knew intimately and pictured with imaginative sympathy and insight the struggle they had to endure in order to survive. The agitational cries are there, the Marxist slogans, but they do not dominate the body of his work. Seen upon the stage, his plays come vividly to life.

Odets' early plays – *Waiting for Lefty* (1935), *Awake and Sing!* (1935), *Till the Day I Die* (1935), *Paradise Lost* (1935), and *Golden Boy* (1937) – are meant to be "proletarian" in content. In *Waiting for Lefty* he devised new techniques (new in the American theater but they had been used by Erwin Piscator in Germany during the twenties) for mass agitation; he planted actors in the theater and allowed them to enter the action as the plot required, thus creating the illusion that the audience was involved in the stormy debate whether to call a strike. Each episode is a little play in itself. Each scene highlights and reinforces the central political theme. For example, in the fifth scene, dealing with the futile efforts of a young actor to find work, the stenographer in the theatrical producer's office hands him a copy of the *Communist Manifesto*, which will reveal to him, she assures him, a new heaven and a new earth and teach him that the meek shall not inherit the earth. The scene ends with the stenographer's missionary summons: "Come out in the light, Comrade." [17] The problem stressed throughout the play is one of economics.

The audience, it is reported, was deeply moved by *Waiting for Lefty* when it was produced by the Group Theater. Audience and actors that first night were in close communion. According to Harold Clurman, a trustwor-

[17] *Sixteen Famous American Plays*. Edited by Bennet A. Cerf and Van H. Cartmell. New York: The Modern Library, 1941, p. 441.

thy because unbiased witness:

When the audience at the end of the play responded to the militant question from the stage: "Well, what's the answer?" with a spontaneous roar of "Strike! Strike!" it was something more than a tribute to the play's effectiveness, more even than a testimony of the audience's hunger for constructive social action. It was the birth cry of the thirties. Our youth had found its voice. It was a call to join the good fight for a greater measure of life in a world free of economic fear, falsehood, and craven servitude to stupidity and greed. "Strike!" was *Lefty's* lyric message, not alone for a few extra pennies of wages or for shorter hours of work, strike for greater dignity, strike for a bolder humanity, strike for the full stature of man.[18]

The attempt to bridge the gap between the auditorium and the stage, however successful it proved that first night in generating a mood of sympathy for the striking taxicab drivers, could not in succeeding performances induce in the audience the illusion that they were, in effect, strikers. That is not how the drama is meant to function, by satisfying "the audience's hunger for constructive social action."

A more eloquent testament of the thirties was *Awake and Sing!*, which, though impregnated with Marxist ideology, was actually an outcry of bitterness against man-made and remediable evils, the response of an outraged conscience to intolerable social conditions. Here no villain spins the plot. Though his plays are instinct with the feeling of revolt, they sound no simplistic revolutionary message, and that is why he was severely criticized by the Communist press at the time for his ideological deficiencies. His commitment was emotional rather than ideological in nature.

Jacob, the grandfather, is the *raisonneur* of the play. Whenever the discussion touches on social or economic issues, he invariably chimes in by saying that if this life leads to a revolution it is a good life; otherwise it is worth nothing. He urges Ralph, his grandson, to wake up and change the world. "Go out and fight so life shouldn't be printed on dollar bills." [19] He pins all his hope for the future on the boy's strength and courage. He points to himself as an example of failure: a man who had wasted the best years of his life in idle talk and empty theorizing. Jacob exhorts Ralph to profit by his mistakes. "This is why I tell you – DO! Do what is in your heart and you carry in yourself a revolution. But you should act." [20] Though this plea is dramatically effective in the context of the play, the epiphany of conversion – young Ralph's awakening – is not convincingly motivated; it is simply tacked on so as to make it possible for the playwright to proclaim his revolu-

[18] Harold Clurman, *The Fervent Years*, pp. 138-39.
[19] Clifford Odets, *Six Plays*. New York: The Modern Library, 1939, p. 48.
[20] *Ibid.*, p. 78.

tionary moral. Ralph, we are to suppose, has transcended his personal desires and frustrations and will throw in his lot with the working class; he will henceforth participate actively in the struggle to change the world so that life will not be printed on dollar bills. And Ralph's decision is meant to communicate the heart of the message and to convince the audience of the necessity for their joining resolutely in the revolutionary struggle!

5. The Philosophy of Commitment Appraised

In retrospect we can see why the campaign to politicalize the American theater failed so badly to achieve its aim. Since we intend to devote an entire section to the literature of commitment, it is perhaps appropriate at this point, even if we anticipate matters a bit, to examine briefly the various and conflicting meanings of commitment. Usually the rhetoric of commitment means a commitment to a particular political cause or movement, a socioeconomic creed, a cult of action of a given kind. It bespeaks a strong desire on the part of the writer to make his work maximally useful in the service of social reform or revolution, though logically it is possible to conceive of a writer committed to Fascism. (The notorious case of Ezra Pound at once comes to mind.) Art thus becomes, by a process of logical extension, a weapon to be employed in the interest of whatever social ideal – freedom, justice, equality, brotherhood, Communism, Fascism, or National Socialism – the writer happens to believe in. In this way he overcomes his feeling of alienation; his work is now inspired and sustained by a sense of social purpose. The Marxist dramatists had to discredit the damnable folly, so they regarded it, of art for art's sake as well as get rid of the enervating, "reactionary" notion that art is fundamentally a form of play, a species of make-believe, a neurotic indulgence, an escape from the challenge of social reality. They summarily rejected the conception that "Art does not make us better citizens, or more moral, or more honest. It may conceivably make us worse." [21] For the Marxist playwright art was real, art was earnest; it could teach, it could shape attitudes and values, it could help transform the structure of society.

When the writer undertakes to force his art to conform to his credal commitment, he runs into serious trouble. He encounters great difficulty in finding an objective correlative for his political convictions. He cannot import ideology into the structure and texture of his work, whether in the drama or fiction, without falling into a propagandistic strain that is alien and inimical to his creative design. The function of art is not to instigate action; it is not to

[21] Morse Peckham, *Rage for Chaos*. Philadelphia and New York: Chilton Books, 1965, p. 313.

be confused with propaganda; it produces profound and indeed incalculable effects, it is true, but not those desiderated by the ethic of commitment.[22]

Commitment, an omnibus and therefore ambiguous term, can be interpreted in a variety of ways. Obviously every man is committed in different degrees to something or other, a moral code, a political program, a religious faith. The word is so all-inclusive in meaning as to lack specificity of content. During the thirties, commitment was for a number of writers an inspiring battlecry; their work stressed the motif of conversion, the necessary transcendence of the ego and its own, the involvement of the individual in a collective fate, the inescapable impact on all men the world over of the class war. The "proletarian" dramatists were committed to the cause of radicalism. As Gerald Rabkin remarks in his book, *Drama and Commitment*: "The 1930's unquestionably represent the high point of Marxist influence on American drama." [23] But this influence was short-lived. With the exception of the plays of Clifford Odets, the "proletarian" drama made no distinctive contribution to the American theater.

[22] "Art is the exposure to the tensions and problems of a false world so that man may endure exposing himself to the tensions and problems of the real world." *Ibid.,* p. 314.

[23] Gerald Rabkin, *Drama and Commitment*. Bloomington: Indiana University Press, 1963, p. 34.

CHAPTER VIII

THE SOCIAL CRITICISM OF JOHN DOS PASSOS

Almost all American novelists have presented the relationship between the individual and society as a struggle between irreconcilables. . . .[1]

1. The Relationship of the Individual to Society

In our evaluation of the first organized effort in the United States to produce a drama of commitment, we have tried to show that from the point of view of aesthetics commitment is a meaningless term. Historically, however, it played an important, if not particularly fruitful role in the creative life of the thirties. It was a fervent moral gesture on the part of intellectuals to set the disjointed world aright. If they accepted the Marxist diagnosis of the breakdown of capitalist society or went even further and joined the Communist Party, it was because Marxism, by promising a humane and just solution of the economic problem, appealed intensely to their ethical concern. Marxist doctrine sounded the keynote of secular salvation. The confident assumption that justified this evangel of commitment was that Communism would not only give birth to a golden age of freedom and social justice for all mankind but also prove a creative bonanza for the writer who, during the transitional stage of the class struggle, sincerely devoted his gifts to the revolutionary cause. This was the mystique that informed the radical writing of the decade. This was the new religion to be embraced, the substance of the true faith. In fact, the dogma became established in some quarters that a writer who did not share this redemptive faith was bound to write badly. This was the period, too, of the United Front, when democratic elements could be wooed and won for the common fight against Fascism.

It is evident that Communism at the time helped to fill a spiritual vacuum. After passing through the Waste Land of the twenties, with its cynicism,

[1] Michael Millgate, *American Social Fiction*. New York: Barnes & Noble, Inc., 1964, p. 203.

disillusionment, and Bohemian irresponsibility, many writers felt the need to believe in something positive and constructive. The Communist Party seemed to satisfy this need admirably. Writing at the end of the decade, George Orwell incisively analyzes the motives that drew many middle-class intellectuals to Communism.

It was simply something to believe in. Here was a church, an army, an orthodoxy, a discipline. Here was a Fatherland and – at any rate since 1935 or thereabouts – a Führer. All the loyalties and superstitions that the intellect had seemingly banished could come rushing back under the thinnest of disguises. Patriotism, religion, empire, military glory – all in one word, Russia. Father, king, leader, hero, saviour – all in one word, Stalin. God – Stalin. The devil – Hitler. Heaven – Moscow. Hell – Berlin.[2]

The middle-class intellectuals who were attracted to this seductive gospel had no knowledge of what politics, particularly revolutionary politics, meant in practice. When they discovered to their cost what the Stalinist regime was capable of – the shifting ideological line geared to expediency, the pacts concluded with the enemy, the betrayal of the Loyalist cause in Spain – they repudiated their allegiance and the epidemic of defections began. Men like Arthur Koestler, Ignazio Silone, Richard Wright had learned their lesson. The confessions of a number of ex-Communists and ex-fellow travelers included in *The God That Failed* seem to bear out Orwell's contention that on the whole

the literary history of the thirties seems to justify the opinion that the writer does well to keep out of politics. For any writer who accepts or partially accepts the discipline of a political party is sooner or later faced with the alternative: toe the line or shut up.[3]

There were many writers on the American scene who, however sympathetic initially to the aims of Communism, could not be made to toe the party line and refused to be silenced. They were too much an integral part of the American tradition, too profoundly imbued with a belief in the ideal of the "open" society, too closely attached to the spirit of liberty without which they could not function creatively, to remain long subservient to an essentially alien ideology. One of these men was John Dos Passos who at first zealously supported the cause but who later swung to the other extreme and bitterly attacked it. His work illustrates a vital aspect of the problem we are concerned with. It deals challengingly with the complex theme of the relationship of the individual to society.

---

[2] George Orwell, "Inside the Whale," in *New Directions*. Norfolk, Connecticut: New Directions, 1940, pp. 231-32.
[3] *Ibid.,* p. 235.

As society grows in magnitude and becomes more completely unified and interdependent in its functioning, the corporate life, as evidenced by its representative institutions (the government, industry, big business), tends to dwarf the stature of the individual. Modern man has after a long historic struggle achieved a measure of individual freedom, and he cherishes it dearly. At the same time he now realizes he is at the mercy of huge impersonal forces which organize his existence on a collective basis. Hence his freedom is curtailed to a point where he can no longer feel that he is responsible for his destiny. His vision of freedom is eclipsed by an awareness of his helplessness in the face of conformist pressures all around him. He is a functional part of a vast social machine and must obey its mandates, forgoing his own desires in the matter. Historical determinism measures out his fate.

The dominance of the collective aspects of man is inherently assured; and with it the gradual conversion of the individual into a frictionless and depersonalized member of the community. For the individual as such will be absorbed in the shadow of his collective self.[4]

This is also the warning sounded by Jacques Ellul in *The Technological Society* and Herbert Marcuse in *One-Dimensional Man*. Writers like Sherwood Anderson, D. H. Lawrence, Capek, John Steinbeck called attention to the menace of the machine, but there was not the same measure of agreement, at least in America during the thirties, on the controversial issue of collectivism.

The novelist, for reasons dictated by the necessity of achieving a structurally unified whole, is compelled to single out one aspect of communal life and show how the individual is shaped and controlled – usually misshaped and harmfully controlled – by the institutional group of which he is a constituent part. The portrait generally drawn is that of a protagonist who, like Kafka's heroes wandering lost in a bureaucratic maze, is no longer master of his destiny; he must subordinate himself to the demands of the group and prove his usefulness to the occupational unit to which he belongs. Whereas in the past the novelist never included society as a character in his fiction since he was inclined to take not only society but its positive values for granted, in the modern novel, especially the modern American novel, society becomes the dominant, if problematical figure besides which the individual characters are reduced to virtual anonymity and insignificance. The vertiginous speeding-up of the process of change, the impermanence of social relationships, the mobility of the class structure, all this has rendered vastly more difficult the problem of the search for identity. Beginning with Dreiser,

---

[4] Roderick Seidenberg, *Posthistoric Man*. Boston: Beacon Press, 1957, pp. 112-13.

David Graham Phillips and Frank Norris, American writers, particularly during the past three decades, have been conspicuously self-conscious in their handling of the social theme.

Many of them seized upon and magnified the deep-cutting conflict between the American Dream and the harsh realities of American life. They exalted the utopian vision and strenuously advocated the ideal of social perfection. When the vision lay shattered, the reaction was one of angry disillusionment. John Dos Passos and John Steinbeck composed novels of social criticism based on moral grounds. As in *The Grapes of Wrath*, the moral rage and resentment sometimes took the form of allegory designed to reinforce the salvationary message of the novel. Some of the aroused social novelists were so earnestly bent on writing realistic exposés of the evils endemic in American society that they often sacrificed depth of insight and understanding to breadth of treatment. Obviously, in choosing all of society as their theme, they labored under a tremendous handicap; they could bring into focus only a fraction of the whole, and even then, so comprehensive was the fraction selected, they got bogged down in a morass of documentary details or they got carried away by their political sympathies. In many cases, they harnessed social description to partisan, doctrinaire ends, instead of making it serve the aesthetic purpose of defining and illuminating "the human predicament." [5]

Another criticism that might be legitimately leveled against the novel of social criticism is that in it society frequently is cast in the role of villain while the heretic, the non-conformist, the rebel, the revolutionary, is hailed as the hero. It pictures a world which alienates the sensitive individual and deprives him of his identity. As portrayed in the fiction of John Dos Passos, John Steinbeck, and Norman Mailer, he cannot find fulfillment in the social life of his time and consequently feels terribly isolated and maladjusted. As Millgate points out: "An attitude of 'protest' has become almost de rigueur for the American writer." [6]

Unlike the proletarian drama and fiction of the thirties, the literature of social criticism in the United States is not directed against society as a whole. Scott Fitzgerald, in *The Great Gatsby*, draws a scathing portrait of the life of the rich and the *nouveau riche* in the twenties, just as in *Tender Is the Night* he uncovers the shabby ethics of the wealthy class and sharply criti-

---

[5] Michael Millgate, *American Social Fiction*, p. 200.

[6] *Ibid.*, p. 203. See *Writers in Revolt*. Edited by Terry Southern, Richard Seaver, and Alexander Trocchi. New York: Berkley Publishing Corporation, 1963. It includes such American writers in revolt as Allen Ginsberg, William S. Burroughs, Edward Dahlberg, and Henry Miller.

cizes the great power they wield so unscrupulously, but he is in no sense a revolutionary. In *U.S.A.*, Dos Passos documents his case against American capitalist society: its adherence to the law of the jungle, the ways in which it undermines the integrity of those who are involved in the all-consuming struggle for wealth and power, the cruelty of an economic system that destroys not only the aspirations of its members but their manhood as well. John Steinbeck, in *The Grapes of Wrath*, tells the story of the Okies who were driven from their land by the erosion of the soil and how the corporations of the East, feeding insatiably on money and investments, take over their farms so that they become homeless migratories heading with desperate hope for the Promised Land of California. But neither Dos Passos nor Steinbeck recommends a revolutionary solution.

The case of John Dos Passos is a puzzling and paradoxical one: his fiction has run the whole gamut of ideological belief, from anarchism to radicalism to ultra-conservatism. He fulminates against the ugliness, the brutish spirit of greed and aggrandisement, and the demoralizing conflicts and calamities of life under industrial capitalism. No novelist of the twentieth century is more earnest and unsparing in his efforts to give an honest and truly representative picture of the internecine conflicts of American society as a whole. In his fiction of the thirties he is clearly in sympathy with reformers and radicals, but he does not endorse their panaceas because of his realization that the social – and the human – problem is too bafflingly complex to be resolved by the magic of some ideological formula. His naturalism is saved from doctrinaire stridency by being filtered through a delicate sensibility and poetic imagination and combined with his desire, that transcends political loyalties and party passions, to see humane values finally established as the norm. That is why he harps so insistently on the fact that life here and now in the United States is mechanized and debased, and that men, crushed by the Juggernaut of finance, are stripped of the last shred of self-respect.

2. The World of Manhattan Transfer

Manhattan Transfer, as it moves in its panoramic description of men and events from 1890 to 1925, makes internal references to politics, scandals, the Stanford White murder, the outbreak of war, the deportation of Communists, and so on. The characters introduced are intended to furnish a cross-section of society within New York City. Members of the various classes, the rich, the business moguls, lawyers, politicians, actors and actresses, theatrical producers, architects, engineers, promoters of wildcat schemes, drifters, Jewish garment workers, victims of the industrial system, are brought in to illustrate the various types of traumas, malaise, misery, and corruption American society inflicts on all those who play the game of life according to its rules and credulously or cynically emulate its ideals. These people, uprooted and isolated, are only mobile masks, animated bodies, atomistic units who, caught up in the frenzied whirl of the acquisitive struggle, never achieve individuality or self-determination. Modern life is too chaotic and too impersonal to be concerned about the fate of individuals. It is society in Dos Passos' fiction that is the all-powerful, the all-conquering protagonist, the *deus ex machina.* The men and women he portrays are, with few exceptions, motivated chiefly by the desire – a socially induced neurosis – to make money and get ahead in the world. Not that these characters cherish no ideals at the start of their career but that their ideals are soon aborted or abandoned. They are forced to compromise realistically with the kind of world they live in. What we get, then, is a cumulative picture of social confusion and corruption, sordid, abysmally depressing.

Manhattan Transfer presents multitudinous facets of the metropolis as seen through a diversified group of minds and temperaments. New York, the cultural and financial center of the nation, symbolizes America in all its tawdry splendor and dynamic wickedness. By giving us a cinematic cross-section of streets, houses, factories, theaters, Dos Passos is able to heighten the cheap glamor and the pathos of frustration of lives spent in this twentieth-century Sodom of stone and steel. He exhibits its crass commercial values in action, its pitiless and unconscionable exploitation of human material. In this harsh world the dreamer is bound to suffer defeat; the strong, the cunning, the unscrupulous triumph, the weak go under. This stupendous melodrama of sex, crime, madness, suicide, wealth, and extreme poverty, Dos Passos never allows us to forget, is enacted beneath the architectural grandeur of skyscrapers. All these people in the novel, the rich as well as the poor, are haunted by the specter of insecurity, fearful of winding up as charity cases, cast on the rubbish heap as worn out and useless by an age of individualism run amok.

Dos Passos' intense moral concern is implicit in practically every scene he presents. This, he is saying wrathfully, is what our present economic order does to people. It robs them of their ideals, their sense of community, deprives them of the capacity to love, forcing them to lead lives of mechanized desperation. They are harried, in perpetual flight, as if a demon were pursuing them, and yet boredom is their immitigable fate, boredom that might culminate in suicidal despair if they had the courage to face the truth about themselves. But they run away in panic from this self-confrontation. Dos

Passos says all this not by overt preachment or the use of propagandistic techniques. He is writing fiction, not allegory. The action reflects from many counterpointed perspectives the hideous and dehumanizing quality of life in our time: the sinister corruption that capitalism breeds, the sense of futility, the curse of alienation. Everything depends on how cunningly one can play the dizzy game of financial speculation, what influence he can bring to bear, what wires he can pull. The unwritten rules indicate that to "succeed" – and "success" is the goal of all striving – one must not be hampered by moral principles or a code of honor. Each man is out for himself, and the devil take the hindmost. This is the criticism Dos Passos directs relentlessly at the society of his time.

The third section, entitled "Dollars," plays ironic variations on the theme of America being the land of opportunity. Jimmy Herf, one of the central figures in the novel, asks at one point, "why in this country nobody ever does anything. Nobody ever writes any music or starts any revolution or falls in love. All anybody ever does is to get drunk and tell smutty stories." [7] Then comes the outbreak of war, the orgiastic dance of death and destruction. The patriotic war songs are fervidly sung. Everyone on the home front is driven mad by the insensate lust for profits while the hospital ships sail furtively into harbor at night delivering their ghastly burden of the crippled, the wounded, and the dying. At the end Jimmy goes off – how far he does not know – but away from this modern Nineveh.

3. The Social Message of U.S.A.

If *Manhattan Transfer* records Dos Passos' rage of repudiation as he contemplates the collective life of America in the version that New York City affords, *U.S.A.*, a striking example of the *roman fleuve*, carries the indictment to even more extreme lengths. This trilogy has of late been dismissed in some quarters on the ground that it is too political in its orientation, too massive in its accumulation of sharply observed naturalistic details, and that it possesses small value as a work of art. This is an ill-conceived and undeserved critical judgment. Dos Passos achieves what he set out to do in *U.S.A.* Ambitious in design, though not on the scale of Jules Romains' *Men of Good Will*, it attempts to create a living image of American society during the first third of the twentieth century.

Published separately as novels, the three parts of the trilogy – *The 42nd Parallel* (1930), *1919* (1932), and *The Big Money* (1936) – constitute a sweep-

---

[7] John Dos Passos, *Manhattan Transfer*. Boston: Houghton Mifflin Company, 1953, p. 193.

ing and impassioned condemnation of American society. But the vastness and diversity of the structure of the story, the host of characters that play a part, large or small, in the unfolding action, the difficulty of tying all the loose strands together in a unified knot, result in a diffusion of dramatic tension. By means of cumulative documentation and constant shifting of focus, Dos Passos undertakes to report the social scene in all its variousness and complexity – the strikes, the financial deals, political bribery and corruption, the war, the effects of Prohibition, riots, the Sacco and Vanzetti case, the life of industry, the October Revolution in Russia, and so on. As in *Manhattan Transfer*, the dominant impression that emerges out of this enormous welter of details is not only depressing but despairing. The American Dream, Dos Passos charges, has been vilely betrayed. The money-changers, the hucksters, the profiteers, the sharpers and swindlers, are in control of the country.

Society is again cast in the role of villain. In the foreground Dos Passos places the dynamic image of America, overwhelming in its immensity; the activities of the individual characters are only of secondary importance or they are brought in to show the economic pressure that makes them wretchedly unhappy and spiritually lost. That is why Dos Passos, in keeping with his central theme, lavishes so much space on the Biographies, the Newsreel, and the Camera Eye that deliberately interrupt the flow of the narrative proper. The author is not interested in weaving a plot but in presenting a huge case study of the effects of economic causation on a cross-section of the American people. The Biographies stand out as vivid commentaries on the life of the country; they provide incisive portraits, invidious or admiring, of the men who crash the headlines, the molders of history, the notables and the rebels, the tycoons, the captains of industry, the inventors, scientists, prophets, and political leaders: William Jennings Bryan, Burbank, Bill Heywood, Ford, Eugene V. Debs, Steinmetz, Theodore Roosevelt, Randolph Bourne, Jack Reed. The Newsreels attempt to capture the movement and mood of events in time in the form of snatches of popular songs, headlines, historic occasions. The Camera Eye is a more complex technique, a stream-of-consciousness, a series of subjective and lyrical impressions, a flow of discrete associations and memories. The Camera Eye passages have but a tenuous connection with the story itself.

If, despite its impressive breadth and scope, *U.S.A.* fails to do full justice to the character of American society, that is because Dos Passos tried to include everything in his trilogy and therefore never achieved the effect of objectivity he aimed at. Despite his assumed stance of naturalistic detachment, he cannot help but reveal his own political prepossessions. The Biographies portray the type of men he admires or detests, just as his Newsreels are carefully chosen to reflect the zany, if not insane, aspects of corporate life in America. That is how he skillfully embodies his social criticism in the texture of the novel. The businessmen, the warmongers, the financiers, the professional idealists, naive or hypocritical, are consistently portrayed in an unfavorable light, while workers, engineers, and Communists (the sincere ones) generally receive some measure of praise. Big Business is singled out as the enemy. It is the socioeconomic system, anonymous, inhuman, inexorable, which, from behind the scenes, really controls the lives of men. The individual is cruelly exploited by capitalism, which has no concern for ethical considerations or human needs.

Whitman in the nineteenth century could still hear America singing; Dos Passos hears only a bitter howl that is both a lament and a chorus of execration. This is a land without a conscience, Dos Passos is saying, these are cities without a soul, inhabited by people devoid of hope and faith. Dos Passos wishes to make his readers realize that the United States is no longer a beautiful and inspiring dream, a splendid democratic ideal, but "a group of holding companies. . . . U.S.A. is a set of bigmouthed officials with too many bank accounts." [8] The total effect of *The 42nd Parallel* is one of extreme disenchantment with America; Dos Passos exposes its superficiality, its vulgarity, its hypocrisy, and flagrant crookedness. Democracy is shown to be a fraud, big business a profitable racket; industry is controlled by buccaneers and their hired thugs. Money is king over the land. The institution of private property is considered more sacred than human life and nullifies the safeguards included in the Declaration of Independence and the Constitution.

1919 continues with more or less the same cast of characters and the same chorus of negative social criticism. Patriotism and profits are booming while war rages in Europe. The biography of Woodrow Wilson portrays him as the man who thought he was God, elected to keep the peace yet hurling the nation into the inferno of war. Coming back from Russia converted to a belief in the new world, Paxton Hibben, the journalist, discovers that there is "no more place in America for change, no more place for the old gags: social justice, progressivism, revolt against oppression, democracy. . . ." [9]

In his fulminations against the horror of war, Dos Passos declares:

War brought the eight hour day, women's votes, prohibition, high wages, high rates of interest, cost plus contracts and the luxury of being a Gold Star Mother.

---

[8] John Dos Passos, *U. S. A.* New York: The Modern Library, 1937, p. vii.
[9] *Ibid.*, p. 184.

If you objected to making the world safe for cost plus democracy you went to jail with Debs.[10]

The Big Money concludes this mammoth trilogy of sorrow, corruption, and defeat. Charley Anderson is the shocking symbol of failure – the brilliant inventor who, finding life joyless and meaningless, connives at his own destruction. With the exception of Mary French, Ben Compson, and Bill Cermak, the characters in *The Big Money* are fighting a losing battle against despair. Thus what we get is a vehement denunciation of the American myth of success. Dos Passos shows this myth, with its phoney emphasis on getting ahead at all costs, to be essentially false by featuring news of strikes, strike-breaking, riots, unemployment, the exploitation of labor at starvation wages. Dos Passos must have hated America and all it stood for when he composed this opus. *U.S.A.* is a searching exposé, all copiously documented, driving home the ugly but incontrovertible fact that the United States in the twentieth century is unconscionable and dehumanized in its passion for profits. *U.S.A.* offers a paradigmatic example of the novel of social criticism.

4. The Recoil from Radicalism

In *The Adventures of a Young Man* (1939), part of the District of Columbia trilogy, the political orientation of Dos Passos undergoes a marked change. Here is an almost complete reversal of form. This novel portrays the career of an earnest but intellectually confused young hero who seeks to identify himself with the working class and fight for its liberation. Glenn Spotwood, a social idealist, is, like Mary French in *U.S.A.*, naive enough to be completely honest and sincere in his intention. It is this very integrity of character that lands him in trouble with the leaders of the Communist Party who think and act only in terms of ideological conformity. Glenn works his head off for the cause, only to be told that he must refrain from criticizing Party decisions and not take actions on his own initiative. That is branded as counter-revolutionary behavior. He soon finds himself thrown out of the Party, stigmatized as a traitor. He decides to volunteer for service in the Spanish Civil War. Even there, while the fighting is going on, he is regarded as a fifth columnist and is thrown into jail on the charge that he is a spy. His "adventure" ends with his death from the bullets of the Insurgents – a death-trap into which the Party leaders had deliberately sent him in order to get rid of him. In addition to thus exposing the time-serving tactics of the Communist Party bureaucrats, Dos Passos draws an unsparing portrait of the radical intelligent-

---

[10] John Dos Passos, *1919,* in *U. S. A.,* p. 246.

sia of the time: the curious cults they worship, the Marxist jargon they love to use.

Dos Passos had by this time rejected the Marxist interpretation of history and society. He returned to the American past not only to gain insight into the present but to recapture the vision of the unbroken continuity of life. In *The Ground We Stand On*, he examines the venerable figures of our national past – Roger Williams, Benjamin Franklin, Thomas Jefferson, and others – who were instrumental in shaping the form and substance of our political creed. Whereas in *U.S.A.* he opposed practically everything America stood for, he is now eager to revise his earlier intemperate judgment and atone for the blindness of his bias. He sees now that Communism in Europe sowed the dragon's seed of bloodshed and fratricide, tyranny and ruin. He now categorically repels the charge that America, the freest country on earth today, is decadent and moribund. On the contrary, this land, heir to a long, honorable tradition of self-government and enriched by a heritage of freedom, is steadily getting to be a better place to live in. The note of social criticism Dos Passos now voices is meant to defend the imperiled cause of freedom, to preserve and perpetuate the democratic faith that will counter the messianic doctrine of Communism.

Midcentury (1961), is, like *U.S.A.*, a sociological documentary in fictional form, but though the technique of presentation remains substantially the same the quality of tone has greatly changed. The heroes have strangely reversed their roles. If employers are shown to be often unscrupulous in running union organizers out of town, hiring company police and thugs to do their dirty work, labor leaders, especially the Communists, are equally venal and corrupt. Dos Passos conducts what amounts to a vendetta against Marxism, Marxists, and the Party henchmen: their quasi-religious worship of history, their demand for unconditional obedience to the Party line. Dos Passos now sees Marxism as a method designed to release "resentment against the established order" [11] and Communists as fanatics who preach class hatred. Dos Passos has obviously shifted his strategy of attack.

He concentrates his fire on the dastardly plotting of the Communists, their control of WPA projects during the depression. He vigorously denounces labor graft and corruption. The honest worker who dares to protest against the racketeering of the union bosses is beaten up or killed, and the courts do nothing to redress the grievances of the victimized workers. *Midcentury* is an exceptional muckraking novel in that its ire is directed against the tyranny of labor unions. The social criticism of Dos Passos has thus taken a new

---

[11] John Dos Passos, *Midcentury*. Boston: Houghton Mifflin Company, 1961, p. 53.

turn. The dread warning he issues is that the country is steadily losing its freedom. He affirms the right of the individual to stand up against institutions that attempt to curb his freedom of thought and action; he believes in salvaging the endangered principle of self-government and in upholding it against the ominously rising tide of collectivism.

CHAPTER IX

THE MORAL COMMITMENT OF JOHN STEINBECK

All fiction, we have agreed, is situated in a social context and focuses on the relationship between the individual and society. The same thing holds true of the drama. Though the genre has a long history behind it and abounds in excellent illustrative examples, the social novel, like the social drama, is difficult to define with precision.[1] The same difficulty attends the attempt to define the political novel.[2] The difficulty is compounded when we endeavor to deal with the more specialized form of the novel of social criticism. Perhaps better than a formal definition will be a close consideration of one specimen of that form, *The Grapes of Wrath*, by John Steinbeck.

A morally rather than ideologically committed writer, Steinbeck has never been a dogmatist and certainly cannot be accused of being a "true believer." If he protests strongly against the evils of modern American civilization – the frenetic pace of industrialism, the supplanting of the working man by the machine, the exploitation of human beings for the sake of financial gain – his protest is made fundamentally in the name of humane rather than strictly political values. Though he has always been on the side of the underdog, his sympathies have not led him to the point, like James Jones in *From Here to Eternity*, of offering simplistic solutions for the ills and afflictions of American society. The proof of his unimpaired integrity as a novelist is evidenced by the fact that he cannot be identified, not even as a fellow traveler,

[1] Warren French uses the term in a restrictive sense. "By 'social novel,' I mean a work that is so related to some specific historical phenomena that a detailed knowledge of the historical situation is essential to a full understanding of the novel at the same time that the artist's manipulation of his materials provides an understanding of why the historical events occurred." Warren French, *The Social Novel at the End of an Era*. Carbondale and Edwardsville: Southern Illinois University Press, 1966, p. 7. French takes up such "social novels" as *The Grapes of Wrath, For Whom the Bell Tolls, The Hamlet*, and other works. Strangely enough, he omits a consideration of Dos Passos' fiction.

[2] See "The Idea of the Political Novel," in Irving Howe, *Politics and the Novel*. New York: Horizon Press, Inc., 1957, pp. 15-24.

with any of the fashionable radical *isms* of the thirties. Nor, despite the growing menace of Fascism during that troubled decade, has he ever lost faith in the essential decency of the human being and his capacity for altruistic behavior. In the worst crisis of adversity, he continues to believe that the generous instincts of man will override his selfishness. If Steinbeck studiously avoids the temptation of indulging in propaganda of one kind or another, he occasionally portrays the human condition by utilizing the resources of allegory. Though this is a weakness that makes itself felt in *The Grapes of Wrath*, it serves his creative purpose in supporting his condemnation of the acquisitive mania of capitalist society and in calling attention to the innate nobility of the common man. As Warren French points out: "An insistence on the primacy of human dignity is the force that has kept Steinbeck from committing himself to some Cause." [3]

In 1936 Steinbeck published *In Dubious Battle*, a novel about a strike that cannot be classified as "proletarian" fiction since it does not espouse a Marxist solution. He does not idealize the character of the strikers nor romanticize their Communist leaders. Then the San Francisco *News* asked him to contribute a series of articles on the problems created by the migrant labor camps in Califonia; thus he became engaged in the task of gathering documentary material that he would later incorporate in *The Grapes of Wrath*. He got to know at first hand the conditions he describes with such vivid authenticity in this novel of powerful social criticism. When it came out in 1939, it aroused a storm of controversy. For it did more than picture with naturalistic verisimilitude and fullness of detail the tragic abuses inherent in a system of virtual peonage; he called for thoroughgoing measures of reform while never advocating resort to revolutionary methods. The existing economic system, which is shown to be outrageously unjust, has to be reconstructed, but he strives to be consistently objective and fair-minded in his presentation of the conflict, even though his sympathies are definitely enlisted on the side of the victims.

Steinbeck is basically a reformer, not a radical, in his outlook, without in any sense scamping his responsibilities as an artist. In *The Grapes of Wrath* as in *In Dubious Battle*, he provides no climax of conversion to Communism, no epiphany of revolutionary violence triumphant. Indeed, the ending of *The Grapes of Wrath* is not really an ending, because it furnishes no clue as to how the complex problem of poverty and labor exploitation is finally

---

[3] Warren French, *John Steinbeck*. New York: Twayne Publishers, Inc., 1961, p. 10.

disposed of, but then Steinbeck is writing fiction, not propaganda. He is not, in any case, required to work out a viable solution. The solution Steinbeck proposes or suggests is implicit in the structural logic of the story: the need for a change of heart, a decisive break away from the tyranny of the cash-nexus and the domination of the self-regarding sentiment until the redemptive truth of brotherhood can be affirmed and fully established. The allegorical message, symbolized somewhat sentimentally in the concluding scene of the novel, is that the anachronistic dream of personal security for the family unit must be replaced by a nobler ideal of human solidarity and mutual aid.

The Grapes of Wrath, like *U.S.A.*, constitutes a brilliant example of the fiction of social criticism, but instead of trying, like Dos Passos, to include all of American life within his compass, Steinbeck seizes on a timely and urgent theme and confines himself to that. He strives to lift it to the plane of universality by depicting the tragedy, not without including welcome touches of comic relief, of uprooted families in Oklahoma and by placing the Joad family in the foreground of his canvas. He makes it clear that these self-reliant, hard-working men and women are not to blame for the disaster that has befallen them: the erosion of the soil, the eviction from their homes, the rape of the land by the tractors. By means of interpolated documentary chapters Steinbeck furnishes the rationale for his blast of social criticism. Like Dos Passos, he emphasizes the fact that in modern times the individual is increasingly at the mercy of vast anonymous and impersonal forces. If the villain of the piece cannot be unmasked and properly dealt with, it is because capitalism, working invisibly but with ruthless efficiency behind the scenes, cannot be identified; it is faceless, mindless, and heartless. The in-between chapters do more than fill in the social background and disclose the widespread misery of the masses; they effectively evoke the mood of desperation of the thirties. Unlike Dos Passos, however, Steinbeck sounds a note of hope and faith in the power of the people themselves to achieve redemption. It is to the aroused conscience of America that he addresses his moral appeal.

And the appeal strikes home because Steinbeck never allows the reader to lose sight of the human element bound up with this national disaster. An earthy, heretical version of Christ, Casy, the preacher, introduces the religious motif. Now that for good reasons of his own he has abandoned his calling as a preacher, he is groping for a new faith; he wants to lead the people, but he does not know as yet where to lead them. He works out his own code of religious values. The call of the spirit, he believes, is nothing but the call of love; he loves people more than he loves Jesus. This conception of Christianity as essentially iconoclastic in its teaching [4] fits in with the theme of the novel. The human spirit, Casy suspects, is nothing apart from the love we feel for all mankind; in short, it is the human spirit that is divine.

The counsel of brotherly love is, as Steinbeck of course realizes, hardly a cure for the economic ills which trouble the nation. The invisible power that rules the country, the holding companies, the banks: this is the inhuman enemy that has to be overcome, but how can the dispossessed farmers vent their hatred and at the same time defend their homes against a destructive force that remains invisible? A bank, a holding company, is not human; it is a monster that must feed on profits or perish. Steinbeck takes pains to describe the nature of these abstract financial transactions that spell the doom of the tenant system; the farmers must vacate their homestead and let the tractors take over. This tearing up of their roots from the soil into which they and their forbears had poured their sweat and blood, this usurpation of the land which belonged to them of right because they had fought for it and worked on it, all this drives home the human side of the tragedy. The bank, unfortunately, has no use for human sentiment and remains unmoved by human suffering. Steinbeck uses the intercalated chapters of exposition to point his moral.

The bank is something else than men. It happens that every man in a bank hates what the bank does, and yet the bank does it. The bank is something more than men.... It's the monster. Men made it, but they can't control it.[5]

Another criticism that Steinbeck levels against society, one that is consonant with his primitivism, is to warn of the grievous loss suffered when the machine, in the name of progress, destroys man's organic relationship to Nature. The tractors, symbols of the technological age, come into the fields and plough up the land; the driver is no longer in life-nourishing contact with the earth; the tractor is indifferent to weather, drought, or rainfall. Under its mechanical ministrations, the crop can grow without the expenditure of human labor. "No man had touched the seed or lusted for the growth. Men ate what they had not raised, had no connection with the bread." [6] All this is the result of the inexorable operation of the economic system whereby one company is controlled by another company, which in turn is owed by some bank in the East.

It is when Casy oberves the plight of these homeless and impoverished

---

[4] Gabriel Vahanian propounds the thesis "that both literature and the Christian tradition, at least in its primitive and essential thrust, are iconoclastic." Gabriel Vahanian, *Wait Without Idols*. New York: George Braziller, 1964, p. x.

[5] John Steinbeck, *The Grapes of Wrath*. New York: The Modern Library, 1939, p. 45.

[6] *Ibid.*, p. 49.

Okies that he receives the call. They will need his help beyond the comfort that mere preaching brings. It is concrete help they require more than the blessings and benefactions of the Holy Spirit. Wherever these displaced farmers travel on the road he will be one of them and share their hardships. If Ma Joad symbolizes Mother Earth, it is Casy who emulates the example of Christ by discarding the old theological trappings. Through this pseudonymous version of the modern Christ Steinbeck preaches the gospel of true human solidarity: "mankind was holy when it was one thing." [7] The holiness was profaned and lost when men became selfish and thought only of securing their own advantage. It is this religious motif of *caritas*, though couched in secular and heretical terms, which informs Steinbeck's vision of social redemption. If these three hundred thousand people on the move are to find salvation, they must unite their forces and, above all, learn to help each other. Like Carl Sandburg in *The People, Yes*, Steinbeck is proclaiming his faith in the indomitable, always striving spirit of the common man.

But if Steinbeck chants a song of affirmation, he also utters a solemn warning of what is to come if the storm clouds on the horizon are not heeded. The chief cause of the present trouble lies in man's need to work, to build a house, to possess something which he can call a home and on which he can lavish his love. Exploited, propertyless, jobless, homeless, the people are beginning to voice their mutinous discontent. What is more, they are slowly discovering the power that inheres in solidarity. The shift from "I" to "we" is a heartening sign that the bonds of brotherhood are being forged. All this portends the shape of things to come in the future. Rendered desperate by their plight, the people on the move along the roads of America are finding out through bitter experience that their strength lies in mutual helpfulness.

Steinbeck is endeavoring to accomplish two things in this novel of social criticism: to dramatize the misfortunes of the Joad family as representative of the misery and suffering endured by hundreds of thousands of dispossessed small farmers, and to trace the root cause of the economic breakdown. What, he asks, is the meaning of the right of ownership? He contrasts the Hoovervilles established on the outskirts of each town with the vast tracts of land that lie unused in the West. The owners of these estates are fearful the migrants may encroach on their property; these ragged, haggard, unfed Okies constitute a dire threat to the haves. But history, according to Steinbeck, teaches a profound and inescapable moral lesson: namely, that repression serves only to stiffen the backbone of the repressed. These three

[7] *Ibid.*, p. 110.

hundred thousand homeless wanderers, "if they ever know themselves the land will be theirs and all the gas, all the rifles in the world won't stop them." [8] Though the owners of the ranches in the West and their armed deputies are determined to break the spirit of these migratories, Ma Joad knows that her people will go on living when the oppressors are gone. As she tells her son: "Why, Tom, we're the people that live. They ain't gonna wipe us out. Why, we're the people – we go on." [9]

Steinbeck exalts the character of these people of the soil, their indwelling dignity and resourcefulness, their grim courage and uncomplaining fortitude, while painting in dark colors the unprincipled selfishness of the rich, so that we get at times what amounts to a sentimentalized black and white composition. It is with prophetic fury that Steinbeck assails American society for the tragedy of waste it allows to take place. Why, he asks angrily, is the fruit rotting in the ground, the coffee burned, the pigs slaughtered and then thrown away while the mass of people are starving?

There is a crime here that goes beyond denunciation. There is a sorrow here that weeping cannot symbolize. There is a failure here that topples all our successes. The fertile earth, the straight tree rows, the sturdy tree trunks, and ripe fruit. And children dying of pellagra must die because a profit cannot be taken from an orange. And coroners must fill in the certificates – died of malnutrition – because the food must be forced to rot.

The people come with nets to fish for potatoes in the river, and the guards hold them back; they come in rattling cars to get the dumped oranges, but the kerosene is sprayed. And they stand still and watch the potatoes float by, listen to the screaming pigs being killed in a ditch and covered with quicklime, watch the mountains of oranges slop down to a putrefying ooze; and in the eyes of the people there is the failure, and in the eyes of the hungry there is a growing wrath. In the souls of the people the grapes of wrath are filling and growing heavy for the vintage.[10]

This is the harvest of wrath that a blundering and iniquitous economic system is storing up for itself. The only way for the people to avoid being exploited and beaten down, Steinbeck reiterates, is to stick together. After Casy, the sacrificial scapegoat, is killed, Tom, hiding in solitude from the arms of "the law," remembers the preacher's words. At this moment of illumination he knows at last that no man is good standing alone. He must carry on Casy's work. "Wherever they's a fight so hungry people can eat, I'll be there." [11] Tom, like Casy, embodies Steinbeck's social evangel: if the

[8] *Ibid.*, p. 325.
[9] *Ibid.*, p. 383.
[10] *Ibid.*, p. 477.
[11] *Ibid.*, p. 572.

people get together they cannot be defeated; they may be pushed back here and there on the far-flung battlefront, but they will always keep marching forward. As Ma Joad declares with unflinching optimism: "We ain't gonna die out. People is going' on – changing a little, maybe, but goin' right on." [12]

The Grapes of Wrath, though heartening in its message, ends on an inconclusive note. We are not told what finally became of these migratories. It is difficult to determine what effect, if any, this novel had in alleviating their burden of misery. All we know is that after the United States was drawn into the Second World War these displaced farmers found jobs in munitions plants and became permanent settlers in the state of California.

[12] *Ibid.,* p. 577.

CHAPTER X

THE SOCIOECONOMIC MOTIF IN THE LITERATURE OF THE ANGRY YOUNG MEN[1]

If we turn now to the literature produced in England in the late forties and the fifties, we observe that the note of social criticism not only persists but grows in intensity. The fever of politics transforms the writer, wittingly or unwittingly, into a partisan and sometimes into a propagandist or self-righteous moralist. As a man he is naturally deeply concerned about the evils of his age, the curse of poverty, the threat of war, the loss of the sense of community, but he realizes there is little that he can do, as an imaginative writer, to change these conditions except to raise his voice against them so as to bear witness. He may lash out at the frequent miscarriage of justice in the land, denounce corruption in high places, call prophetically for a change of heart that will make possible the building of the ideal society, but it is doubtful – and he knows it – if his work will of itself usher in a wave of reform. As Auden wrote in his "New Year's Letter" for 1940, after repudiating the categorical imperatives of Marxism, "art is not life and cannot be/A midwife to society." Nevertheless, many modern writers, especially among the so-called angry young men of England, are not discouraged by this handicap from expressing their passion for social justice.

Nothing is more revealing of the relationship between literature and society and, in particular, between literature and the vicissitudes of history than the change in tone and content in English fiction produced after the Second World War. A new generation of novelists emerges, different in outlook and radically different in the social values they espouse. They challenge the right of class distinctions to exist. The structure of society: that is their theme and the object of their attack. They hale society before the bar of justice and then proceed to recite their grievances and present their proposals for reform. What their protagonist generally wants is his rightful

[1] This chapter is an expanded and revised version of an article by the present writer, "The Literature of the Angry Young Men," *The Colorado Quarterly,* Spring, 1960, VIII, pp. 293-303.

share of the good things of life. Often he is bitter, railing against a world that he cannot control.

Novel after novel deals with the story of class mobility, the struggle to move upward in the social and economic hierarchy. This is the theme of *The Red and the Black*, the theme, too, of *Jude the Obscure*, both novels of trenchant social criticism, but there is an important difference to be noted. The contemporary world is vastly more complex and more confusing. If the latter-day hero is more sophisticated or cynical, he is not at all certain of his place or function in the world. Everything has been thrown into a fluid state: class categories, moral values, lines of conduct. "Since the end of World War II, however, many young writers have been attempting to return to a traditional nineteenth-century theme, the theme of how a man works his way through society, with a characteristic twentieth-century lack of assurance about what the man or the society is really like." [2] The element of class conflict looms large; it is the system that the hero rebels against. Though these writers owe much to their predecessors, they did strike out on new paths. They describe the difficult quest for selfhood in a mass society. Their attitude is often irreverent, opposed to religion and directed against the Establishment.

Descendants of the lower middle or working class families, these writers at least accept their world, even though they protest vehemently against the socioeconomic system that prevents them from coming into their heritage. Though some are filled with unconcealed resentment, the majority simply want a chance to prove themselves in the struggle for advancement under equal conditions; they wish to institute a social order that will provide an open and equitable market for talent. Not that they share a common political platform, but the dominant attitude seems to be that some far-reaching social reforms must be instituted if the members of the younger generation are not to drift idly, their aspirations frustrated, their God-given energies wasted.

In some respects they resemble the beat generation in the United States in their cult of the Outsider, their interest in Sartrean Existentialism (though that interest is held in check by their pragmatic English temperament), and in their search, on the part of a few, for a religious synthesis, but they evince none of the extremist defiance that characterizes the beat writers. The socialism that some espouse is balanced by the sober realization that a rigidly egalitarian society offers no incentive for men of superior intelligence and ability. But in general they seem to be agreed on one issue: they are resolved

---

[2] James Gindin, *Postwar British Fiction*. Berkeley and Los Angeles: University of California Press, 1962, p. 4.

not to sing the old tunes of accommodation to the *status quo* or subscribe to the myth that God's in his heaven and all is right with the world. Critical in outlook, toughened by the realities of the wartime conflict, they are suspicious of utopian promises and programs, whether these be Marxist or Christian in inspiration. They have been shaped, though in different ways, by the same confluence of forces that gave rise to the beat generation: the experience of the Second World War, the collapse of faith in the messianic dream of Communism, and a more realistic, even disillusioned attitude toward the cult of progress that would usher in a paradisaical future. That is why they distrust panaceas and reject the salvationary mystique of the proletariat. They refuse to be fooled a second time. Their ingrained idealism, however negative in expression, nevertheless breaks out in their attack on the established social system and in their desire to play a constructive role in a world that is so lacking in the things that matter most to them. Whereas members of the beat generation, thoroughly disillusioned, attempt to live recklessly in the moment, fleeing the vicious competition of the marketplace and aligning themselves with the marginal men of American society, the angry young men of England crave to participate actively in the remaking of their world.

Their creative contributions have filled the literary atmosphere of the fifties with the noise of strident controversy. Their work reveals a fairly consistent pattern of negation. What binds this divergent group of writers together in uneasy fellowship is a sustained mood of disgruntled opposition. They will not accept the effete and discredited traditions of the past nor will they compromise with the values of the established order. A few still believe in the possibility of reform and recommend the application of socialist principles. But on the whole what identifies these writers is their hostility to caste-lines. Outspoken in their social criticism, they are determined to force the cosy "insiders" out of their privileged position of financial security; they ridicule the shams and shibboleths of the ruling class in England, their religion of respectability, their worship of success, and their demand for conformity. They have mobilized their resentment and use it with damaging effect in assault after assault on the bastions of the Establishment. It is this chronic distempered tone of social criticism which explains why they were called angry young men, though the term has a wide range of meaning. According to Kenneth Allsop in *The Angry Decade,* which is subtitled "A Survey of the Cultural Revolt of the Nineteen-Fifties," the term angry young men

carries multiple overtones which might be listed as irreverence, stridency, impatience with tradition, vigour, vulgarity, sulky resentment against the cultivated and a hard-boiled muscling-in on culture, adventurousness, self-pity, deliberate disengagement from politics, fascist ambitions, schizophrenia, rude dislike of anything phoney or fey, a broad sense of humor but low on wit, a general intellectual nihilism, honesty, a neurotic discontent and a defeated reconciled acquiescence that is the last flimsy shelter against complete despondency – a widely ill-assorted agglomeration of credoes which, although without any verbal coherence, do belong to this incoherent period of social protest.[3]

In this amazing farrago of contradictions – revolt and defeated acquiescence, protest and schizophrenic disengagement from the hurly-burly of politics, nihilism and fascist ambitions – a number of motifs stand out. Primarily what these angry young men want to do is to topple their elders from the seats of power. They are frankly eager to take over, and they are prepared to do so without apologias or a display of good manners. They are releasing their hitherto bottled-up hostility – a form of *ressentiment* – against a society that rewards the second-rate and neglects those endowed with original minds. In a period of intellectual exhaustion and cultural inertia, they feel they have something vital to say and they have hit upon striking ways of making themselves heard.

One of their irascible spokesmen is Jimmy Porter, the hero of *Look Back in Anger*, who is at odds with the world he lives in. Though unlike Joe Lampton in *Room at the Top* he is not striving for success, he is badly maladjusted in his egotistic insistence that the wrongs of society are specially designed to frustrate him. He had married a woman belonging to a higher class, and he can neither forget nor forgive the fact that her parents, especially the mother, had done everything in their power to drive him away. In their eyes he was but a vulgar young man, without money or impressive social background. He had tasted suffering and deprivation as well as social rejection. He had watched his father die. He learned at an early age what it meant to be angry and resentful and yet feel his own helplessness. His pent-up anger explodes in the last act when he cries out:

I suppose people of our generation aren't able to die for good causes any longer. We had all that done for us in the thirties and forties, when we were still kids. . . . There aren't any good, brave causes left. If the big bang does come, and we all get killed off, it won't be in aid of the old-fashioned, grand design. It'll just be for the Brave New-nothing-very-much-thank-you. About as pointless and inglorious as stepping in front of a bus.[4]

As they recall the time of the general strike, the despair of the depression years, the horror of the Second World War, the members of the generation

---

[3] Kenneth Allsop, *The Angry Decade*. New York: British Book Centre, 1958, p. 10.
[4] John Osborne, *Look Back in Anger*. New York: Bantam Books, 1950, pp. 104-105.

to which Jimmy Porter belongs yearn nostalgically for the golden age of security England once enjoyed. England had emerged from the war drained of its energy, stricken with a malaise of futility. At this time there arose a band of young men from working class origins who were bent on pushing their way upward to the topmost peaks of power. Though they have been afforded the opportunity of gaining a higher education, they are not grateful for favors received, for they still do not feel they "belong." They cannot be satisfied with what they have achieved; there are still formidable barriers, in the form of traditionally preserved class distinctions, which stand in their way. They are caught between two worlds, that of their former plebeian or lower middle class status, which they have left behind them, and that of the new and higher social order which does not, they insist, actually accept them. Then, too, as they look back upon their own past, they are troubled by a rankling sense of guilt for having cut themselves off from their class roots at the same time that they despise the vulgarity and coarseness of the life led by the poor. Success, they therefore conclude, is the only valid ethic of justification, and success, if it is to be evaluated realistically, must be measured in terms of money.

Though they detest snobbery and demagogic appeals and are simply bored by the dialectics of the class struggle, they take a lively interest in economic matters, but it is predominantly a practical interest: they are concerned chiefly about themselves, their professional career, their income, their advancement. Whereas the hero of *Room at the Top* is intent on achieving success at all costs, other heroes, unable to devote themselves seriously to business affairs, have seceded, as it were, from society and resigned themselves to a state of indifference. Both types of protagonists are infected with a cynicism born of critical disenchantment with the way society is run. Though Kingsley Amis's heroes sympathize with the underdog, they arrive at no economic or political solution. The attitude which seems to prevail is that one is well advised to be a realist and zealously watch out for his own interests. The problem is how to "live" right now, how best to come to terms with conditions as they are. Either that or relapse into Oblomovian apathy. Even the English working class, according to Richard Hoggart's study, *The Uses of Literacy*, are overcome by the same feeling of uselessness. Why save for a future that they may never live to see, a future that may never come? Their mildly hedonistic philosophy is supported by a deeply felt conviction that the truly big rewards are not theirs to strive for. Therefore, why worry? Their idea of freedom, which is always that of freedom from, is carried to such an extreme that they refrain from condemning anything at all. Everything is relative. Unlike the angry young men, however, they seem to believe that the easiest way out is to conform. But they share a number of attitudes with the angry young men, particularly in their distrust of all "higher" values. They suspect that everything is a fraud or a racket. Like many of the intellectuals during the past thirty years, they are suspicious of authority and fearful of letting their emotions go.[5]

Fully to understand the nature of the phenomenon the angry young men represent, we must examine briefly the condition of England at the time they appeared on the literary scene. The new generation that sprang up between the wars did not experience the misery and humiliation of chronic unemployment. Though they occasionally knew joblessness and poverty, most of them were able to acquire a coveted university degree and rise appreciably in the scale of wealth and power. Indeed, quite a number of them gained the positions of leadership they so eagerly craved. Yet they could not wipe out the record of their past, for that would mean repudiating a precious part of themselves. In his autobiography, *Time and Place*, George Scott declares: "There is no shame in birth, environment or poverty; there is shame only in trying to deny their realities." [6] A man's a man for all that.

The social criticism of the new generation of English intellectuals is summed up in the cry that it is time for a change. When the elders of the tribe reproach them for their lack of political enthusiasm, their failure to commit themselves, they reply that, having benefited enormously from the experiences of their fathers, they prefer to keep their feet planted in the good earth. No more quixotic adventures in social idealism for them! Violent enthusiasm can be a dangerous thing. Why turn the world upside down with utopian schemes? It is evident, however, that a social revolution of tremendous proportions has been peacefully wrought in England. This accounts in part for the singular obsession of a goodly number of intellectuals from humble backgrounds with the dynamics of wielding power, their aggressive demands for some degree of representation in the councils of the mighty.

Why this overwhelming preoccupation with symbols of power, status, prestige, and success? Because the memory of their comparatively inferior social origins continues to haunt them. They have not completely thrown off the proletarian or petty bourgeois traits which, like a physical birthmark, serve to betray them. Though they are not to the manner born, they do not abandon their quest for social acceptance. Their aim is to demonstrate to the skeptical that talent of a higher order is to be found outside the cadres of the social elite. It would be a mistake, if we judged them by these

[5] Richard Hoggart, *The Uses of Literacy*. London: Chatto and Windus, 1957, pp. 87-88.

[6] George Scott, *Time and Place*. London: Staples Press Limited, 1956, p. 26.

ambitions, to assume that they have sold out to the powers that be. Their hope is actually that of establishing a truly classless society, without invidious distinctions of rank. A ruling group must, however, be put in charge, but only on condition that it is held open to all those who possess the requisite ability.

What this indicates clearly enough is that the reformist zeal of the thirties has come to an end: the generous idealism, the larger hope, the willingness to make sacrifices for the sake of the future. The grim lesson taught by the thirties deters the young intellectuals from engaging in any crusading folly. In this respect they are reacting to the pressures of contemporary history and reflecting the views of their class. They had seen the leaders of the Soviet Union betray the original purpose of the Revolution. The politics of Communism lacked common sense and good judgment. The English writers of the fifties are not inflamed with desire to overthrow capitalist civilization. Stemming as they do from proletarian or lower middle class roots and therefore knowing whereof they speak, they contemptuously debunk the myth of the proletariat acting as the saviors of society. They know full well the character of the working class: its vicious temper, its rancorous envy, its hatred of excellence in others. As these young intellectuals adjusted themselves to the realities of the postwar world, they came to the conclusion (with the exception, of course, of men like Raymond Williams and Arnold Wesker) that the Socialist ideal was a lost and hopeless illusion. A Socialist administration would merely entrench a bureaucracy in power.[7]

The Welfare State has brought with it a large measure of disappointment. The intellectuals who benefited from the largesse provided by the State found that vertical mobility was indeed possible but only upward to the middle class, not beyond. According to one contributor to the volume, *Convictions*: "All this has bred in the intellectual milieu a ferocious hatred of equality and a desperate, almost comic, quest for the traditional certitudes of a hier-

---

[7] This view is not shared by Raymond Williams who as a Socialist affirms that Socialism carries on the struggle for human liberation. In his book, *Modern Tragedy*, he deals with the problem of revolutionary commitment. "It is undoubtedly true that a commitment to revolution can produce a kind of hardening which even ends by negating the revolutionary purpose.... The enemies of the revolutionary purpose then seize on the evidence of hardening and negation: either to oppose revolution as such, or to restore the convenient belief that man cannot change his condition, and that aspiration brings terror as a logical companion." Raymond Williams, *Modern Tragedy*. Stanford: Stanford University Press, 1966, pp. 81-82. See also his political novel, *Second Generation*, which marks a belated and distinctive contribution to the literature of the angry young men. It presents the theme that each man is responsible for the whole of society, either by accepting the *status quo* or by endeavoring to change it for the better. The hero at the end decides that the system can and must be changed.

archical society." [8] The ironic result is that the revolutionary fathers have bred a generation of bitter counter-revolutionaries. Not that they wish to wreck the Welfare State and revert to the free-for-all competition that prevails under a laissez-faire economy. As George Scott affirms:

We are looking for a way in which the humanitarian instincts may be combined with the encouragement of ambition, that hard work and talent may receive its proportionate reward, that old and injurious prejudices may be discarded to make room for those new concepts of modern society which alone can ensure not merely Britain's survival, but the common advancement of her people. [9]

This envisions a modest enough program. It calls for the recognition of men of letters and those possessed of an assured capacity for leadership. It also makes the point that the potentialities of these men have been inhibited by their attitude of skepticism toward all that is false and phoney in English corporate life.

To some degree this explains the addiction of the angry young writers to the vein of comedy, the genre in which Kingsley Amis and John Wain display their greatest aptitude. Their satire, which is a form of attack by means of humorous derogation, is instinct with irony and even charged with elements of burlesque and caricature as it portrays life in a society that is without firm moral standards. Their fictional heroes either forge shrewdly ahead or else refuse to become involved in the economic struggle. Some of them, in fact, long for the good old times that are irretrievably gone and align themselves ideologically with the right wing but even they are not to be counted as party men.

Nothing illustrates more aptly the astringent mood of disenchantment with the dirty business of politics than the pamphlet, *Socialism and the Intellectuals*, by Kingsley Amis, author of *Lucky Jim*. It gives a candid and informed analysis of the reasons that led a number of English writers to disassociate themselves from both reformism and revolutionary extremism. Amis frankly confesses his ignorance of matters political. Son of an office worker, winner of a scholarship to one of the Oxford colleges, he had during his undergraduate days been converted to Marxism, but this ideological infection did not last long. Though he votes Labor, he belongs to no political organization. If the intelligentsia of the fifties are not impelled by any revolutionary fervor, it is because, Amis contends, the intellectual is not by nature and vocation a political animal. George Orwell's *Nineteen Eighty-Four*, when it came out in 1948, disillusioned the young with Communism and opened their eyes to the realities of political power. (Here is a signal

[8] Norman MacKenzie (ed.), *Convictions*. London: MacGibbon & Kee, 1959, p. 214.
[9] George Scott, *Time and Place*, p. 192.

instance of a novel indirectly exerting a marked social influence.) Since what moves men in politics as in economics is the pull of self-interest, Kingsley Amis distrusts the motives of both professional idealists and prophets of reform.

Kingsley Amis's novel is frequently quoted, and always admiringly, as an excellent example of the critical and at times even contumacious attitude toward English society characteristic of the angry young men. But the satire, however damaging, is carried out in a spirit of fun. Here is a young academic, a tyro in his field, who cannot seriously join in the ritualistic goosestep and mumbo-jumbo required of him. Whenever he is put to the test, he follows his honest impulses and thereby ruins his chances for advancement. He is too decent a chap at heart, fundamentally too sensitive, not to protest in his own "subversive" way against all that is fake and pretentious in the college community; he cannot survive in this stuffy, hypocritical atmosphere. The sum and substance of his objection to the academic life is that it is insufferably boring. He is basically too rebellious a character to sink back contentedly into academic harness. His moral values, though he has not formulated them clearly, are there to guide him in a pinch, and his moral values categorically reject the society around him. "All positive change was good; standing still, growing to the spot, was always bad. . . . The one indispensable answer to an environment bristling with people and things one thought were bad was to go on finding out new ways in which one could think they were bad." [10] *Lucky Jim* gives expression to an irrepressible spirit of intransigence.

The exemplary novel of the angry young men is *Room at the Top*, by John Braine. It is exemplary in that it sounds many of the leading social motifs of the group. Here is Horatio-Alger type of fiction rendered in sophisticated and ironic terms, the American drive for success projected against the contemporary social background of England. John Braine introduces the young conquering hero, who has been a flier in the Second World War and who feels keenly the stigma of his lower class origin. When he assumes his new job, he moves to a part of town where huge houses stand, with spacious drives, cultivated hedges, and parked expensive cars – the visible honorific symbols of the kind of life he would like to enjoy. After his first taste, on a modest scale, of the luxuries of the upper class world, he resolves to dedicate himself to the religion of Mammon.

Room at the Top furnishes a documented and vividly dramatized picture of the hero's single-minded obsession with the cash-nexus; his is a class-

---

[10] Kingsley Amis, *Lucky Jim*. New York: The Viking Press, 1958, p. 132.

consciousness which is resentful because it craves to possess what it envies in the members of the ruling class. If Joe Lampton had money he would not feel inferior. He has come a long way since 1941, when his home was blown to bits, yet he remembers what is father had told him: "There's some things that can be bought too dear." [11] Looking back over the road he had traveled to reach the top, he comes to understand that the young Joe Lampton could feel deeply and relate to people with genuine spontaneity, whereas now, as a successful man, he is cut off from others by his very success. Not that he is in the least tempted to live like the poor and the downtrodden, though there are times he wishes that he harbored such a wish. He has made his choice as to which of the two worlds he cared to live in:

The world of worry about rent and taxes and groceries, of the smell of soda and blacklead and No Smoking and No Spitting and Please Have the Correct Change Ready and the world of the Rolls and the black-market clothes and the Coty perfume and the career ahead of one running on well-oiled grooves to the knighthood. . . .[12]

At the end he marries the boss's daughter, achieves the glory of success, and feels utterly despicable for what he had to do in order to gain this coveted prize. This novel plainly stresses the price one has to pay in striving to rise high in the business world while at the same time giving a glowing account of the pleasures and privileges the ownership of wealth bestows.

Thus the English novel of the fifties is very much of this world wordly, satiric in its thrust, stressing the follies and flagrant contradictions of society. Engaged in a quest for identity and higher status, the hero becomes aware of the costly price he must pay for the wages of success, the loss of innocence, and pays it, though not without severe conflicts of conscience. Or else he stubbornly resists conscription by the Establishment and pays the penalty for his contumacy. If *Room at the Top* represents one pole of this quest, *Hurry on Down* and *Happy as Larry* represent the other. In *Hurry on Down,* by John Wain, Charles Lumley, like Joe Lampton, realizes that one needs money and influence to get ahead, to enjoy "the finer things of life," swanky bars and exclusive hotels, beautiful women, suburban homes, but he retains his integrity by refusing to pay the price. It is not in his nature to resign himself to the economic or matrimonial yoke. He resents being pigeonholed, finger-printed, regimented. What is middle-class-respectability, however highly touted, but another euphemism for enslavement to a job. Most men, he observes, wear the uniform and badge of their occupational class, whereas what Charles wants above all things is to be classless, independent, not

[11] John Braine, *Room at the Top*. Boston: Houghton Mifflin Company, 1957, p. 80.
[12] *Ibid.,* p. 196.

caught up in the hideous swindle of bourgeois existence. If he despises the values of the middle class, he is equally repelled by the vulgarity of the workers. Thus he wanders in no-man's land, belonging to no group, uncommitted, a man without a future.

Published in England in 1959, *Hurry on Down* relates the picaresque story of his efforts to break out of his bourgeois background: how he sets up in business as a window cleaner, a driver of motor cars, a dope runner, a bouncer in a night club, a gag man for a radio show, but no job can hold him down for long or curb his rebellious craving for freedom. The moral of this hilarious satiric tale, the gist of its social criticism, is plain: to make one's way in the jungle of the business world one must be prepared to sell his soul. *Hurry on Down* dwells pointedly on the misery and wretchedness of the competitive struggle, the spiritual abasement and the cunning casuistry of compromise required, before one can win a secure place for himself in the hierarchical social order. Though intensely class-conscious in content, this novel, too, voices no desire to overturn society. Unlike the snobs who worship the gilded idol of success, Charles Lumley would keep his soul unmortgaged, and that, precisely, is his mortal offence in the eyes of the enterprising middle class: he lacks ambition, he is not even trying to get ahead. His major crime is that he belongs nowhere. He is neither a tradesman nor a Bohemian, but the man without a job or a bank account has no identity whatsoever.

In their world, it was everyone's first duty to wear a uniform that announced his status, his calling and his ambition: from the navvy's thick boots and shirtsleeves to the professor's tweeds, the conventions of clothing saw to it that everyone wore his identity card where it could be seen.[13]

In a series of lively, facetious, but revealing scenes the novel depicts Charles Lumley's struggle for independence outside the class framework. Gradually he discovers that the world of business is a whited sepulcher, a ghastly lie, designed to conceal corruption, prostitution, swindling, and racketeering. In a number of key passages the aggrieved and unaffiliated hero, obviously speaking for the author, delivers his attack on a society that is ruled rapaciously by Mammon.

Money. The network everywhere: no, a web, sticky and cunningly arranged. You were either a spider, sitting comfortably in the middle or waiting with malicious joy in hiding, or you were a fly, struggling amid the clinging threads.[14]

Charles Lumley identifies himself with the fly and feels, even as he is being pulled apart and devoured, only contempt for the spider. At the end, rejecting the pernicious myth of success, he severs all the ties that bind him to

[13] John Wain, *Hurry on Down*. London: Secker & Warburg, 1959, pp. 9-10.
[14] *Ibid.*, p. 76.

society. What he really wants is not self-sufficient poverty or sleek contentment but the right to live his own life as he sees fit, to put himself beyond the arena of struggle.

The running fight between himself and society had ended in a draw; he was no nearer, fundamentally, to any *rapprochement* or understanding with it than when he had been a window cleaner, a crook, or a servant.[15]

But it is made abundantly clear, as his adventures in life are about to start again, that he will never give in.

The Contenders, also by John Wain, is a novel based on the theme suggested by the epigraph, a quotation taken from Anthony Trollope: "Success is the necessary misfortune of human life, but it is only to the very unfortunate that it comes early." *The Contenders* is a high-spirited exposé of the absurdities of the competitive mania. The story is about Robert, the artist, and Ned, the energetic businessman, who are constantly competing against each other, while Joe Shaw, the confidant, is, as he himself humorously declares, a non-competitive creature who is clearly cut out to play some mediocre role. In school as in later life, the novel points out, the gospel taught is: compete and succeed and thou shalt be saved. Competition is the perfect training for careerists, and competition need not be confined to business affairs; it can take the form of social or sexual or personal aggrandisement.

The account of the intensive competition between Robert Lamb and Ned provides the staple entertainment of the novel. Robert succeeds as an artist but success spoils him. Joe observes what this frenzied struggle for success does to people, how it undermines their character, turning all their human relations into calculated moves, so that they look upon marriage, for example, as a kind of investment or business deal. Joe Shaw is struck by the fact that his friend Ned regarded women as instruments of prestige, just as Don Juan treated them as instruments of pleasure. Joe has no liking for the breed of moneyed men. A businessman, he says, "is distinguished from other people, not by his being busy while they are idle, but because he is in it for the money rather than for the sake of whatever it is he's doing." [16] That is what the novel is about: the failure of worldly success. The bitch goddess has become a vampire that sucks men's blood dry.

In all these strictures on the failings of contemporary English society, John Wain writes not in a mood of anger (in his autobiography, *Sprightly Running*, he summarily disposes of the label, "Angry Young Man," that had been applied to his work) but in a spirit wholly dedicated to the truth. And it is this spirit that held him back from subscribing to any set political pro-

---

[15] *Ibid.*, p. 239.
[16] John Wain, *The Contenders*. New York: St. Martin's Press, 1963, p. 155.

gram, because that would lead him to oversimplify. "A programme is an abstraction from human experience, and the truth is always richer, more various, and more contradictory than an abstraction." [17] Here is a forthright social critic who believes that life is inescapably tragic.

No shallow optimism, no easy faith that humanity will be happy when this or that piece of social engineering has been completed, or when we have finished our conquest of Nature.... The longest journeys are made within the self. The solitude that can exist within the human mind is more absolute than the emptiness of interstellar space. That is why I care nothing for technology, nothing for science. With all their improvements they can never touch anything but the surface of human life. The same problems face every man, and they always begin again. There are many ways of making life more tolerable, but none of ridding it of its basically tragic quality.[18]

Inherent in this tragic vision is the realization that in a world governed by the cash-nexus, the non-conformist is bound to be a victim. Thomas Hinde, in *Happy as Larry* (an ironic title like Samuel Beckett's *Happy Days*), presents an anti-hero who is virtually immobilized by a sense of futility. Here is the rebel who refuses to be bought off, who will take no part in a game that is not only rigged but rotten through and through; he washes his hands of the shameful business of selling one's labor in the open market. Why should one use up one's time and talent in some tedious, meaningless occupation in order to earn enough to pay the landlord, the grocer, the baker, and the butcher? He will not allow himself to be sold into economic servitude. His freedom as an artist (he wants to become a writer) is frustrated by the demands of a materialistic society that is geared principally to utilitarian ends.

Hinde's fiction is unsparingly negative in its social criticism. Even his humor is mixed with gall, and his farcical scenes are intended to highlight the incredible hypocrisy and selfishness of the human animal. The plot, in its mixture of bitter cynicism and despair, is unrelieved by any touch of compassion except for those who suffer hopelessly and without illusion. What we get is a composite picture of English society infected with the leprosy of the lie, a society, righteous in its rhetoric, whose religion is grounded in work, the job, a steady and, whenever possible, lucrative source of income. Those who try to be honest are persecuted because they disturb the established order of things. Larry Vincent, the hero of the novel, has ceased to care what happens to him. After perceiving the pointlessness of life, he has died within. He cannot take his own writing seriously. He feels he should make the effort to create but he can find no good reason why he should do so. The world is a crooked, dismal, oppressive place to live in. And he clings to

[17] John Wain, *Sprightly Running*. New York: St. Martin's Press, 1963, p. 207.
[18] *Ibid.,* p. 262.

his conviction that a regular job is not necessity but only an excuse for living.

Despite this counterpointed note of nihilistic futility, most of the younger novelists of the fifties and early sixties welcome the Welfare State, and why not? And yet, thought they have won many of the prizes for which they so strenuously competed, they do not rejoice in their success. Though they prefer to think of themselves as realists who are suspicious of idealistic theories and programs that purport to solve all social problems, they somehow continue to feel guilty for not keeping up the mental fight until they have built Jerusalem in England's green and pleasant land. This internal conflict makes for tension in the fiction they produce but it also blunts the edge of their criticism of society. Though not in itself highly creative, their work, satiric in aim and ironic in tone, was an inverted expression of protest, "a stage of dissent from old formulations," in which "contempt, sickness and anger were the predominant impressions." [19]

For truly representative examples of the literature of protest we must turn to some of the twentieth-century novels and plays which condemn the barbarism of the age: its resort to the cataclysmic violence of war, its invention and use of the atom bomb, and the nihilism that justified the practice of genocide.

[19] Raymond Williams, *The Long Revolution*. New York: Columbia University Press, 1961, p. 352.

CHAPTER XI

THE CALL OF CONSCIENCE

A power can be overthrown only by another power, not by principles, and no power that can confront money is left but this one. Money is overthrown and abolished only by blood. *Life* is alpha and omega, the cosmic onflow in microcosmic form.[1]

1. Introduction

The literature of social protest is a branch of the literature of social criticism. Indeed, much, if not most, of the literature of social criticism represents some form of protest. Consequently such works as *We, the People, Awake and Sing!* and *The Grapes of Wrath* could be legitimately included in this section. The categories overlap, but we have preferred to treat separately those plays and novels that focus their attention on a particular social evil: war, the tragedy of life shut up in a concentration camp, the practice of genocide. In order to conserve space, we have had to be highly selective in our use of representative material. Were we to attempt to consider the full body of twentieth-century literature that protests against various manifestations of social evil – corruption in business and high places, the Sacco-Vanzetti case, the muckraking exposé of the meat industry, discrimination against the Negro, anti-Semitism, and so on – we should have to compose a book of encyclopedic proportions.

In seeking to explore the relationship between literature and society, we are faced again and again with the question basic to our inquiry: in what way does literature affect the ongoing process of social change? If literature leaves its impact, whatever that may be, upon society, it is nevertheless clear that society to a marked degree shapes the form as well as content of literature. Society provides the substance and structure of the plot, the *mise en scène*, the characters, the actors, the director, and even (Marxist spokesmen argue) the logic of the denouement, the resolution of the conflict. In-

---

[1] Oswald Spengler, *The Decline of the West*. Translated by Charles Francis Atkinson. New York: Alfred A. Knopf, 1926, II, 507.

deed, many sociological critics contend that society is the generative context of value, the source of everything that man has achieved through the ages: culture, civilization, law, language, philosophy, music, letters, and art. Hence, according to this view, literature is best studied and understood in its social and historical setting, as a symbolic response to the urgent needs and problems of the age. The Marxist aesthetic goes further and holds that the writer, himself a social being, inevitably interprets his world in the light of his class affiliation. However individualized his work, it is invariably the product of a number of interrelated external influences: economic, social, political, and ideological.

There is much to be said for this point of view: the literature of a country must be situated in its cultural and historical context; it does not come into being and flourish in a vacuum. For example, in nineteenth-century England, when Utilitarianism was in the saddle, free competition was considered an eminently desirable state of affairs. What contributed to the material welfare of society and the State was also regarded as a positive good promoting the full development of the individual. In the United States, to take another example, the theme of loneliness became a perennial and obsessive theme as industrialism spread and the individual became depersonalized, absorbed in the efficient function of the productive machinery of the land.[2] The realities of the American scene conditioned in part the kind of novels and plays that were composed and the underlying conflicts they dealt with: public morality in business and politics versus private morality, instinct versus mechanization, spontaneity pitted against the repressive ethic of conformity. In story after story Sherwood Anderson portrayed characters, cut off from Nature, struggling to keep their identity and fulfill their aching need for love in an industrialized environment concerned exclusively with acquisitive ends. Faulkner describes how the Snopes clan invade the South like a plague of locusts and cunningly take possession of whatever they can lay their hands on. Increasingly, one motif that crops up in the American literary tradition is that of the lonely individual who seeks to maintain his integrity in a hostile society. Not surprisingly we hear the plangent roar of dissent, voices raised in opposition to the religion of success and the idolatrous cult of what the beat generation calls Moneytheism.

Such correlations can of course be impressively documented, but what they often leave out of account is the disconcerting fact that more or less the same social conditions call forth strikingly different reactions on the part of wri-

---

[2] For an illuminating analysis of the theme of isolation in the American novel, see Edwin T. Bowden, *The Dungeon of the Heart*. New York: The Macmillan Company, 1961.

ters. Gorky and Andreyev, both contemporaries, responded differently to the revolutionary challenge of the Russian masses. Historical determinism is inadequate in its attempt to explain the emergence, uniquely individual-ized, of a literary masterpiece. Kafka, Poe, Ionesco, Samuel Beckett, D. H. Lawrence, Aldous Huxley, Pasternak, James Joyce – surely the artistic effectiveness of their work cannot be measured simply in terms of the social and economic conditions that existed in their lifetime.

The writer who explores the psychological depths and moral dilemmas of the subjective world acknowledges the reality of society, but he also goes beyond its constraining limits. A Kafka, a Joyce, a Samuel Beckett or Iones-co is not led astray by the pull of politics, the ideological passions of the hour. For them the imagination is the living truth, and dreams are an essen-tial part of reality. The metaphysical vision tempers their delineation of man caught in the cross-currents of the temporal. They find existence alien, in-comprehensible, and frightening. Kierkegaard speaks for them when he writes:

I stick my finger into existence – it smells of nothing. Where am I? How came I here? What is this thing called the world? What does this word mean? Who is it that has lured me into the world? Why was I not consulted, why not made acquainted with its manners and customs...? How did I obtain an interest in this big enterprise they call reality? Why should I have an interest in it? Is it not a voluntary concern? And if I am to be compelled to take part in it, where is the director? I should like to make a remark to him. Is there no director? Whither shall I turn with my complaint? [3]

This strikes a recognizable, if still muted, chord in nineteenth-century lite-rature but one that becomes a full-throated cry of anguish in the twentieth century; it heralds the intensification of Cartesian consciousness, the upsurge of subjectivity, the Existentialist revolt. Is this solely the outcome of history? Are the writings of Kierkegaard no more than a conditioned response to the determinants of his age? [4]

Literature is not merely a mirror held up to society, a faithful image of social conditions as they exist. No, it creates an imaginative world of its own, it explores areas of spiritual experience that overtly or by indirection ex-pose the lacks and limitations of social reality. Even Socialist realism is ruled by the optative mood and violates its own aesthetic principles by going

[3] Sören Kierkegaard, *Repetition*. Translated by Walter Lowrie. Princeton: Prince-ton University Press, 1946, p. 114. Quoted in J. Hillis Miller, *The Disappearance of God*. Cambridge: Harvard University Press, 1963, p. 9.

[4] "Surely the sense of history is one of the causes of the experience of existential isolation, but withdrawal into the privacy of consciousness can also lead to an aware-ness of historical contingency." J. Hillis Miller, *The Disappearance of God*, p. 99.

beyond what is to a categorical vision of what ought to be. Literature thus often serves as a medium of protest against the abandonment or desecration of the ideal. There is no denying the fact that literature through the ages, from Sophocles and Aeschylus to Shakespeare and Cervantes and the modern writers, serves to "criticize" social reality, but the point at issue is how this criticism is embodied, apart from the equally complex problem of the effect it produces. This "criticism" is voiced in a way that fails to conform to any current political or sociological formula. In examining the finite world of people and events from a number of varied and incongruous perspectives, it breaks up the so-called "normal" universe of perception and belief.

But in an age overshadowed by the imminent danger of an atomic Armageddon, the writer feels compelled to break out of his ivory tower and sound his cry of warning. He protests against the dehumanization of man by the machine and the horror of nuclear warfare. Particularly in a time of crisis is the writer drawn as a matter of conscience to the art of preachment, composing manifestoes bidding his readers and fellow literati defend this or that menaced ideal. When Fascism was on the march in Europe and the United States was about to become involved in the Second World War, a group of alarmed intellectuals arose to attack the literary naturalism, stridently negative in tone, of the twenties.[5] In 1940 Archibald MacLeish published his polemic, *The Irresponsibles*, anathematizing the literary men of his land who had remained culpably silent while Fascism was threatening to destroy the foundations of Western culture. MacLeish urged American writers to gird their loins and take part in the crucial task of defending democracy. Implicit in his jeremiad, of course, is the assumption that literature is an integral part of the social process, perfectly capable, and legitimately so, of influencing the course of its development.

Imaginative literature, however, cannot adapt itself to the time-bound demands of national policy without betraying its *raison d'être* and debasing its value as art. Instead of becoming politicalized and exploited for the sake of redressing some special case of inhumanity or injustice, it must, as the irreconcilable voice of protest, bear witness to the disparity between conditions as they exist in the always imperfect present and the elusive but always sought-for ideal. Addressed to the conscience of mankind, it holds up a vision of life that is essentially different from the dominant view of social reality. "In its advanced position," as Herbert Marcuse says, "it is the

[5] For a spirited reply to these attacks, see James T. Farrell, *The League of Frightened Philistines*. New York: The Vanguard Press, 1945.

Great Refusal – the protest against that which is." [6] It calls for the fullest harmonious development of human potentialities, even if that seems "unrealistic" in the light of what is possible at the time. The *status quo* cannot be maintained. Change is necessary for the health of society as a whole as well as for the health of the individual, especially today in a social order which functions with mechanical efficiency and yet is subject to recurrent explosions of destructive irrationality. A world which periodically wages war must not be allowed to go unchallenged.

Blinded to his true interests, his material needs abundantly satisfied, twentieth-century man, as we have seen in the previous chapter, is inclined to approve of the welfare state and identify himself with the politics of production. He becomes, as Herbert Marcuse points out, one-dimensional in his thinking, a willing cog in the service of the industrial machine. There is no longer a province jealously preserved for private needs, no longer a dynamic state of tension and conflict between the individual and society. The individual becomes a grammatical fiction. The unanimist is obliged to create his massive novels without introducing a central character. As Jules Romains puts it:

A century ago it may not have been absurd to make the whole life of the city gravitate around a single individual and associate everything with the experiences of one man. Today, in my belief, it would be rather ridiculous.[7]

Though he cannot dispense with the use of individual characters, they are kept subordinate to the composite portrait of society as a whole. Collective life, this French novelist is convinced, cannot be effectively rendered in terms of the consciousness of a single individual. And Nathalie Sarraute, in *The Age of Suspicion*, cogently argues that the death of the self in modern fiction reflects the liquidation of the self in mass-society.

In picturing the gap between the ideal and the real, in protesting against the intolerable contradictions of his society, the writer must not labor under the illusion that his work will of itself produce the desired result. The best he can hope to achieve by the mediation of his art is to induce his readers to look into their heart and determine their degree of guilt for what has befallen them and their world. Literature, even in its symbolic quest for the ideal, is social in character in that it is addressed to an audience and presumably exercises some measure of influence.[8] We shall endeavor to trace the

---

[6] Herbert Marcuse, *One-Dimensional Man*. Boston: Beacon Press, 1964, p. 63.

[7] Jules Romains, *Men of Good Will*. Translated by Warre B. Wells. New York: Alfred A. Knopf, 1934, p. ix.

[8] As T. S. Eliot remarks in "Religion and Literature": "The author of a work of imagination is trying to affect us wholly, as human beings, whether he knows it or

extent of that influence in the body of protest literature in the twentieth century, especially as it bears upon the tragic problem created by war, the atom bomb, and the horror of life in a concentration camp.

2. *The Syndrome of Guilt and Atonement*

I am responsible for all the evil that is perpetrated in the world, unless I have done what I could to prevent it, even to the extent of sacrificing my life. I am guilty because I am alive and can continue to live while this is happening. Thus criminal complicity takes hold of everyone for everything that happens.[9]

The fires of literary protest in our time are fueled by the writer's sense of guilt for the man-made calamities that afflict the people of the earth. Just as the scientist, despite his unswerving devotion to the truth, is not exempt from obeying the ethical mandate (a problem that C. P. Snow takes up in *The New Men* and Duerrenmatt in *The Physicists*), so a philosopher like Karl Jaspers comes to feel that he is personally responsible for everything that happens in the world. The *social* problem of guilt and responsibility is, however, too vast and too complex to be handled adequately by the literary imagination. The powers at work on the lighted stage of history, powers that often work invisibly behind the scenes, are too abstract to be brought within the confines of art. Hence the writer concerns himself with the struggle of conscience, the syndrome of individual rather than collective guilt. When the Second World War was over and the totalitarian terror had been brought to a close, works of drama and fiction appeared – Sartre's *The Condemned of Altona*, Camus's *The Plague*, and Hochhuth's *The Deputy*, for example – which focused their attention on the crucial question of individual guilt. The guilt was not to be denied; the memory of the millions of victims killed in crematoria as well as the millions slain on the field of battle was not to be erased. Besides, the atomic bomb presented a real threat to the possibility of human survival.

The logic of the world situation was such at the end of the war that many writers began to feel they were powerless to act.[10] During the fifties they probed more deeply the problematical character of the self, since they could not hope, as literary men, to resolve the power-conflicts of the age. Living

not, and we are affected by it, as human beings, whether we intend to be or not." Morton Dauwen Zabel (ed.), *Literary Opinion in America*. New York: Harper & Brothers, 1947, p. 621.

[9] Karl Jaspers, *Tragedy Is Not Enough*. Translated by Harold A. T. Reiche, Harry T. Moore, and Karl W. Deutsch. Boston: Beacon Press, 1952, p. 53.

[10] See Charles I. Glicksberg, "What Can the Intellectuals Do?" *The Western Humanities Review*, No. 1, Summer, 1954, VIII, pp. 201-208.

as they did during an historical period that has been called variously the age of anxiety, the age of unreason, the age of suspicion, and that might with equal appropriateness be called the age of guilt, they stressed heavily the motif that we are all responsible for the disasters that have overtaken us and for the even worse disasters to come. Kafka, in *The Trial*, drew the pattern for this universal neurosis of guilt. His work communicates an oppressive feeling of anxiety accompanied by a haunting sense of guilt. He deals obsessively with the theme of the violation of "the Law," though it is hard to make out what "the Law" commands. Nevertheless, it must be obeyed. Failure to do so, whatever the reason, is invariably punished. In his story, "In the Penal Colony," Kafka describes a machine which inscribes upon the body of the prisoner the exact nature of his transgression. His flesh is made to bear the imprint of his guilt.

If the writers of the fifties felt keenly their helplessness in the face of world problems, this did not lessen their sense of guilt or their desire to protest against conditions as they were. They had before them the inspiring example of the commitments their fathers made during the embattled thirties. There is an ache of longing, a note of envy and frustration, in Jimmy Porter's voice in *Look Back in Anger* as he recalls the brave causes the previous generation had to fight for, while the men of the fifties had nothing but their own cynicism to feed on. The civil war in Spain generated an outburst of revolutionary enthusiasm during the heyday of the United Front. The conscience of young writers then spoke out with prophetic assurance as they dedicated themselves to the task of laying the foundations of a new, ultimately classless society. In his introduction to the verse anthology, *New Signatures* (1932), Michael Roberts declared:

I think, and the writers in this book obviously agree, that there is only one way of life for us: to renounce that system (monopoly capitalism) now. . . .[11]

But Julian Symons makes this revealing confession:

"Someone must have been telling lies about Joseph K. for without having done anything wrong he was arrested one fine morning." One hardly needs to read further than the opening sentence of *The Trial* to understand why Kafka exerted so much influence over English prose writers in the late Thirties. Like Kafka's heroes they were aware of guilt without being able clearly to discover its nature; like them, they were in rebellion against the authority which they respected, and to which they desired to submit.[12]

Their attitude toward authority was ambivalent. They wanted to obey the

---

[11] Julian Symons, *The Thirties*. London: The Cresset Press, 1960, p. 19.
[12] *Ibid.*, p. 152.

commands of the Communist Party, which was supposed to represent the inexorable will of history, but something within them made them resist Party decisions and controls. Their participation in the Spanish Civil War turned out unhappily. The defeat of the struggle in Spain, coupled with the outbreak of the Second World War, brought on a wave of disillusionment with Communism.

In fact, after the Second World War, writers, as writers, shied away from political commitments. The writers of the West, in their shifting pattern of ideological alignment, demonstrated that the voice of conscience is ambiguous in its pronouncements. This was evident in the reversal of their attitude toward leftwing politics. Whereas Sartre preached the need for literature to support the cause of Communism and in his play, *Dirty Hands*, exalted the character of the Communist at the expense of the irresolute and ineffectual middle-class intellectual, the French new novel was not politically oriented. Robbe-Grillet declares that the fiction he and the others in his group produce does not "serve a political cause . . . even a cause that seems to be a just one, even if in our political life we fight for its triumph." [13] The politics of the left and the right, the various shades of opinion in the spectrum of allegiance, the conflicting imperatives in the ethic of commitment, all that did not matter; what mattered was the perfection of the work in its revelation of the truth of the human condition.

But the chorus of protest continued, each writer protesting in his own way against the flagrant social evils of his time. From the time of Dada to the stormy debut of *The Deputy*, from the plumbing of the depths of the Surrealists to the production of *Rhinoceros* and *Mother Courage*, modern literature has cried out against the dehumanizing character of Western civilization. Those who could not appeal to God's justice or mercy had to address their appeal to the court of world conscience.

Literature is thus invested with a moral as well as social function, and it is this function which raises a thorny problem in aesthetics. It brings up the perennially puzzling question, a question which has engaged the attention of thinkers from Plato to Tolstoy and T. S. Eliot: what is "the value" of literature? What "good" does it accomplish? For whom, for what purpose, does the writer create his work?[14] It is, of course, a mistake to consider literature as solely or chiefly a moral utterance. Certainly the moral value of a work cannot be separated from its embodiment as art. Nevertheless, aesthe-

[13] Laurent Le Sage, *The French New Novel*. University Park: Pennsylvania State University Press, 1962, pp. 10-11.

[14] See "For Whom Does One Write?" in Jean-Paul Sartre, *What Is Literature?* Translated by Bernard Frechtman. New York: Philosophical Library, 1949, pp. 67-160.

tic values do not function autonomously in a vacuum. Though writers may not agree on what is "moral," just as they do not agree necessarily in their political views, they are moralists, though in subtly differentiated ways, even when, like Baudelaire and Genet, they embrace the extremity of evil.

Morality in literature, however, always runs the danger of overreaching itself, of falling into the heresy of the didactic. Though it cannot beat its wings in the intense inane of irresponsible freedom, it is more than morally declarative. It does not consist of an imaginatively embellished series of ethical or political propositions. Such an envisagement of the aim and function of literature reduces it to the narrowness of allegory or preachment. As Vincent Buckley declares in *Poetry and Morality*:

It seems to me foolish to ask poetry to console or sustain man, to integrate or harmonize him, to "save" him; for each of these ways of putting it really means to redeem him from the limitations, the impotence and terrors, attendant on his actual state in the world.[15]

This sums up nicely the predicament of the writer who wishes to transcend the limitations of the word and to convert his art into a magical instrument for eliminating the evils of the world.

The moral ideal assumes a bewildering variety of forms in life as in literature, but it is generally invoked when man finds himself in an extreme situation: thrust into the maelstrom of war or incarcerated without reason in a concentration camp and facing death in a gas oven. Even an Eichmann on trial professes his adherence to the Kantian categorical imperative. The beleaguered Jews of the Warsaw Ghetto were convinced that the world would rush to their rescue once it learned of the genocidal atrocities the Nazis were committing. Their faith in a universal standard of justice and respect for life sounds pathetic in the light of the historical facts as they later became known. As Hochhuth points out in his play, the Nazis discovered to their gratification that they could carry out their mass murders with impunity. It was only after the hostilities ended that the ghastly truth about the crematorial horrors were brought to light.

---

[15] Vincent Buckley, *Poetry and Morality*. London: Chatto & Windus, 1958, pp. 23-24.

CHAPTER XII

THE NEMESIS OF WAR

It is evident to me, not only that I must die once, that is to say, when I have reached the limiting point of natural death, but also that I am face to face, at every moment of my life, now and always, with the immediate possibility of death.[1]

The literary protest against war (there are few writers today who are inclined to chant its heroic virtues) is essentially a protest against death. The art of mass slaughter perfected by technological means has brought home to twentieth-century man the realization that in the next world war possibly all of human life may be wiped out on this planet. This is not merely a statistical summing up, an actuarial count, but a grim existential fact that concerns every living being who faces the threat of atomic extinction. It is not only, as in past wars, millions of soldiers who will perish on far-flung battlefields; civilization as a whole will be destroyed. It is therefore not surprising that death, with its attendant nihilistic strain, provides the chief absorbing theme of literature in our time. As Frederick J. Hoffman reveals in *The Mortal No*, it brings into focus the haunting question of the ephemerality of historic time versus eternity and makes man poignantly aware that he lives in a fleeting, precarious present. How is the writer to cope with this challenge? He is driven to condemn the recurrent epidemics of violence, the dance of death over fire and water and in the air that is more horrible than the worst nightmares conjured up by the mind.

How shall modern man make his peace with death that comes not in the fullness of time but with cataclysmic suddenness? How shall he resign himself to the knowledge that in the imminent future – he cannot tell how soon the hour of doom will strike – he and his kind will utterly cease to be? The danger of atomic annihilation weakens the assurance of vicarious immortality through the germ-plasm, the biological perpetuation of the species, for

[1] Paul-Louis Landsberg, *The Experience of Death: The Moral Problem of Suicide*. Translated by Cynthia Rowland. New York: Philosophical Library, 1953, p. 6.

once the atomic bombs begin to explode the world of man with all its historical records and precious artifacts will be destroyed. A new frightening dimension is added to time and life. The certainty that death conquers over all
things strengthens the conviction that death is the supreme evil.

In this crisis the literary mind is often tempted to simplify the problem
and cry out there must be no more wars, and many writers utter this piercing
cry, but this fails to solve the problem. Modern man keenly feels his helplessness in this situation; he is incapable of preventing the fate – and yet it
is of his own making – that is about to befall him. The writer, too, as he
struggles to impose the order and unity of art on the chaos of life, wonders
what he can possibly do to put an end to the ghastly horror of war. The First
World War unleashed a wave of revulsion. The millions of dead who died
in vain, the millions of the wounded, the starvation among the people of
Europe, the senselessness of the conflict and the anticlimax of the aftermath
– all this triggered the mood of disillusionment that characterized the reaction of the creative elite during the twenties. The fighting achieved no
positive results. It did not make the world safe for democracy and it did
not bring the blessing of assured peace. As Ezra Pound wrote with under-
standable bitterness in "Hugh Selwyn Mauberley":

> Died some, pro patria, non "dulce" non "et decor"...
> walked eye-deep in hell
> believing in old men's lies, then unbelieving
> came home, home to a lie,
> home to many deceits,
> home to old lies and new infamy;
> usury age-old and age-thick
> and liars in public places.

But it was Ernest Hemingway, not the angry and eccentric Ezra Pound,
who served as the spokesman of the lost generation. In *A Farewell to Arms*
he told the truth about the costly blunders and demented butchery of war.
Like Pound he protested against the patriotic lies the leaders fed the populace. His hero, Frederick Henry, had seen nothing sacred in war, "and the
things that were glorious had no glory and the sacrifices were like the
stockyards at Chicago if nothing was done with the meat except bury it." [2]
But Hemingway had no redemptive message for his time; in the general collapse of values in his age he voiced his belief in personal courage, the code

[2] Ernest Hemingway, *A Farewell to Arms.* New York: The Modern Library, 1929,
p. 196.

of honor among the initiated, as the only virtue that can give man a sense of dignity as he marches to his death.

There were numerous other writers – Remarque, Stefan Zweig, Arnold Zweig, Barbusse, Richard Aldington, Siegfried Sassoon – who could not rest until they had communicated their vision of the meaningless tragedy of war. The war was a traumatic experience for those who had believed fervently in the publicly proclaimed ideals of progress, democracy, world peace, and the brotherhood of man, in the name of which the war had ostensibly been fought. They returned from the war uprooted, spiritually shaken, to carry on their life once more in a world that lay in ruins. But they could not forget, and the memory of the past, frightful, guilt-haunted, led some writers to seek to grasp the meaning behind this outbreak of homicidal madness. They hoped that by their realistic debunking of the romantic notions of war they might be able to prevent it from happening again. Unfortunately their protest against the insanity of war could achieve but little. The best they could do was to utter a solemn warning or voice their pity at the monstrous waste of human lives, and all for what?

Chlumberg, a French dramatist, was gripped by an idea that came to him suddenly: what if all the dead should rise up and return to the world which they had died to save? His play, *The Miracle at Verdun*, highlights the contrast between the callous heedlessness of those living in the present and the passionate concern of the dead who had been slain in the war. The time is August 1934, twenty years after the onset of the First World War. The dead who have risen discover that their ordeal in the Gehenna of battle, the agony of killing and dying, was all for naught. One soldier finds that the factory where he had been formerly employed has been converted to the manufacture of double fuses for the coming war. Another learns that his son is being trained to kill in battle. In the last scene, the character who lives through this fantasy in his dream, hears a German father teaching his son that a soldier's death is the most beautiful death of all.

In defeated Germany the postwar years gave rise to major dramatic works of protest by Expressionists like Georg Kaiser and Ernst Toller. The experience of disaster intensified in the Expressionists their rejection of nationalism and their call for spiritual transformation, the preliminary step in the work of bringing a better world to birth. The reign of Mammon and the tyranny of the machine, they insisted, must be abolished and make way for the brotherhood of man. Ernst Toller, the activist who believed in political solutions, was no doctrinaire prophet. He could find no words strong enough to denounce the actions not only of the militarists but also of those radical agitators who preach the class war and instigate the workers to revolt even when the cause is hopeless. Like Karl Jaspers, he was convinced that all men are responsible for the crimes that are committed on earth. He condemned those who advocate the use of force. He belongs to those visionary writers whose conscience bleeds for the man-made suffering that exists in the world and who take upon themselves, directly as well as vicariously in their art, the burden of guilt for the evil their fellow men perpetrate. In his desire to make the gospel of love and human brotherhood prevail, he was willing to politicalize his plays. In 1923 he wrote:

There are no plays without political bearings. Drama is the presentation of the relation between men as social beings. Only the bourgeois believes that there can be a society devoid of social and political ties.[3]

As a dramatist Toller wished to use the theater as a medium not for the dissemination of propaganda but for spiritual awakening and enlightenment. He spoke out in behalf of the inarticulate and oppressed and strove like Brecht to arouse a direct response in his audience, but his technique was radically different. He tried to achieve his ends through Expressionist rather than doctrinaire means. The four plays he wrote in prison – *Transfiguration* (1917), *Masses and Man* (1921), *The Machine Wreckers* (1922), and *Hinkemann* (1932) – contain the heart of his message. They are plays of inspired social protest. No orthodox Socialist, Toller believed that the love of man transcended and could defeat the forces of hatred in the world. When some critics assailed *Masses and Man* on the ground that it was tendentious, he replied:

There is only one form of tendentiousness which the artist must avoid, and that is to make the issue simply between good and evil.

The artist's business is not to prove theses but to throw light upon human conduct. Many great works of art have also a political significance; but these must never be confused with mere political propaganda in the guise of art. Such propaganda is designed exclusively to serve an immediate end, and is at the same time something more and something less than art. Something more because, at its best, it may possibly stimulate the public to immediate action; something less because it can never achieve the profundity of art, can never awaken in us the tragic sense of life, or, as Hebbel put it, "rouse the world from its sleep." [4]

Toller, a sensitive Jew who regarded himself as essentially a German writer, was deeply shaken by the events of the First World War. The war was his university, giving him insight into the malign instinct of hatred that impelled

[3] Ernst Toller, *Looking Through the Bars*. Translated by R. Ellis Roberts. New York: Farrar & Rinehart, 1937, p. 302.

[4] Ernst Toller, *Seven Plays*. New York: Liveright Publishing Company, 1936, p. 280.

not only the leaders, both the Junkers and Communists, but also the masses who furnished the cannonfodder. It taught him once and for all that it is a ghastly perversion of the truth and a crime against mankind to glorify the fact of war. Like Hemingway, he unmasked the hypocrisy of the officially proclaimed idealistic war aims. Men lost their identity as well as their humanity fighting in a war which had no meaning: "We were all of us cogs in a great machine which sometimes rolled forward, nobody knew where, some times backwards, nobody knew why." [5] After Toller had fallen ill and was finally discharged as unfit for further military service, he brooded feverishly on his agonized memories of the war. What did it all portend? How could this apocalypse of slaughter be halted? Wherein was to be found the cure for this destructive mass psychosis? He came to the conclusion that more than political reforms had to be instituted if peace was to be permanently established; the whole world and particularly the heart of man would have to be transformed. In *Transfiguration,* Toller, through the *persona* of his protagonist, voices his gospel of redemption.

Friedrich, the hero, a tormented, alienated Jew, is struggling hard to end the split in his being. At first he desires to inspire his fellow citizens to defend their country with their lives, though he wonders uneasily if there is not a higher loyalty than the call of patriotism. When he learns that the war is actually being fought for safeguarding the profits of capitalism, he abandons his work as a sculptor and sets out alone on the quest for identity. Before he can identify himself with humanity he must find himself, discover the meaning of his life. In anguish he cries out:

a millon shattered arms are stretched towards me. The agonizing cries of a million mothers echo in my ears. Where? Where? The unborn children whimper. The madmen cry. Oh, holy weeping! Speech defiled! Mankind defiled! ... For our country's sake! Oh, God ... can it really be? Can a country really ask this much of us? Or has our country sold its soul, sold it to the State? Sold it in a dirty business speculation? Perhaps the State is a pimp, and our country a whore to be sold for any brutal lust − blessed by that procuress, the Church! [6]

Friedrich, the impassioned apostle of a spiritual revolution, is seeking to remove all the barriers that prevent the real self in man from reaching fulfillment. In his final speech he proclaims his faith that men can still be human if they preserve their belief in themselves and in humanity and bring the war to an end.

The plea went unheeded. The war did not end until the defeat of the

[5] Ernst Toller, *I Was a German.* Translated by Edward Crankshaw. New York: Morrow, 1934, p. 90.

[6] Ernst Toller, *Seven Plays,* p. 85.

German forces was assured. Then came the disastrous aftermath: inflation, hunger, widespread misery and want, and the rise of the Brown Terror. The triumph of Nazism trampled under foot and bestially defiled everything Toller had fought to achieve. His people, the Jews of Germany, were rounded up and thrust into concentration camps. He left his native land. When he beheld what was happening in the world, how love turned to demonic hate, how the German culture of which he had been a part regressed to the law of the jungle, he had no more desire to remain alive. He made his final gesture of protest: he committed suicide in New York in 1939, just before the outbreak of the Second World War. He had labored to halt the relapse into barbarism, he had endeavored to bridge the gap between art and prophecy, but his protest was unable to alter the course of historic events.

A little more than twenty years elapsed between the end of one war and the beginning of the second. The worst came to pass. The vision of a redeemed humanity that Toller had held up was dissolved in the smoke issuing from the crematoria at Auschwitz and the atomic conflagration of Hiroshima and Nagasaki. No age is without its troublesome problems, its conflicts and crises, but ours is peculiarly and unprecedentedly an age of catastrophe. The specter of universal disaster is no longer remote but frighteningly imminent. What compounds the evil is that for the first time in the annals of history man realizes his helplessness in the clutch of social, economic, and technological forces too complex and too abstract for him to grasp, much less control. He craves peace and security but wars unpredictably break out and there is seemingly nothing he can do to stop them. In such a truly desperate climate of thought, the writer either refuses to participate in the legalized ritual of mass murder, the politics of fratricide (witness the current spread of protests and demonstrations among intellectuals against America's role in the war in Vietnam), and devotes himself single-mindedly to his creative work until doom overwhelms the world, or he takes upon himself the mantle of Jeremiah and, like Toller, attempts to utilize his art as a form of prophecy and protest.

Whenever an age suffers a radical and traumatic reversal of its traditional way of life, as happened since the time of the First World War, the world of the imagination suffers a corresponding shock. Writers caught in this impasse are bound to ask themselves what purpose their art can possibly serve in a world which periodically consigns millions of young men to death. War, the Nemesis of history, the orgiastic involvement in a collective Dance of Death, nullifies the worth and negates the validity of the artistic enterprise. Besides, society, once it loses its faith in the future of mankind and the continuity of the race, is really in no condition to encourage the development of letters and art, though it may continue to pay assiduous lip-service to the intrinsic values of culture. The literature of the past fifty years has undergone a series of revolutionary transformations as it sought to assimilate and give expression to new areas of experience. Free association, the stream of consciousness, the interior monologue, the logic of the dream, the resources of fantasy, irony, and farce, broke open new vistas of time and tapped hitherto unexploded sources of anxiety and *Angst*. The writers of our time

have responded in an untraditional manner to the wars and revolutions, to the statistical tabulations, the advertising slogans and the Geiger-counters. The resulting changes in our literature have transformed not only manner and style; they have driven to the very core of literary expression, metamorphosing literature itself.[7]

Here is further evidence that literature is profoundly affected by major changes that take place in the social sphere.

By the time the Second World War was fought, the trappings of war had lost all their romantic glory. The dirty business of defeating Hitler had to be finished, but there was little sense of triumph in the accomplishment. The literature born of this struggle was ideologically confused in content. Whereas the writers thrown up by the First World War, men like Remarque, Hemingway, and Barbusse, were in rebellion against what they considered a betrayal of the cause of mankind, the writers of war novels in the late forties and fifties generally lacked this rebellious spirit. According to Malcolm Cowley, "many of the novelists are really disillusioned this time, instead of being rebellious. . . ."[8]

For many writers the only refuge against the unleashed fury of war was to retire within the fastness of the self, but even this hideout could offer no protection against atomic bombs. Death, by becoming technologically efficient, sealed the doom of the individual hero. In modern technological society, as Ernst Juenger maintains in his novel, *The Glass Bees*, individualism is an anachronism. In an age of massive concentrated power, words such as honor and loyalty have lost their meaning; "even war was no longer war."[9] The cavalry is replaced by fighting machines: the tanks and airplanes. Soldiers, too, have become mechanized; the struggle for power is now waged with deadly scientific weapons. Juenger feels that technology itself, like warfare, is a force that makes for destruction. He is protesting against the me-

[7] John McCormick, *Catastrophe and Imagination*. London and New York: Longmans, Green and Company, 1957, p. 2.

[8] Malcolm Cowley, *The Literary Situation*. New York: The Viking Press, 1954, p. 40.

[9] Ernst Juenger, *The Glass Bees*. Translated by Louise Bogan and Elizabeth Mayer. New York: The Noonday Press, 1960, p. 42.

chanization of life to a point where "technics have become destiny." [10] Norman Mailer, in *The Naked and the Dead*, also pictures the ruinous consequences of the struggle for power, but his major stress is placed not on the horror and inhumanity of war but on the danger posed by Fascism. General Cummings, the commander of the troops in this sector of the Pacific, insists that technology demands coordination; "the majority of men must be made subservient to the machine. . . ." [11] Man's deepest urge, he is convinced, is to seize and exercise power. But the ending of the novel shows that the General does not know all the answers. The world does not turn Fascist.

The literary protests against war continue in undiminished volume, but their sense of urgency is increased by the knowledge that in the next war waged by the great powers atomic armaments may be used.

[10] *Ibid.,* p. 106.
[11] Norman Mailer, *The Naked and the Dead*. New York: The Modern Library, 1948, p. 177.

CHAPTER XIII

THE ATOMIC HOLOCAUST

Your first thought upon awakening be: "Atom." For you should not begin your day with the illusion that what surrounds you is a stable world. Already to-morrow it can be "something that only *has been*": for we, you, and I and our fellow men are "more mortal" and "more temporal" than all who, until yester-day, had been considered mortal. . . . For if the mankind of to-day is killed, then that which *has* been dies with it; and the mankind to come too. . . . The door in front of us bears the inscription: "Nothing will have been"; and from within: "Time was an episode."

Gunther Anders, "Commandments in the Atomic Age." [1]

WAKE BEFORE BOMB? How did one do it? Was it ever advisable? The past, whether one liked it or not, was all that one actually possessed: the green stuff, the gilt-edge securities. The present was that moment of exchange – when all might be lost. Why risk it? Why not sleep on the money in the bank? To wake before the bomb was to risk losing all to gain what might be so little – a brief moment in the present, that one moment later joined to the past. Nevertheless . . . it was a wonderful sight. There was this flash, then this pillar of fire went up and up as if to heaven, and the heat and light of that moment illuminated for a fraction the flesh and bones of the present. . . . To wake before the bomb was tricky business. What if it scared you to sleep?

Wright Morris, *Lone Ceremony in Tree*.[2]

All the terror of a supernatural power which comes to punish and destroy mankind has now attached itself to the idea of the "bomb"; and this is some-thing an individual can manipulate. It lies in his hands. An earthly ruler can now unleash destruction surpassing all the plagues with which God visited the Egyptians. Man has stolen his own God. He has seized him and taken for him-self his armoury of doom and terror.

Elias Canetti, *Crowds and Power*.[3]

---

[1] *Burning Conscience*. New York: Monthly Review Press, 1962, p. 11. For a thoroughly documented and convincing refutation, as given in *Burning Conscience,* of Claude Eatherly's guilt and expiation for the crime of having dropped the atomic bomb on Hiroshima, see William Bradford Huie, *The Hiroshima Pilot*. New York: G. P. Putnam's Sons, 1964.

[2] Wright Morris, *Lone Ceremony in Tree*. New York: Atheneum, 1960, p. 32.

[3] Elias Canetti, *Crowds and Power*. New York: The Viking Press, 1962, p. 468.

In "The End of the Survivors," the Epilogue to *Crowds and Power*, Canetti sums up his message. Power is concentrated in crowds – the East stands opposed to the West. Both are armed with the latest technological weapons for the showdown. Whereas wars in the past could last a hundred years, then four or five years, now the damage inflicted can be so devastating that there can be no protracted conflict. What is frightening is the knowledge that the leader of the contending nuclear powers can push a button that will set all this off. He is the technological wizard who by a spoken command can wipe out the peoples of the earth – and do so at a distance. But history has been speeded up to a point where retaliation comes immediately. As a result the leader, no longer sure of his survival, has grown fearful. If he is in command of weapons that can wreak death at tremendous distances, so is the enemy. Like the mobilized crowd who carry out his orders, he is exposed and vulnerable. There is no place where he can hide.

There is nowhere the new weapons cannot reach, including whatever refuge he may make himself. His greatness and his invulnerability have become incompatible. He has over-reached himself. Rulers tremble today, not, as formerly, because they are rulers, but as the equals of everybody else. The ancient mainspring of power, the safe-guarding of the ruler at the cost of all other lives, has been broken. . . . Today either everyone will survive or no-one.[4]

Having lived through the Second World War, the survivors now face the prospect of atomic annihilation. The realization that the rulers, despite the enormous power they wield, are no longer invulnerable, that everyone or no one will survive in the holocaust, is no consolation. In this frightful impasse modern man is at a loss what to do, and the writer who is his spokesman is at a loss what to say. Never before in the history of civilization has the individual been stricken by so complete and demoralized a sense of his own impotence. He seeks survival in a spirit of stoical courage even as he is caught up in a hurricane of events that seem to be beyond the control of reason. What in this crisis of the imagination can the protest of the writer hope to accomplish? Once the war breaks out, as it threatens to do at any moment of extreme international tension, he knows that no humanitarian appeals will deter the leaders of the world from unleashing their atomic weapons against "the enemy" before he seizes the initiative. The writer may voice his protest, but he is powerless to rebel. Against whom is he to rebel when virtually all of society is infected with this destructive mania? His only recourse, he feels, while yet there is time for reflection, is to retreat into himself and thus, if possible, keep himself immune from the collective madness of his age. Stand-

4 *Ibid.,* p. 469.

ing aloof from society, he judges it harshly, no longer bound by its atavistic passions. In this hour of tragic self-confrontation, he feels compelled to express his ultimate concern. He is driven to do whatever is humanly possible to prevent this dangerous situation from getting out of hand, though he suspects that all action is futile.[5]

Today there is only one theme that concerns mankind and especially the literati: the peril posed by the threat of nuclear warfare. The danger is no longer localized; it is total. It is this unprecedented world crisis which constitutes "the greatest of all menaces to the future of mankind." [6] If the atom bombs stored in the arsenals of the major powers are allowed to explode on target – and the target is always the frail, vulnerable body of man – all of life on the surface will be destroyed. Obviously the literati, unlike the political scientists,[7] have no solutions to offer; they are not oracles who can descry the shape of the future and prescribe sure-fire remedies for the political and economic ills of the world, but they do take themselves and their creative work seriously as the responsible voice of conscience. They strive to make the world of man realize the full meaning of the threat carried by the atom bomb; they reveal the hideous anxieties and grisly fears that gnaw at the vitals of modern man as he contemplates the possibility, now imminent, of extinction. In a world which may go up suddenly in atomic smoke, to speak of sacred ideals is a source of ludicrous embarrassment. To invoke the humanistic traditions of the past, to preach the necessity for moral restraint, to call on the name of God when man has usurped the prerogative of God and "taken for himself his armoury of doom and terror," all this is idiotically irrelevant. There is not sufficient time at present for philosophical parleys or religious conferences or talking marathons at the United Nations. The only premise that can be taken for granted is that the race wishes to survive, and that the only absolute evil is that which leads to death and destruction. It is on this premise that the writer bases his jeremiad.

In this emergency situation, what can the writer *do* by the labor of his pen? Shall he become an embattled propagandist and transform literature

[5] See José Ferrater Mora, *Man at the Crossroads*. Translated by Willard R. Trask. Boston: Beacon Press, 1957.

[6] Karl Jaspers, *The Future of Mankind*. Translated by E. B. Ashton. Chicago: The University of Chicago Press, 1961, p. 4.

[7] Max Lerner ends his detailed analysis of the world political situation on a note of courageous but ambiguous hope. "Of one thing I am certain. At some point man will fashion something like the collective policing agency, with a monopoly of the more lethal weapons, which I have described as crucial for survival. There is only one question: Will it be before, or will it be after, the great 'Death-happening' of an over-kill war?" Max Lerner, *The Age of Overkill*. New York: Simon and Schuster, 1962, p. 308.

into an instrument of political commitment in behalf of life? It is foolish to demand of the writer what he, as writer, is not capable of giving. He is not a scientist or political expert or social engineer. As far back as 1888, Chekhov cogently rebuked those who insisted that the writer offer a constructive solution to the problems of society.

... I always insist that it is not the business of the artist to solve questions which require a specialist's knowledge. It is wrong for an artist to take up matters he does not understand. Specialists exist for special questions; it is their business to judge of the commune, the future of capitalism, the evil of drink, of boots, of the diseases of women. ... An artist can judge only of what he understands; his sphere is as limited as that of any other specialist – this I repeat and on this I always insist.[8]

If the writer is thus limited to raising questions and not in a position to provide categorical answers, the questions he raises may nevertheless embody a protest against those forces that are hostile to life. Though knowing that life is essentially tragic, he produces work that is an affirmation of life and a celebration of human greatness.[9] Man, a mortal atom in the vertiginous flux of things, knows he is sentenced to die, but for this very reason he has hitherto been driven to utter an everlasting Yea to life. It is this instinctive love of life that has of late been weakened. Intolerably heightened by the prospect of the atomic smash-up, modern man's obsessive awareness of the imminence as well as finality of death seems to have paralyzed his powers of affirmation.

The dominant symbols of doom in the literature of the fifties and sixties are not to be lightly set aside as nightmares conjured up by a morbidly beset imagination. They are symptoms of a moral despair when mankind as a whole comes to believe there is no way out of the trap. Either the anachronistic passion of nationalism, together with the ruinous wars to which it gives rise, will be overcome or else the abortive experiment of history, only a few millennia old, will reach its end and mankind will become extinct or regress to the diabolical state that Aldous Huxley depicts in *Ape and Essence*. Beckett, in *Endgame*, shadows forth a world that is already dead, a world in which the game of life is over.

It cannot be said that literature did not sound its apocalyptic warning

---

[8] Anton Chekhov, *The Life and Letters of Anton Tchekhov*. Translated and edited by S. S. Koteliansky & Philip Tomlinson. New York: George H. Doran Company, n. d., p. 126.

[9] "Every really great drama expresses ... amid the apparently inescapable, mutual destruction of men, an *affirmation of life*. It is a *glorification of human greatness*." Georg Lukács, *The Historical Novel*. Translated by Hannah and Stanley Mitchell. London: Merlin Press, 1962, p. 122.

long before the atom bomb was actually invented and put to use. In *The Absolute at Large*, Karel Capek describes the outcome of an invention that can exploit the energy resident in the atom. Satirizing the malefic cult of efficiency that governs technological production Capek predicts a time will come when all atomic machines will be destroyed. In *An Atomic Phantasy* he constructs an ingenious tale about a man who experiments with explosives and discovers "Krakatit," a substance that can wipe out armies and cities with one spectacular lethal blast. The inventor, an eccentric scientist, refuses to be corrupted by offers of vast sums of money; he will not be guilty of increasing the murderous potential of modern warfare. First published in England in 1925 under the title of *Krakatit*, this novel warns against the dangerous folly of indulging in scientific *hubris*. Carried away by his intemperate pride of knowledge and his technological mastery, man is now in a position not only to damage irreparably the fabric of civilization but to destroy the entire race. Humanity inhabits a planet which is a powder magazine that may be set off and explode at any moment. Prokob, the inventor, knows, even if no one else realizes it, that man dwells in an ocean of immeasurable forces and, what is worse, that this explosive energy is present in man too.

Are the scientists, as Aldous Huxley charges, to blame for bringing us to this pass? In his novel, *The New Men*, C. P. Snow propounds the thesis that scientists, as distinguished from engineers, are not a breed apart, concerned solely with their experimental work in the laboratory; they are morally sensitive, responsible individuals who are opposed to allowing the government to exploit their discoveries for destructive military ends, but there is, he points out, a limit to what they can do individually or as a group.[10] Snow speaks of the scientists, specifically the physicists, as "rebellious, questioning, protestant, curious for the future and unable to resist shaping it." [11] They are determined to put a stop, if they can, to the inhuman misuse of science. "For any cause on earth, they could not bear to destroy hundreds of thousands of people at a go." [12] The powers that be pay no heed to their moral protest and the atom bomb is brought into action, not once on Hiroshima but again on Nagasaki. In the light of these tragic events, what is the implicated scientist to do? "Either you retired and helped to leave your country defenceless. Or you made a weapon which might burn

[10] This is amply confirmed by the contribution of scientists to the volume edited by Morton Grodzins and Eugene Rabinowitch, *The Atomic Age*. New York and London: Basic Books, Inc., 1953. See also J. Bronowski, *Science and Human Values*. New York and Evanston: Harper & Row, 1965.

[11] C. P. Snow, *The New Men*. New York: Charles Scribner's Sons, 1954, p. 176.

[12] *Ibid.*, p. 178.

men, women and children in tens of thousands. What was a man to do?" [13] The hero of the novel, a physicist, refuses to compromise, but his act of renunciation does not in the least alter the character of the power structure.

The advent of the atom bomb, the deadly fruit of the mobilized labor of science and technology, reveals how helpless the individual, be he scientist or poet or layman, is to affect the inexorable logic of events. He needs to believe that he has a personal stake in the life of society, but society has become scientifically so specialized and complex in its organization that his sense of helplessness is intensified to a terrifying degree. He has lost his autonomy, his conviction that he is primarily responsible for the things that happen in the world. He is far from indifferent to the issue that confronts him, but increasingly he comes to perceive that there is nothing he can do to right what is wrong. Science and technology, the huge and complex machinery of politics, have forced him to surrender his personal judgment of international affairs and place his trust in the hands of the proper authorities.[14] He is pulled in two opposed directions. He has derived many remarkable benefits from the contributions of science and yet he is beginning to look upon it with suspicion and even hostility as the potential enemy of life. He is part of the very society against which he is forced to protest. He wants to be a member of society, "to belong and to conform. And at the same time, he wants to be a person, to act out his will and to break the constraints of society." [15] Especially when these constraints, gone berserk, threaten to kill off the race of mankind.

We have already seen how a number of writers among the beat generation revolted against society in America. They found a scapegoat in the military State and in the coercive society which tramples what is uniquely human and creative in man under foot. They struggle to affirm their individuality and the only way of affirmation open to them, they believe, is that of rebelliousness, even though they know that their social protest will do no earthly good. They expect no miracle to happen that will radically reverse the deathward drift of history. They continue to direct their attack on the madness of war, pointing out in fiction and fantasy, in parable and allegory, that reliance on the resources of technology and on scientific coordination and control is not enough to save the world and insure the survival of the race.

Other writers, more disciplined in their art, use the metaphor of madness as an ironic means of dealing with the theme of the present peril of nuclear

[13] *Ibid.*, p. 215.
[14] See Glynne Wickham, *Drama in a World of Science.* London: Routledge and Kegan Paul, 1962.
[15] J. Bronowski, *The Face of Violence.* London: Turnstile Press, 1954, p. 55.

warfare. In the extravagant dramatic fable, *The Physicists* by Dürrenmatt, the action takes place in a madhouse; the setting is meant to suggest the condition of the world today. If, as Dürrenmatt tells us in his stage directions, the play observes the right restrictions imposed by the three Aristotelian unities, that is because a classical restraint is necessary for a theme that portrays madmen plotting the destruction of the world by atomic bombs. Tragedy, Dürrenmatt is convinced, is rare, if not impossible in the present age, since the individual feels utterly helpless as he confronts events of a magnitude and complexity that are beyond his powers to cope with.

In his reflection on the insane play of world politics, Dürrenmatt scores some of his most telling points. He stresses the fact that the State has ceased to be identifiable; it has become an anonymous machine, a highly efficient corporate bureaucracy. It is hard to know what goes on behind the scenes, who makes the decisions; the leaders are mere figureheads. The mighty have not fallen; they have simply vanished from the stage. Their place is taken by technological forces.

The state has lost its physical reality, and just as physics can now only cope with the world in mathematical formulas, so the state can only be expressed in statistics. Power today becomes visible, material only when it explodes as in the atom bomb, in this marvelous mushroom which rises and spreads immaculate as the sun and in which mass murder and beauty have become one. The atom bomb can not be reproduced artistically since it is mass-produced. In its face all of man's art that would recreate it must fail, since it is itself a creation of man.[16]

In the light of all this it is not surprising to find that Dürrenmatt believes that comedy, not tragedy, is the dramatic form best suited to the spirit of the times, for whereas tragedy presupposes a formed world comedy presents a world that is topsy-turvy, ready to fall apart. Then, too, tragedy depends on a fixed body of moral values, but in our benighted world of flux

there are no more guilty and also, no responsible men. "We couldn't help it" and "We didn't really want that to happen." And indeed, things happen without anyone in particular being responsible for them. Everything is dragged along and everyone gets caught somewhere in the sweep of events. We are all collectively guilty.... Comedy alone is suitable for us. Our world has led to the grotesque as well as to the atom bomb.[17]

But if pure tragedy is denied us, the possibility of the tragic vision is still available to us by being wrested out of comedy. It does not follow, Dürrenmatt contends, that comedy is the expression of despair, though some indi-

[16] Friedrich Dürrenmatt, "Problems of the Theatre," in Robert W. Corrigan and James L. Rosenberg (eds.), *The Context and Craft of Drama*. San Francisco: Chandler Publishing Company, 1964, p. 265.

[17] *Ibid.*, p. 267.

viduals may confront the world with despair. It is possible to face the world in a spirit of endurance and to portray man as a courageous being.

It is this spirit, tempered with the acids of irony, that informs *The Physicists*. The three patients housed in the "villa" or mental institution are all physicists, each one for reasons of his own pretending to be mad. Johann Wilhelm Möbius, the chief character, has been confined in this place for the past fifteen years. He intends to remain mad because he realizes the disastrous consequences that would follow the publication of his scientific thinking. He prefers to remain in the madhouse, for there he is at least safe from the clutches of power-crazed politicians. It is out of a basic sense of moral responsibility that he abandoned his professional career, his family, his craving for fame, and chose the path of madness. As he says:

In the realm of knowledge we have reached the farthest frontiers of perception. We know a few precisely calculable laws, a few basic connections between incomprehensible phenomena and that is all. The rest is mystery closed to the rational mind. We have reached the end of our journey.... Our knowledge has become a frightening burden. Our researches are perilous, our discoveries are lethal. For us physicists there is nothing left but to surrender to reality. It has not kept up with us. It disintegrates on touching us. We have to take back our knowledge and I have taken it back.[18]

The solution he proposes to the other two physicists is that they all remain in the madhouse. In this time of peril scientific genius must go unrecognized. Möbius declares: "We are wild beasts. We ought not to be let loose on humanity." [19] All three decide to remain: they will be mad but innocent.

If Dürrenmatt rubs in the culpability of atomic scientists, urging that it is better for them to choose a life of self-imposed madness than to bear guilt for the crime of wholesale murder, Walter E. Miller, Jr., in *A Canticle for Leibowitz*, stresses the religious spirit, though not too hopefully, as the only force that can withstand the destructive element in man. The author pictures life for us after the Atomic Armageddon. The novel reminds us of the monsters brought to birth as the result of genetic damage caused by radiation. There are ruins of fallout survival shelters in the desert, mementoes of the horror that had once befallen the earth. The monks in the desert chant their prayer to avert this diabolical evil:

> From the place of ground zero,
> *O Lord, deliver us.*

[18] Friedrich Dürrenmatt, *The Physicists*. Translated by James Kirkup. New York: Grove Press, Inc., 1962, pp. 80-81.
[19] *Ibid.*, p. 83.

From the rain of the cobalt,
O Lord, deliver us.
From the rain of the strontium,
O Lord, deliver us.[20]

These are the terrors that haunt the mind of the holy men: the fallout, the misbegotten monsters.

The survivors reconstruct what must have happened during the cataclysm that devastated the earth: the use of atomic weapons that could instantly wipe out a whole nation. That is how the Age of Destruction emerged: cities were reduced to rubble and ashes, the land was littered with the dead bodies of men and animals; the forests were blasted; the fields lay withered, turned to desert tracts. The air was poisoned. The few who survived fled in terror from the holocaust, their hatred directed against the rulers who used these lethal weapons and against those who had invented them. The Age of Simplification began. All books and records were burned. Mass murders took place. The homicidal madness, born of collective hatred and fear, was transmitted to the next generation. No one literate was spared. Only Father Isaac Edward Leibowitz, a scientist, received permission to found a monastic community, the aim of which would be to preserve human history for the future. The members of this saintly community labor to save human culture from extinction. Unfortunately Leibowitz is caught and killed, dying a martyr's death.

Scholars later try to reconstruct the science of the past by studying the documents Leibowitz left behind him. It is hard for the scholars to believe that the illiterate, sodden peasants of the present age are descended from a race of men who were technological wizards, masters of the unleashed energy of Nature, inventors of airplanes, thinking machines, and rockets to the moon. How could such a mighty and enlightened civilization have committed virtual suicide? There is the mystery. But the monks in the desert community endure. A Dark Age seems to be ending. Twelve centuries have passed during which time the monasteries kept the flame of knowledge burning. The abbot knows that secular truths are ephemeral. Even culture is short-lived. Only the religious vision can save man from perishing in the flux of the temporal.

There is always danger. There are warriors in the land whose leaders seek power. They care not for the Christians who seek to bear the burdens of the world on their shoulders, nor for the pernicious doctrine their Church teach-

---

[20] Walter M. Miller, Jr., *A Canticle for Leibowitz.* Philadelphia and New York: J. B. Lippincott Company, 1959, p. 26.

es, namely, that each man is accountable for the deeds of all. The fight with the Devil goes on, as of old, but now the Devil is synonymous with Fallout. History is about to repeat itself; the technological triumph will result in another destructive contest for power. All this is anathema to the abbot. How could man knowingly turn against his conscience and deny his sense of human responsibility? The men in power, however, are not to be stopped; they have forgotten the terrible lesson of the past.

Then comes the age of spaceships, the age of unlimited power. Here is a race ambitious to conquer the planets and the stars. Nothing is going to deter them from consummating their mad dream, not Hiroshima, not entropy. The atom race is on again. The manufacture of nuclear arms is prohibited but it goes on just the same. There is going to be war. Lucifer walks the earth, Lucifer, the fallen angel, symbolizing the atom bomb. The people are about to destroy the world once more. In despair the abbot asks where the truth lies.

A protest of a different kind, more timely and topical in its appeal, is delivered in the novel, *Fail-Safe*, by Eugene Burdick and Harvey Wheeler. It argues a supposititious case. Suppose the future of mankind is at stake, dependent on the decisions made by the Rulers of the United States and Russia. An error intrudes in the computerized machine, but the machine, with its men, follows orders blindly: the instructions, carefully checked, read unmistakably that they are to unload their atom bombs on Russia. The officer in charge of the planes winging their way eastward cannot be reached. The planes sent out to pursue them and, if necessary, destroy them, are too late. Nothing can be done. In this situation will Russia instantly retaliate?

The irony of the situation is that the machinery of war devoted to defense and attack is supposed to be fool-proof. No accident can, theoretically, mar its perfect functioning at all times. But the impossible happens and disaster, global disaster, impends. What in such an emergency is to be done? There is no easy, assured solution to the problem. Here is a fictional, melodramatized version, based on actual material and living contemporaries, of what might happen if in only one crucial instance the computers go wrong. Accidental war, desired perhaps by none, may break out as the result of the increasing complexity of the mechanical organization of the State. In *Fail-Safe* the plot is not drawn from the realm of fantasy; it constitutes a real possibility. The authors maintain that theirs is substantially a "true" story. "The accident may not occur in the way we describe but the laws of probability assure us that ultimately it will occur." [21]

We are introduced to the War Room of the Strategic Command in order

[21] Eugene Burdick and Harvey Wheeler, *Fail-Safe*. New York and London: McGraw-Hill Book Company, Inc., 1962, p. 7.

to give us some idea of the ramifications of technology, the enormous amount of applied knowledge and skill required for this computer age. The Fail-Safe point is "a fixed point in the sky where the planes will orbit until they get a positive order to go in. Without it they must return to the United States. This is called Positive Control. Fail-Safe simply means that if something fails it is still safe. In short, we cannot go to war except by a direct order." [22] The machinery of communication and command is supposed to be infallible, but it proves otherwise. A malfunction causes a failure in communication, and the bombers streak off to attack Moscow.

The novel emphasizes the point that the machine has gotten out of hand. We have perfected the science of intercontinental missiles. Technicians are in charge of a world of the absurd, working underground, perfecting missiles. They estimate the number of people – probably a hundred million, perhaps more – who would be killed in a full-scale nuclear war between the United States and the Soviet Union. One expert – Groteschele – argues that the best advantage is to be gained by the country which is most fully armed for defense and retaliation. He still thinks in terms of victors and vanquished. He is opposed by Emmett Foster, a liberal who advocates unilateral disarmament. War, he holds, is obsolete in this age. No culture can survive a nuclear holocaust. He paints a dreadful picture of "A culture with most of its people dead, the rotting smell of death in the air for years, its vegetation burned off, the germ plasm of survivors contaminated." [23] Betty, General Black's wife, interrupts the debate to maintain that man himself has become obsolete. "His damned brain has gotten us into this mess because of its sophistication and we cannot get out of it because of his pride. . . . And he cannot tap the truth of his viscera because that, for a specialist, is the ultimate sin." [24] She goes on to say that man has become a passive and impotent spectator in the theater of the world.

The two evil forces he has created – science and the state – have combined into one monstrous body. We're at the mercy of our monster and the Russians are at the mercy of theirs. They toy with us as the Olympian gods toyed with the Greeks. And like the gods of Greek tragedy, they have a tragic flaw. They know only how to destroy, not to save.[25]

The catastrophe is bound to come.

Fail-Safe is a thesis novel of ideas, with the ideas vividly dramatized and counterpointed in a pattern of suspense-laden action. The theme hinges on

[22] *Ibid.*, p. 40.
[23] *Ibid.*, p. 97.
[24] *Ibid.*, p. 97.
[25] *Ibid.*, p. 98.

the possibility that the slightest miscalculation in adjusting and installing a Fail-Safe black box could bring about an atomic war. No machine is perfect, immune against some unpredictable breakdown. The mistake the leaders make is to put their complete trust in the Fail-Safe mechanism, the computerized system.

These literary protests show how hard the writer struggles to make some morally meaningful sense of life lived under the shadow of the atom bomb. The bomb, like any other technological invention, is not the spawn of the Devil. It is man who has created it and it is man who is capable of putting it to use. Political scientists talk of enslavement, surrender, the loss of leadership, if the nations of the free world were to destroy their atomic arsenal, whereas what the people long for is a lasting peace so that they can live their lives without fear of annihilation. As Denis de Rougemont wrote immediately after the attack on Hiroshima: "If the Bomb is left alone, it will do nothing, plainly. It will stay quietly in its crate. . . . What we need to control is man."[26]

But who is to control man? How is he to control himself? The nihilism practised by the German nation under Hitler was expressive of a total contempt for the sacredness of human life. If millions can be killed off unconscionably and with impunity, then the literary outcry of condemnation carries no weight. Everything hinges on the possession of naked power. As Spengler declares with magisterial finality: "It is *life*, not the individual, that is conscienceless." [27] The will to power is then the only reality. This was the moral situation writers had to deal with as the ghastly record of mass killing in German concentration camps came to light after the end of the Second World War.

[26] Denis de Rougemont, *Man's Western Quest*. Translated by Montgomery Belgion. New York: Harper & Brothers, 1957, p. 145.

[27] Oswald Spengler, *The Decline of the West*. Translated by Charles Francis Atkinson. New York: Alfred A. Knopf, 1926, II, p. 443.

CHAPTER XIV

THE KINGDOM OF NIGHTMARE AND DEATH

1. The Totalitarian Terror

The literature of the holocaust is a retrospective form of protest. The crime has already been committed; the millions of the dead, victims of the Nazi genocidal plan, cannot be brought back to life. No amount of reparations can hope to atone for this monstrous letting of blood. The guilt of those directly or indirectly associated with the crime of genocide remains, and they, like the survivors among the intended victims, must make the effort to understand what aboriginal taint in humankind was responsible for this gratuitous outbreak of homicidal passion. Why did the conscience of the world remain silent while these atrocities were taking place in the abattoirs of Europe? Why did this relapse into barbarism occur in the twentieth century and in, theoretically, the most enlightened nation on earth? To a number of present-day German writers it seemed as if the race had gone mad and they use the metaphor of madness to account for this saturnalia of blood and death. But then the metaphysical question obtrudes itself: were the Germans alone to blame or was the rest of the world implicated in this crime of genocide? The postwar writers voice their protest against the inhumanity of man to man by bearing witness to the agonizing truth of the horror.

Not that writers have been culpably silent in this age of crime and catastrophe, but for the most part their work conveys the same unrelieved mood of despair. Their attitude, like that of their *personae*, is passive and spectatorial. If the protagonists that Aeschylus presents in the *Choephori* blunder through the night of life, seeking to expiate the curse on the house of Atreus, the gods are working behind the scenes to uphold the law of justice so that the order of the universe will not be overthrown. But in the brave new world as portrayed in *Nineteen Eighty-Four, Caligula, The Condemned of Altona*, and the literature of the concentration camp, the Erinyes do not function as the agents of the gods and justice is not done. The perversity of evil goes unchecked and unpunished. Modern man is trying to learn how to live without God, alone in a universe that is unmoved by the calamities that befall him. The nightmare of history cannot save him. The cause of idealism, he feels, is discredited and bankrupt.

These are the obsessional neuroses from which he suffers and which are abundantly reflected in the literature of his time. If like a Karl Jaspers or a Sartre the writer today believes that he is responsible for everything that happens in the world, he is at a loss how to voice and implement his concern. Dismayed, uncommitted, infected by a radical skepticism, in the name of what categorical imperative is he to speak? All he is sure of is that the human animal, "the poor, bare, forked animal," as demonstrated by the lurid, blood-soaked history of the recent past, is capable of any infamy. Never before in the annals of the world have abominations occurred on such a vast and deliberately planned scale. The Nazi regime, in its systematic attempt to degrade the image of man, gave expression to a diabolical rage for unmotivated destruction. The quality of sheer horror, amoral and psychopathological, that dominates life in the twentieth century is communicated with hallucinatory vividness by a nihilistic novelist like Louis-Ferdinand Céline, an anti-Semite who as far back as the twenties called for the extermination of the Jews.

Céline justified his work on the ground that the truth, no matter how revolting, must be told. His fiction reveals the degrees to which the conscience of mankind has broken down. If the gods are dead, the men who have installed themselves in the seats of the mighty are even more callous than the old gods in their disregard for the value of human life. George Orwell, in *Nineteen Eighty-four*, paints a grimly realistic picture not only of what modern man can become but what he already is. He projects a dramatic portrait of conditions that exist today. If this world he portrays of Thought Police in action, children spying on and betraying their parents, organized hate sessions, seems like a grossly exaggerated fantasy, it pales in comparison with the real horrors that were enacted in Nazi Germany and Stalinist Russia. Underground imprisonment, sadistic tortures designed to break the spirit of a man, a reign of terror: these were some of the means employed against those accused of being guilty of a thought crime. The torture is administered in graduated doses of increasing strength until the victim's mental resistance is crushed. Power in the totalitarian State is absolute, an end in itself. How, Orwell asks, can this type of despotism be defeated by the frail and vulnerable spirit of man?

This was the substance of Orwell's bitter outcry against a society that practiced the art of wholesale murder and rendered the individual subservient to the will of the State. As an integrated part of mass society, the individual surrenders his moral autonomy and feels free to commit the most frightful crimes. As Alex Comfort declares: "We are living in a madhouse whenever society is ... regarded as a super-individual. We are living in a madhouse now." [1] Writers were compelled to ask themselves why it was that the twentieth century became an age of premeditated and "legally" justified murder. On what grounds, Camus asks in *The Rebel*, do men arrogate to themselves the right to kill? The murder of millions of Jews dealt the final blow to the conception of man as a rational being. The triumph of Nazism in Germany, the land of Lessing, Goethe, and Schiller, the atrocities committed at Auschwitz and Belsen, the "liquidation" of the Jews in the Warsaw Ghetto, these, apart from the inferno of the Second World War, demonstrated the powerlessness of literature to halt the tidal advance of barbarism.

2. The Fire Raisers

In *The Fire Raisers*, a mordant parable of our time, Max Frisch discloses by what sinister, blackmailing means the yoke of Nazism was clamped around the neck of the German people. Wrathfully he prophesies the coming of doom unless we change our ways instead of cravenly compromising with the forces of evil. He calls his play "a Morality without a Moral," but the moral is present just the same, only it offers no consolation, no crumb of comfort. He has no confidence that the lesson of history will teach mankind the necessary wisdom. The action speaks for itself. The chorus with its leader emulates the Greek model, but what a startling change is evident in its strategy of appeal. It guards the city vigilantly against fire, hoping to extinguish the first few sparks before they burst into flame. Not every fire that starts, the Chorus Leader, who is the chief of the Fire Brigade, points out, is "the work of inexorable Fate." [2] In Brechtian fashion the Chorus spells out the true meaning of Fate: those monstrous events which assail the people are labeled Fate to prevent them from examining the causes which brought them into being. They are wrought by human hands, they are the pernicious deeds committed by fellow citizens. Resignation is fatal. Stupidity leads to death. Rousingly the Chorus declaims its message:

> It is unworthy of God,
> Unworthy of man,

---

[1] Alex Comfort, *Art and Social Responsibility*. London: Falcon Press, 1948, p. 22.
[2] Max Frisch, *Three Plays*. Translated by Michael Bullock. London: Methuen & Co., Ltd., 1961, p. 3.

> To call a stupidity Fate
> Simply because it has happened.[3]

It condemns this type of fatalism as abject, unbecoming the race of man, the inheritor of the earth and the fruits thereof.

Frisch, like Brecht, is convinced that the only literature worthy of our age of crisis and catastrophe is the literature of exhortation. Art as a purely aesthetic phenomenon is a luxury the contemporary mind can ill afford. But unlike Brecht, Frisch's impulse to preach is checked by the realization that art abhors the didactic. Hence his morality play, while it deals with urgent social themes, is balanced by a note of ironic complexity, as if the author were aware beforehand of the powerlessness of art to set the disjointed world straight. He makes it clear, for example, that there are no absolutes he can invoke; there is no standard of justice that is universally binding. If the world of man should decide to destroy itself, if the edifice of civilization that has thus far succeeded in surviving the buffeting of time should be consumed by an atomic holocaust, then there is nothing to be done. It will happen, but at least mankind, if any survivors are left to mourn in the cemetery of the earth, will be unable to complain that it has not been warned.

Gottlieb Biedermann is Frisch's version of Everyman, the personification of blind selfishness, the successful businessman who is interested only in holding on to his possessions. When he encounters the perpetrators of evil, he does not oppose them but instead tries to appease them. When the arsonists frankly tell him what they are up to, he refuses to believe them. Intimidated by Joe Schmitz, the fire raiser, he allows him to sleep in the attic. With fine scorn Schmitz remarks: "Most people nowadays believe in the Fire Brigade instead of in God." [4] Once Herr Biedermann shelters Joe Schmitz and feeds him, that is the beginning of the end. The Chorus exposes the fatal flaw of the faint-hearted who are naively impelled to deny the reality of evil. The parallel with what happened in Nazi Germany during Hitler's rise to power is not to be missed.

Once Schmitz and his accomplice take possession of the attic, they make their preparations to burn the house down, not even taking the trouble to conceal their nefarious activities. Though Biedermann protests furiously because of the noise his uninvited guests had made during the night rolling drums of petrol, he can do nothing with either of them. Though they assure him that the drums contain gasoline, as the label plainly states, Biedermann remains convinced that this is only a practical joke. He will not believe the

---

[3] *Ibid.*, p. 4.
[4] *Ibid.*, p. 9.

truth even when it stares him in the face. He is drawn into the very net he is seeking to escape.

When the Chorus calls his attention to the drums in his attic and warns him that the peril is imminent, he becomes angry and insists on his right to do as he pleases in his own house. But the smell of gasoline definitely pervades his house. When he declares he does not smell anything, the Chorus Leader replies: "So used already is he/To evil stenches." [5] That is the point exactly: those who strive at all costs to maintain the *status quo* cannot avert the disaster that threatens to overtake them. So it turns out. The Chorus rings down the curtain as a fiery explosion breaks out:

> What all have foreseen
> From the outset,
> And yet in the end it takes place,
> Is idiocy,
> The fire it's too late to extinguish
> Called Fate.[6]

In *The Fire Raisers* (1958), Frisch adds his voice to the debate that is still raging over the question of who was responsible for the rise and triumph of Fascism. Corrupt business deals, collusion, bribery, rampant selfishness, these brought on the debacle. We feel the impact of Frisch's profound concern over the tragic problems that bedevil his age, but we also sense his despair over the moral cowardice and incorrigible stupidity of the race. He can strike no hopeful note. As he writes in his *Tagebuch:*

As a playwright I would consider my task thoroughly fulfilled if one of my plays could succeed in so posing a question that from that moment on the audience could not go on living without an answer – without their own answer, which they can only give through their own lives. . . . Every human answer as soon as it transcends a personal answer and pretends to general validity will be questionable. . . .[7]

3. The Apocalypse of Destruction

Modern literature, though it grappled courageously with the theme of horror, has thus far failed to capture the full, underlying meaning of the apocalypse of destruction that struck our age, just as it failed by its protests and appeals to alter the tragic course of history. Camus, in *The Rebel*, voiced his faith in

---

[5] *Ibid.*, p. 35.

[6] *Ibid.*, p. 62.

[7] Quoted in Alex Natan (ed.), *German Men of Letters*. Volume III. London: Oswald Wolff, Limited, 1964, p. 319.

the unconditional value of human life, the one absolute which, if resolutely defended, can defeat the universe of the absurd, but even this absolute was rendered null and void by the reality of the Nazi concentration camps and death factories. The concentration camp, supplied with efficient gas chambers, was the fitting, if ghastly, symbol of the plague of nihilism that raged in the twentieth century. Confronted with this plague, literature was reduced for a time to appalled silence. The genocidal crimes carried out on orders given by the Nazi leaders were so incredible that the protestations of innocence of the war-criminals when they were brought to trial seemed more convincing than the reports of the survivors. Neither reportage (like *Notes from the Warsaw Ghetto*) nor drama (like *The Deputy*) nor fiction (like *Missa Sine Nomine*) could hope to do justice to the experience millions of men, women, and children had passed through in the concentration camps and the death houses of Europe.

In her brilliant documented study, *The Origins of Totalitarianism*, Hannah Arendt points out that the mechanical, cold-blooded policy of extermination could never be fully grasped by the imagination.[8] These wanton massacres, this huge organized industry for the manufacture of corpses, how could all this be brought within the compass of rational understanding? For these victims were condemned to die without reason by men in power whose nihilism eradicated entirely the concept of guilt.

The extermination camps – where everything was an incident beyond the control of the victims as well as the oppressors, where those who were oppressors today were to become victims tomorrow – created a monstrous equality without fraternity and without humanity, an equality in which dogs and cats could have easily partaken, and in which we see as in a mirror the horrid image of superfluousness.[9]

If life is thus insanely degraded, if human beings are treated as so much expendable flesh to be turned into ashes, then not only literature but all culture stands forth as a pointless endeavor, a diabolical joke, a cruel lesson in the dialectic of self-deception. Seen in retrospect, the reality of the extermination camps and the horrid image of superfluousness they projected, reinforced the conviction that there is nothing tragic in the fate of man.

How could the men and women trapped in the universe of the concentration camp emerge as tragic figures? Enclosed behind electrified wires, they were selected to die in crematoria without even the pretence of a trial. The concentration camps were ideal laboratories for the purposes of barbarism.

[8] Hannah Arendt, *The Origins of Totalitarianism.* New York: Harcourt, Brace and Company, 1951, p. 416.
[9] *Ibid.,* p. 430.

In them the inmates, no longer human beings but tatooed numbers, could be transformed into abject beasts or corpses. The number of those who perished in Auschwitz and Maidanek, Dachau, Belsen, and other camps were more than five million, but what do figures alone matter? The atrocities inflicted on the flesh and spirit of these victims are beyond the reach of statistical description. One eye-witness report tells of a horrible massacre that took place in the Ukraine. The men, women, and children, five thousand of them, all Jews, were forced to disrobe by an S.S. man carrying a riding whip. The report given at the Nuremberg trial goes on to say:

Without screaming or weeping, these people undressed, stood around in family groups, kissed each other, said farewells and waited for a sign from another S.S. man, who stood near the pit, also with a whip in his hand. During the fifteen minutes that I stood near the pit I heard no complaint or plea for mercy. . . .[10]

At the edge of the pit, smoking a cigarette, sat an S.S. man who did the shooting with a tommy gun, while below him the corpses lay tightly wedged together, a few bodies still moving.

The literature of horror,[11] composed after these horrible events had become part of the historical record, did not need to press home its accusation. The documentary data had been conscientiously gathered and filed away in archives: the grisly pile of statistics, the first-hand accounts furnished by eye-witnesses, the confessions, personal histories, affidavits, the reports of psychiatrists, the movies that were taken on the spot at the time the survivors were rescued. In these pictures we can see the heaps of the dead frozen in ghastly postures, the pits of lime which served as a common grave for all those who were slaughtered, the lamp shades made of human skin, the sight of the survivors, rickety, stomach bloated, the eyes bulging in emaciated faces, the light of the spirit dead within. Small wonder that many writers drew back in despair from the task of capturing imaginatively the hideous truth of a world dedicated to the God of Death. The truth must be made known, but what was the truth? The burden of collective guilt for these monstrous crimes must be borne, but who was guilty? When life in the Warsaw Ghetto was drawing to a close, the surviving Jews discussed the question of what was the most important message to send if someone could be smuggled out as a messenger to the world outside. "Everybody agreed that the most

---

[10] William L. Shirer, *The Rise and Fall of the Third Reich*. New York: Simon and Schuster, 1960, p. 961.

[11] See Marie Syrkin, "The Literature of the Holocaust," *Midstream*, May 1966, XII, pp. 3-20.

important thing was to arouse the world to the horror of the organized extermination we are now suffering." [12]

The survivors who later wrote about their experience did not cry out for
revenge. Why, most of them asked, did all this happen? Who was responsible? Why did God remain silent? In seeking an answer to these questions,
they were forced to modify radically their views on the basic nature of man.[13]
Above all, they were forced to re-examine and revise their conception of
God and His relation to mankind. Ignaz Maybaum, in *The Face of God
After Auschwitz*, describes how he spent some time in a concentration camp
and lost his mother and two sisters in the holocaust; nevertheless he retained
his faith in God. He is fully aware of the enormity of what took place at
Auschwitz and other death-camps; it marks a decisive turning point in the
history of the human imagination. "Auschwitz is the truth, the truth which
reveals such monstrosity that the word tragedy becomes a white-washing
lie." [14] The horrible truth that Auschwitz disclosed bears upon all of life and
all the injustices that occur in the world. The reality of Auschwitz confirms
Maybaum's conviction that humanism is impotent in the face of such atrocities. "Humanism without belief in God, scientific philosophy without the
aid of faith lead to nihilism. This nihilism leads to Auschwitz." [15] He does
not avoid the religious question, why did God permit six million victims to
be sacrificed? He rests his faith in the transcendent, in the sphere beyond
history. Man is the creature of God and Jewish man believes in the coming
of the Messiah. Death is not the end. These were the very problems – faith
and the loss of faith in God, the collapse of humanism, the problem of guilt
and moral responsibility, the reality of evil – literature had to deal with as
writers struggled to interpret and protest against the implications of this age
of horror.

4. The Novel as Epilogue and Epitaph

If the dead have not yet found a Dantesque voice that will speak for them,
it is because no writer can compose a *Divine Comedy* in our time. The best
the writer can do is to bear witness. In *Forests of the Dead*, Ernst Wiechert
gives a personal account of his refusal to collaborate with the Nazi regime;

[12] Emmanuel Ringelblum, *Notes from the Warsaw Ghetto*. Edited and translated
by Jacob Sloan. New York and London: McGraw-Hill, 1958, p. 291.
   [13] See Bruno Bettelheim, *The Informed Heart*. Glencoe, Illinois: The Free Press,
1960.
   [14] Ignaz Maybaum, *The Face of God After Auschwitz*. Amsterdam: Polak & Van
Gennep Ltd., 1965, p. 48.
   [15] *Ibid.*, p. 70.

he preferred persecution and imprisonment to the ignominy of keeping silent. This sensitive and compassionate autobiography is not only an indictment of the bestial cruelty of his captors but a splendid tribute to the innate decency of the victims who were his comrades in the universe of the concentration camp. Informed by moral passion and a religious reverence for the truth, *Forests of the Dead*, like David Rousset's *The Other Kingdom*, is but the prelude to the Symphony of Death that will one day be composed.

While waiting for the dread summons to come – the imperious knock on the door, the search, the arrest – Ernst Wiechert brooded on the betrayed and defiled idea of justice. From all parts of his accursed land there came to him the call of despair, the piercing screams of distress, but there was nothing he could do to help these unfortunate ones. Each day marked another obscene triumph of brute force, the obliteration of all sense of moral responsibility "This was the age of barbarism, the kingdom of the Antichrist." [16] How could the law, either human or divine, prevail if those into whose hands it was entrusted failed to honor it?

Only after Wiechert was thrust into a concentration camp did he learn the full meaning of the horror to which his people were being subjected: the dreary emptiness of time, the tortures inflicted upon the inmates and the hatred that burned in them like a devouring flame, the numerous suicides, the deaths that occurred daily and that became an all too familiar reality. It was then Wiechert began to wonder whether God had indeed died. This led him inevitably to the question of ultimate meaning: if through the ages force proved victorious over right and there was no redress, no final reckoning, then what was the purpose of his life on earth? To what moral certitudes could he cling in these dark, God-forsaken days of confinement? Nevertheless, he did not lose his faith. Though living in this hell ruled over by Nazi devils armed with whip and club and gun, he felt convinced that the Third Reich bore within itself the seeds of dissolution. "No culture could be raised on human blood."[17] Though the internees were now brutally beaten, starved, shot to death or despatched in droves to crematoria, the spirit of humanity, he believed, would assert itself in the end. A man of indomitable faith, he felt that the decent people were those incarcerated in the concentration camps.

Man's longing in the camps went out for man, and both together longed for freedom. More even than for freedom from their shackles, they longed to see the dignity of man restored, no matter into what belief they should finally merge.[18]

[16] Ernst Wiechert, *Forest of the Dead,* Translated by Ursula Stechow. New York: Greenberg, 1947, p. 7.
[17] *Ibid.,* p. 77.
[18] *Ibid.,* p. 119.

As if realizing that he could not possibly communicate the full reality of the horror, Wiechert in his novel, *Missa Sine Nomine*, limits this part of the narrative to flashbacks that describe the effect the experience of confinement in a concentration camp had on the hero. He is a nobleman, one of three brothers, who had dared to speak against the regime and was consequently arrested. We see him returning to his castle, now confiscated and in ruins, walking like one who had come back from the dead. He feels cut off from both man and God. Corrupted by dwelling four years in a world of hate-charged violence and demented evil, he knows himself to be unclean. "It had not sufficed to live in purity and quiet and 'to do nothing'. He had closed his eyes against the evil of the world, and the evil had found him defence-less." [19]

Though Wiechert condemns the outbreak of violence in the modern world, he does not single out the defeated Germans for special castigation while whitewashing the motives and actions of the victors. All are equally guilty, especially those who in the hour of victory conduct elaborate trials and build concentration camps for "the beasts" who had carried out these crimes against humanity. The solution, Wiechert holds, lies in forgiveness, not in gratifying the spirit of revenge; in pity born of the insight that evil is permanently rooted in the nature of man and as such can be combated by self-less humility but never eradicated. For power rules the world of our time, and that power is being used amorally.

Man had become a murderer without passion, without even being at all worried about it.... They might talk and write for years now about guilt and atonement, about freedom and the rights of man. But he who got power would always do the same – more carelessly still – more thoroughly perhaps.[20]

Those who had no power were at the mercy of the powerful. They could no longer appeal to the tribunal of the law or the judgment of God. Wherever they turned their eyes there was no Heaven above them, only the vast, terrifying emptiness of space.

All the victims of these years had stretched out their hands to the last second while they screamed or prayed under the gallows, under the axe, under torture. Nobody had grasped their outstretched hands. Even in death they remained outstretched, open, twisted, alone.[21]

These despairing meditations of the hero voice the religious concern of the author. He is convinced that "the victory of the heart was the only one which

---

[19] Ernst Wiechert, *Missa Sine Nomine*. Translated by Marie Heynemann and Margery B. Leonard. London: Peter Nevill, 1963, p. 24.

[20] *Ibid.*, p. 43.

[21] *Ibid.*, p. 44.

could master the demons." [22] The true victory, he insists, belongs to the humble, those whose hearts are purged of hatred and whose faith enables them to conquer fear. Pity is the answer. "He who has pity has atoned for everything." [23]

Thus we get the Christian message of forgiveness. Wiechert's protest is balanced by his understanding that hatred springs from the extremity of fear.

If only the smallest group of people succeeded in conquering the fear of man, the fear of hunger or of violence: the fear of the dreadful emptiness into which the West was now sliding; the fear of the mere fact of a simple existence into which man is thrown, as a piece of wood is thrown into a whirlpool: then had been won the most that could ever be won in this world.[24]

If that spiritual victory were won, then the need "to kill time" would vanish as well as the enervating fever of restlessness that held men in its grip. "For they wished to kill time, because they felt that time, which could not be stayed, carried them into nothingness." [25] Mechanization, the flight of airplanes, the explosion of rockets and atom bombs, all these brought mankind nearer to the final terror of annihilation. The answer to this terror is to be found not in collective groups, but in the regeneration of the individual, in the affirmation of the human heart.

Night of the Mist, by Eugene Heimler, is another grimly told tale, one of many that have appeared in recent years, that picture life in a concentration camp. The Nazi tanks and armored cars arrive and the round-up begins. Rumors of the fate awaiting the Jews quickly spread: rape, imprisonment, torture, death. On the train ride to the concentration camp the victims are deprived of water, go mad in their misery, or are crushed to death. For the inmates at Auschwitz the days pass without count. The sense of time is anesthetized. Reality and unreality are confusedly mixed together. The barbarous, exhausting routine of camp life has to be endured; those who cannot keep up the pace must die. By night the chimneys of the crematoria send up their flames and smoke. In this efficiently run inferno all moral values are ignored, the promptings of conscience stamped out. Even the sight of corpses soon loses its initial shock of horror.

There are times when the protagonist is overcome by the need to puzzle out the meaning of it all. How account for these disastrous events, how interpret the mysterious ways of fate. He used to pray, but his faith was

---

[22] *Ibid.*, p. 107.
[23] *Ibid.*, p. 254.
[24] *Ibid.*, p. 306.
[25] *Ibid.*, p. 306.

undermined by what he witnessed and had to suffer during his stay in Auschwitz and Buchenwald.

Auschwitz had dealt the first great blow to my former belief in God. The thousands of pitiful creatures stumbling towards the crematoria, the hatred and the amorality, the cruelty and death, had unleashed a profound feeling of doubt within me. If all this was possible, if men could be herded like beasts towards annihilation, then all that I had believed in before must have been a lie. There was not, there could not be a God, for He could not tolerate and condone such godlessness.[26]

Despite this feeling that overcame him, he often prayed to God, thanking Him for keeping him alive. "I felt that God frequently works out His plans through human beings, and that if only we listen to human words and voice, we can often hear Him speak." [27]

What is striking about these stories of life in a concentration camp is that the protest they register consists not of strident accusations but of efforts to understand the ways of God and the true nature of man. What is equally striking about this literature of horror is that the personal records read like fiction and the fiction often reads like an imaginatively compiled documentary. For that was the difficult problem the writers had to struggle with: how to justify this outburst of gratuitous evil and make it seem credible. In *Night*, Elie Wiesel recounts the series of dreadful misfortunes that befell his fellow Jews in Hungary. Like the world at large, the Hungarian Jews could not get themselves to believe in the frightening rumors they heard. The massacre of an entire people – that was pure melodramatic invention! When the blow finally fell, when their worst fears were realized, they yielded passively to the insane designs of their executioners. As François Mauriac asks in his foreword to *Night*, how could God's chosen people bear up under these calamitous events? How could their faith endure under the stress of suffering that surpassed anything that Job had to undergo? For the religious faith of Elie Wiesel, who had been brought up devoutly on the teachings of the Talmud, collapsed when he witnessed this appalling reign of evil. The logic that supported his conclusion was incontrovertible: if God existed, He could never have permitted this to happen; therefore, God did not exist.

The boy who tells the story of *Night* rebels against the faith of his fathers. Was not God silent while all these infamies were carried out? He is not yet able, however, to cast off the long-instilled habit of prayer. But he knows that the memory of his first night in camp – the smoke pouring out of the

[26] Eugene Heimler, *Night of the Mist*. Translated by Andre Ungar. New York: The Vanguard Press, Inc., 1958, p. 102.
[27] *Ibid.*, p. 173.

crematoria, the children whose bodies had been reduced to ashes – will remain with him forever. "Never shall I forget these moments which murdered my God and turned my dreams to dust. Never shall I forget these things, even if I am condemned to live as long as God Himself. Never." [28] And yet at night in Auschwitz the inmates still talked of God's inscrutable ways, the sins of the chosen people, the coming of the Messiah, the hope of deliverance in the future. By this time the young lad is no longer capable of prayer. "I did not deny God's existence, but I doubted His absolute justice." [29] In the concentration camp death by hanging was the penalty for any serious infraction, for the slightest sign of insubordination, and the internees were taught a salutary object lesson by being made to parade before the body of the victim on the gallows. When one man asks, "Where is God now?" the boy hears a voice within him answer: "Where is He? Here He is – He is hanging on this gallows. . . ." [30]

In two other novels, *The Town Beyond the Wall* and *The Gates of the Forest,* Elie Wiesel continues to debate the issue of evil with God. How, he asks, can man believe in a God who is responsible for the slaughter of the innocent, for the lives of the millions of Jews that went up in the smoke of the death-factories? And his heroes refuse to believe but they persist in conducting a dialogue with a non-existent God. Either God is responsible or He is indifferent or He is cruel. It cannot be true that He does not know what is going on. Unless – there is always another possibility – He is punishing the Jewish people for a purpose that is beyond their comprehension. Perhaps they have sinned.

In a style that is mystical and hallucinatory Wiesel bears witness to the blood-madness of his age that resulted in the death of man. As the chief character in *The Town Beyond the Wall* says: "*You had* to be crazy to hope for a victory of the spirit over the forces of evil . . . you had to have lost your reason, or sacrificed it, to believe in God, to believe in man, to believe in a reconciliation between them." [31] If the horror of the holocaust is Wiesel's sole theme – it is his creative obsession, coloring and conditioning everything he has written – he does not attempt to overwhelm the reader with a minutely detailed account of the torture the inmates of concentration camps had to endure or with morbidly visualized scenes of what took place in the gas chambers and crematoria. His impassioned protest reaches to the heart

[28] Elie Wiesel, *Night.* Translated by Stella Podway. New York: Hill and Wang, 1960, pp. 44-45.

[29] *Ibid.,* p. 53.

[30] *Ibid.,* p. 71.

[31] Elie Wiesel, *The Town Beyond the Wall.* Translated by Stephen Becker. New York: Atheneum, 1964, p. 47.

of the matter. If the earth of Europe has been transformed into huge ceme-
teries that is because this is an age of madness.

It has descended upon us, not like lightning but like the plague. We've returned
to the Middle Ages.... Only now neither the priests of the Inquisition nor the
victims understand what drives them to act or in what god's name the fires are
lit. It's a universal eclipse. Everything's falling apart; past, future, present, hope,
humanity, progress, all these are nothing but words.... It's the end of the
world....[32]

The human spirit is extinguished; man is dead. The enormity committed by
this generation exceeds that of all the Sodoms and Gomorrahs of the past.
This is the generation of the guilty. "We all have a share in the crime, even
if we combat it; there's no escape from the trap. There's the madness of our
generation, complicity between executioners and victims, imposed upon the
latter without their being aware of it." [33]

The memory of the horror has not been forgotten. One of the characteristic ways of facing it was to despair not only of God but of humanity as well.
In *The Tin Drum* Günter Grass exposes the innate temptations to evil of the
race, tears off the masks of goodness from the face of mankind. Romain
Gary, in *A European Education*, adopts a different outlook. He does not
say that the beast in man triumphs and evil reigns supreme. He believes that
the spirit of man, no matter how cruelly oppressed, rises superior to the force
of tyranny. Though he protests against the rise of barbarism, horror in his
novel is negated by hope, brute strength is overcome by an indomitable feeling of fraternity, the nothingness of death transcended by a redeeming act of
faith. Like *A European Education*, *The Last of the Just* attempts to impose
a higher meaning on the modern experience of horror by invoking the name
of God. The result unfortunately is that the novel is bathed in an atmosphere of perfervid sentimentality. It ends symbolically with the smoke rising
from the crematoria and the largely rhetorical affirmation

that Ernie Levy, dead six million times, is still alive somewhere, I don't know
where.... Yesterday, as I stood in the street trembling in despair, rooted to the
spot, a drop of pity fell from above upon my face. But there was no breeze in
the air, no cloud in the sky.... There was only a presence.[34]

The literature of protest, as it comes to grips with this unprecedented theme
of horror let loose in the world at large, seeks to discover some principle of

[32] Elie Wiesel, *The Gates of the Forest*. Translated by Frances Freynaye. New
York and Chicago: Holt, Rinehart and Winston, 1966, pp. 120-21.

[33] *Ibid.*, p. 129.

[34] André Schwartz-Bart, *The Last of the Just*. Translated by Stephen Becker. New
York: Atheneum, 1960, p. 345.

justification, some transcendent moral meaning, to determine who are the guilty. If there is no commanding world-spirit, if history responds to no universal law, then the way things turn out depends on the decisions individual men make. The responsibility for resisting evil is thrown upon the individual conscience. Thus the evil was not confined to those who did the actual killing. The question of guilt involved not only members of the National Socialist Party but the whole administrative apparatus: professors, doctors, lawyers, businessmen and industrial leaders, everyone. For that matter, did not the rest of the world react with embarrassed silence, disbelief, and inaction when it received news how the Nazis were solving the Jewish problem?

Who was innocent, who was guilty? It is impossible for modern man to avoid being implicated in the mass murders of his time. "Since all contemporary action leads to murder, direct or indirect, we cannot act until we know whether, and why, we have the right to kill." [35] If millions of people not at all involved in the war, women, children, the aged, could be slain indiscriminately and with impunity, what basis was there for assuming that a world conscience exists? In her Epilogue to *Eichmann in Jerusalem*, Hannah Arendt argues that the attempt to exterminate the Jewish people was a crime not only against them but against humanity as a whole, of which the Jews are a part. It is only fitting that the most powerful indictment to date of these crimes should be delivered by a German, Rolf Hochhuth, in *The Deputy*.

5. *Christianity and Genocide*

Here is a play of protest that raises the question of conscience rather than legality in passing judgment on the German people for the crimes they committed. Though the Pope is made to appear the chief culprit, *The Deputy* is really an attempt to define in dramatic terms the complex categories of guilt and innocence. Why, it inquires, did the rest of the world, especially the Catholic Church, remain silent while these wholesale murders were being carried out? This is what the play is about. The first scene opens at the Papal Legation in Berlin in August 1942, where the problem of how the Church shall deal with Hitler's *known* plan of genocide for the Jews is being discussed.

Kurt Gerstein, Obersturmführer in the S.S. arrives, breathless, with the shocking news that the concentration camps in Poland are daily putting ten thousand Jewish victims to death by gas. The Nuncio refuses to listen, but Gerstein insists on reporting his incredible tale of death factories in opera-

[35] Albert Camus, *The Rebel*. Translated by Anthony Bower. New York: Alfred A. Knopf, 1954, p. 12.

tion. He pleads that the Vatican must intervene at once, but the Nuncio declares he is utterly without authority to interfere. Gerstein (who is not a Catholic) cannot comprehend this attitude. He shouts:

> Authority! Here in Berlin you represent
> the – the Deputy of Christ,
> and you can close your eyes to the worst horror
> that man has ever inflicted upon man.[36]

Unable to control his feelings, he insists that it is the duty of the Pope to speak in the name of the world's conscience. Why, he asks in anguish, has the Vatican concluded a pact with Hitler? Why was the Concordat signed with a nation of murderers? Pointing to the painting of the Crucified Christ, he exclaims bitterly that Christ was authorized while His Deputy remains culpably silent.

The powerful emotions and the violent controversies the play aroused spring in part from the fact that it is based on documentary evidence. This is not simply a "literary" protest. It is a thesis play in which "real" historical characters, not only the Pope but Adolf Eichmann, appear. Hochhuth discloses that an efficient expediter of death like Eichmann was in fact a nonentity, a loyal but mediocre cog in the Nazi bureaucratic machine; it is hard – as Hannah Arendt, too, demonstrated – to picture him as the archfiend. Hochhuth says that "it took study of the documents to unmask him as the most diligent shipping agent who ever labored in the employ of Death." [37] Hochhuth paints other revealing character portraits: for example, that of the Doctor, a nihilist, who has gone beyond good and evil. He is the one who with his little swagger stick in hand "selects" his victims in Auschwitz. Yet outwardly there is nothing sinister about him. The stage directions describe him as cool, cheery, self-controlled, the incarnation of Absolute Evil – "far more unequivocally so than Hitler, whom he no longer even bothers to despise – which is his attitude toward all members of the human race." [38] The embodiment of the Devil, he takes genuine pleasure in his professional work as the inhuman agent of Death.

In pitting the forces of good against those of evil, Hochhuth endeavors to keep the balance even. Gerstein, the true Christian, is contrasted with an amoral type like the Doctor. It is possible for Gerstein to escape from Germany, but he refuses to leave while these mass murders are going on. He is secretly harboring a Jew in his Berlin apartment. When the Doctor visits Gerstein, whose loyalty he suspects, the latter makes an effort to play his

[36] Rolf Hochhuth, *The Deputy*. Translated by Richard and Clara Winston. New York: Grove Press, Inc., 1964, p. 24.

[37] *Ibid.*, p. 29.

[38] *Ibid.*, p. 31.

assumed role convincingly. He does not deny that he is a Christian but one can be a Christian and still harbor doubt. The Doctor, who is well aware of the horror he calls forth in the humane and religiously committed Gerstein, quotes Otto Weiniger: "The principle of evil is despair/at giving life some meaning." [39]

Then Riccardo, the hero of the play, calls on Gerstein, bringing the heartening message that the Vatican will help him and the intended victims of Hitler's genocidal mania, though he has no express authorization to do so. By this time Gerstein is inclined to be skeptical. Months have passed, the reports of the gassing of Jews have been fully confirmed, but the Pope has failed to act. Gerstein cannot understand the reason for the delay. He greatly admires the heroic example set by Pastor Niemöller, who is a prisoner in a concentration camp. That is why, as a member of the Confessing Church, he decided to join the S.S. He knows he is playing a dangerous game, but this is what he feels compelled to do: to help destroy the dictatorship from within. Human rights are more binding than oaths of loyalty to the State. Hitler is not Germany. Gerstein realizes that he will not survive the work he has to perform.

> "A Christian in these days *cannot*
> survive if he is truly Christian." [40]

Riccardo questions how it came about that a highly cultured nation like Germany, the country of Goethe and Schiller, Beethoven and Mozart, could revert to such a state of barbarism. Gerstein replies that the Germans are no worse than other Europeans. This is clearly Hochhuth's position and that of others like Wiechert. The scoundrels, those who fomented and those who succumbed to the evil of nihilistic hatred, are to be found everywhere – in Holland, in France, in the Ukraine, in Poland, even though it is true that the Germans bear the greatest burden of guilt.

The Deputy demonstrates the limitations that beset the literature of protest. The best a writer can do in this genre is to harrow the conscience of his audience, to hold up a magnifying mirror to the glaring contrast between the morality society preaches and its flagrantly immoral behavior. He must expose and denounce with scorn and indignation the discrepancy between the officially cherished ideal and the lamentable social reality. The satirist, too, focuses attention on disparities of this kind, but he works his effects mainly by making people laugh at the follies and vices depicted, whereas the issues Hochhuth is concerned with are literally matters of life and death and therefore too tragic to be laughed at.

[39] *Ibid.*, p. 72.
[40] *Ibid.*, p. 79.

The third act of *The Deputy* quotes from an underground pamphlet commenting on the astonishing fact that the world knows what is going on, the mass liquidation of the Jews, and yet keeps silent; even the vicar of God remains silent. The citizens of Rome who are Jews are being hunted down in the very vicinity of the Vatican, but Riccardo's plea for action by the Church falls on deaf ears. Though the Cardinal, a wily politician and experienced diplomat, condemns the murders committed by the Nazis, he has no intention of recommending that anathema be pronounced by the Church against Hitler, for that would mean helping the Bolsheviks. He looks upon Hitler as a bulwark against the spread of Russian Communism, as God's appointed instrument to achieve the unification of the West. Gerstein reminds him that "God would not be God if He made use of a Hitler..." [41]

Riccardo has by this time been reduced to a state of desperation. Though as a priest he is forbidden to use violence or to resist it, he is free to take upon himself the role of martyrdom and share the fate of the victims. He will wear the star of David and pretend he is a Jew. How can the Church be idle while Jews are being herded into the gas ovens at Auschwitz? He screams his protest:

> We are *priests*! God can forgive
> a hangman for such work, but not a priest,
> not the Pope! [42]

It is the moral issue that Hochhuth stresses throughout the play. He arranges events dramatically so as to make it seem that a forceful protest by the Pope might have brought Hitler's genocidal program to a halt. In the fourth act the conflict comes to a head. The Pope refuses to condemn Hitler's atrocities, though he knows that Jews are being gassed. After Riccardo makes his impassioned appeal, the Pope tries to explain what motivates him to keep silent. Christian Europe cannot be saved unless the Holy See acts as the mediator. If Hitler were overthrown, the military front would collapse and Russian troops would march into Berlin. The Pope declares that he will pray for the Jews and issue a proclamation in their behalf, but what he dictates to his Scribe is only an innocuous message couched in grandiloquent rhetoric.

The last act attempts to suggest rather than picture realistically the horror of life in the concentration camp. Hochhuth is fully aware that these events resist the efforts of the imagination to comprehend them and make them seem credible. As he says:

[41] *Ibid.*, p. 148.
[42] *Ibid.*, p. 155.

We lack the imaginative faculties to be able to envision Auschwitz, or the destruction of Dresden and Hiroshima, or exploratory flights into space, or even more mundane matters such as industrial capacity and speed records. Man can no longer grasp his own accomplishments.[43]

Documentary naturalism was consequently out of the question. Nor could brilliant flights of metaphor, which might possibly prove fitting if he were composing an elegy for the millions of victims, serve Hochhuth's dramatic purpose. The particular truth he wished to body forth on the stage could not rely on the striking force of metaphoric implications alone.

For despite the tremendous force of suggestion emanating from sound and sense, metaphors still screen the infernal cynicism of what really took place – a reality so enormous and grotesque that even today, fifteen years after the events, the impression of unreality it produces conspires with our natural strong tendency to treat the matter as a legend, as an incredible apocalyptic fable. . . . No matter how closely we adhere to historical facts, the speech, scene, and events on the stage will be altogether surrealistic. For even the fact that today we can go sightseeing in Auschwitz as we do in the Colosseum scarcely serves to convince us that seventeen years ago in our actual world this gigantic plant . . . was built especially in order that normal people . . . might kill other people.[44]

We witness the debate that takes place between Riccardo, the priest who has come to sacrifice his life, and the Doctor, the Mephistophelean nihilist. Like Goetz in Sartre's *The Devil and the Good Lord*, the latter is challenging God to combat, provoking Him so outrageously that He will be compelled to give an answer:

> Even if only the negative answer
> which can be His sole excuse, as
> Stendahl put it: that He doesn't exist.[45]

The Doctor persists in his diabolical baiting of the priest, sneering at his faith. Why did God remain silent while the Doctor was consigning souls for shipment to Heaven? Neither God nor history, the Doctor gloats, can possibly justify the evil practiced on earth.

> The truth is, Auschwitz refutes
> creator, creation, and the creature.
> Life as an idea is dead.
> This may well be the beginning
> of a great new era,

[43] *Ibid.*, p. 222.
[44] *Ibid.*, p. 223.
[45] *Ibid.*, p. 247.

a redemption from suffering.
From this point of view only one crime
remains: cursed be he who creates life.
I cremate life. That is modern
humanitarianism – the sole salvation from the future.[46]

Hochhuth saves this scene from lapsing into melodrama by making the Doctor a cunning and clever dialectician; even though he is a nihilist infected with a morbid hatred of life, he is no hypocrite; he openly accepts the conclusion to which his reasoning leads. He has no use for religion or metaphysics. He recognizes only the fact of power. He finds Hitler, whom he does not respect, more to his liking than a philosopher like Hegel. Though he suffers from boredom, he assures Riccardo he feels no remorse, no sense of guilt. The play ends with Riccardo's death and a voice announcing that the Pope has refrained from protesting the deportation of the Jews.

In an appendix to the published play, "Highlights on History," Hochhuth informs the reader that he respected reality in his work, but what was this reality that he so scrupulously respected? The facts in the case, as he himself admits, outrun the power of the imagination to assimilate them. It is the facts themselves that have to be interpreted – and judged. Hochhuth makes a strategic mistake in placing the blame entirely on the Pope and thus simplifying the complex problem of guilt.[47]

If this whole section gives the discouraging impression that the writers were largely ineffectual in protesting against the evils of their day, they were not remiss in their duty as writers. They did everything in their power, not only by public speeches, petitions, pamphlets, newspaper articles, but also by their imaginative work, to call attention to these evils. If they could not help to change conditions, their outspoken protests provoked wide and intense discussion and awoke the slumbering conscience of mankind.[48] Fundamentally

---

[46] *Ibid.,* p. 248.

[47] In *The Catholic Church and Nazi Germany* Gunter Lewy declares that there is no way of proving or disproving Hochhuth's arguments that if Pope Pius XII had protested the massacre of the Jews he might have saved many lives. "Whether a Papal decree of excommunication against Hitler would have dissuaded the Führer from carrying out his plan to destroy the Jews is very doubtful. A revocation of the Concordat by the Holy See would have bothered Hitler still less. However, a flaming protest against the massacre of the Jews, coupled with the imposition of the interdict upon all of Germany or the excommunication of all Catholics in any way involved with the apparatus of the Final Solution would have been a far more formidable and effective weapon." Gunter Lewy, *The Catholic Church and Nazi Germany.* New York and Toronto: McGraw-Hill Book Company, 1964, p. 303.

[48] See *The Deputy Reader.* Edited by Dolores Barrancano Schmidt and Earl Robert Schmidt. See also *The Storm Over the Deputy.* Edited by Eric Bentley.

their protest was based on moral and religious rather than political grounds. In our next section we take up a group of writers who believe in the function of literature as a revolutionary weapon. All of them were Communists or Communist sympathizers at the time and drew heavily on Marxist doctrine in formulating an aesthetic of "commitment."

PART III

THE LITERATURE OF SOCIAL COMMITMENT

CHAPTER XV

THE POLITICS OF THE WRITER [1]

In a political age literary criticism which attempts to leave out politics inevitably becomes detached from reality. A literary criticism which brings in politics, however, is obviously open to the dangers of becoming doctrinaire, passion-blinded or corrupt. These are dangers; the unreality which comes from "leaving politics out" – when dealing with writers profoundly affected by politics – is not a danger but a certain calamity.[2]

For quite some time in the twentieth century we have heard the demand put forth, though with varying degrees of urgency, that the writer shoulder his burden of political responsibility and play his part in helping to solve the troubled problems of the world. The rallying cry for a literature of social commitment is still being sounded not only in Soviet Russia and the countries of Eastern Europe but also in France by such influential spokesmen of the left as Sartre, Louis Aragon, and Roger Garaudy. This call to arms, this attempt to mobilize the genius of literary men in behalf of some liberal, radical, or humanitarian cause, has its historical antecedents. The gospel of commitment was preached zealously by nineteenth-century Russian critics such as Chernyshevski, Dobrolyubov, and Pisarev, by Zola after his conversion to Socialism, and by a host of embattled writers in England and the United States during the thirties. The social implications of this militant aesthetic are put forth in blunt, categorical terms: the artist, the creative person, is called upon to abandon his anachronistic refuge in Axel's castle and grapple manfully with the hydra-headed evils of his age. The cult of art for art's sake is denounced as an expression of footloose and irresponsible individualism, the mark of the beast. Irresponsibility of this kind, it is charged, converts the artist into an alienated Bohemian without roots in the life of his own culture; if he is convinced of his own unique genius and the imperative

---

[1] Based in part on an article by the present writer, "Literature and Society," *Arizona Quarterly*, Summer 1952, VIII, pp. 128-39.

[2] Conor Cruise O'Brien, *Writers and Politics*. New York: Pantheon Books, 1965, p. 142.

necessity for cultivating it to the highest possible stage of perfection, that is because his work is concerned not with the fate of society but only with the inflation and aggrandisement of his own precious ego.

We are confronted here with a basic confusion of categories. It is possible for a writer like Shakespeare, Proust, and Genet to be largely or wholly unpolitical in his orientation and yet, by projecting in his writing an image of what is false and corrupt in the society of his day, reveal his conception of an ideal social order. According to this view, every writer, even if he be asocial in his outlook, passes judgment, implicit or explicit, on the life of society. The revolt, for example, of the members of the Beat generation, their refusal to participate in what they call the rat-race of American life, represents an extreme act of social criticism, and this criticism, though chiefly negative in character, is reflected in their fiction and poetry. But this is scarcely enough to satisfy the criteria of commitment formulated by the literary Marxists. This is not at all what they have in mind. Vociferous advocates of an aesthetic doctrine of social commitment, they argue that the writer must respond positively to the challenge posed by his socioeconomic environment. Only by affiliating himself with "the universal democratic humanism" that Communism is supposed to embody will his life gain unity of purpose and his work be imbued with vital collective meaning. If this role entails that he become a propagandist, that is a consummation devoutly to be wished, for all art is essentially propaganda.

The philosopher-king whom Plato exalted, the leaders of the Church Militant, and the Commissar of our day entertain strikingly similar views on the function of literature, regarding it as at bottom an agent of moral enlightenment and persuasion. Plato would drive out the poets from his utopian commonwealth on the ground that they harmfully aroused the passions of men and scandalously libeled the gods. The Church harbors no distrust of literature *per se* except that it condemns those books which in its judgment are flagrantly immoral or blasphemous. The Communist Party when it wields absolute power in the State, arbitrarily censors or bans those literary productions which deviate from the paths of ideological orthodoxy. Indirectly all three, Plato, the Church, and Communism, acknowledge the disturbing, subversive influence of literature; all three assume it can be used for "good" or "evil" ends, and each in its own way seeks to control this instrument of moral suasion.

It is enormously revealing how in times of crisis the men in positions of power want to exploit the services of the writer – and recruit him naturally on the right side. The temptation is strong to make him serve the best interests (but who is to define them and *how* are they best served?) of society or the State. To be sure, many writers have earnestly spoken up in behalf of movements designed to promote the cause of social justice. We have already discussed the protests, the criticism made by such writers as Shaw, Dos Passos, Ernst Toller, Max Frisch, Dürrenmatt, and Hochhuth, but these were not Party men. The writer best benefits society not by dragging politics in but by retaining his individual freedom, his right to criticize society when it falls short of the ideal. He should be bound not by ulterior considerations but solely by the compelling truth of his personal vision, even if this results in the nightmares of perversion of a Marquis de Sade or the nihilistic ironies of a Samuel Beckett. Only in an atmosphere of freedom can the redeeming truth be told. In voicing his vision of the truth of life, whether like Flaubert he uncovers the crass boredom and banality of middle-class existence or like William S. Burroughs pictures the opposition of the individual to a technologically controlled society, the writer is doing his share in disclosing the weaknesses of a corrupt social order.

To display the truth, even a limited aspect of the truth, is to elevate a criterion against which falsehood must be judged and condemned. In this way, any artist is an agitator, an anarchist, an incendiary. By expressing an independent standard of value he attacks the principle of authority; by portraying the truth according to his own vision he attacks the factual manifestation of authority.[3]

During times of war, however, when the life of the nation is at stake and all energy must be concentrated on the task of defeating the enemy, the effort is made to transform literature into an ideological weapon, a means of bolstering morale. For example, during the Second World War, when the United Nations were making common cause against Germany, a number of writers in the United States rushed to the defense of democracy. But the experience of the war itself produced a more sober and profound reaction. On far-flung battlefields, in lonely outposts of the Pacific, while flying long hours on reconnaissance in Africa or engaged in dangerous missions to bomb Berlin, men, coming face to face with the ultimate realities of life and death, achieved a deeper understanding of themselves in relation to the universe. The writers who knew the reality of war at first hand strove to rid themselves of deceptive ideals and get down to the fundamental truth of being. The eschatological vision of Marxism, the pipe dream of founding the classless State, went up in the smoke of burning cities; the ravaged battlefields of Europe and the inferno of concentration camps simply added to the growing sense of horror. In "New Guinea Letter," Karl J. Shapiro states the meaning the war had for him. Trapped in a jungle hot and teeming with tropical vegetation, he won-

[3] George Woodcock, *The Writer and Politics*. London: The Porcupine Press, 1948, pp. 17-18.

ders whether men are now more closely united as brothers and arrives at wryly negative conclusions. War solves no problems, it only creates new ones. Whereas Archibald MacLeish urgently declared in 1941 that "There is no possible substitute for Utopian thinking," [4] Shapiro would do away with all ideological nostrums and come to terms with enduring realities, with men as they are. In accents instinct with the irony of disenchantment he formulates his new faith:

> Give me a future you can't dream up,
> Men as they are, as they were begun
> With a nice right emphasis on Number One.
> Keep to the Left but if it gets hectic
> Take a powder on Papa and the dialectic.

He concludes his "poetic letter" with an expression of his need for privacy, so that he may retrace his steps and find "The start of the maze within my mind,/The exquisite pattern of mankind."

What then, it is appropriate to ask again, is the function of the writer in society, what is his relation to politics? As a writer he has but one compelling duty: to report the truth of life as honestly and completely as he can, without distortions or *parti pris*. If he portrays the world of man as he genuinely experiences it and as it is refracted through his individual sensibility and imagination, his work will contain its own social and political overtones of meaning, but these will not be externally imposed. They will not constitute a formal ideology. There is no need in imaginative literature for overt political commitments. The writer's proper job is not to preach the class war or provide his readers with revolutionary slogans. His primary allegiance belongs to his art. He is above the battle only in the sense that he judges all the participants in the life-struggle, whatever the particular banner under which they fight, by the same strict laws of the imagination. His party, in short, includes all of humanity; his vision extends beyond all geographical frontiers and class lines.[5] The greater the writer the more difficult it becomes to determine what system of politics he espoused. Though Shakespeare "had very strongly a conception of what is good in society," [6] it is impossible to say what religious or political views he held. What political message did Proust set forth in *Remembrance of Things Past*? Or Kafka in *The Castle*? Or Joyce in *Ulysses*? If politics and freedom of mind are, as

---

[4] Archibald MacLeish, *A Time to Speak.* New York: Duell, Sloan, 1941, p. 23.

[5] See Julien Benda, *The Betrayal of the Intellectuals.* Translated by Richard Aldington. Boston: The Beacon Press, 1959.

[6] Edwin Muir, *Essays on Literature and Society.* London: The Hogarth Press, 1948, p. 32.

Valéry maintained, mutually exclusive,[7] so are politics and the freedom of art.

One of the astounding features of the twentieth century is the degree to which a band of "committed" writers, fired by their vision of Communism triumphant the world over, were willing to give up their creative freedom for the sake of transforming literature into a vehicle for ideological preachment. Dispensing with the vestigial and "reactionary" function of "bourgeois aesthetics," they take on the role of midwife of the ideal society to be ushered in. The literary tradition of the past is ignored to make way for work that is freighted with "the right" kind of social message. They felt spiritually justified in their switching of roles. Their writing was now invested with prophetic urgency; it could shape the future, remake the world. What they failed to realize is that though the writer remains an integral part of society, his values are not identical with the temporal interests or goals of that society, be it capitalist or Communist in structure. Even when the writer is sincerely committed to a particular set of political beliefs, he nevertheless owes an obligation to the art he practices.

Communism is a secular religion whose ideal of Kingdom Come is situated in time and on earth. Universal in its claims, it is binding in its imposition of duties on the individual who embraces it. Most of the writers in Russia were inspired by the Communist faith, and that faith originally consisted of a selfless desire to make sacrifices for the sake of an oppressed group, the proletariat. But once the Communist Party firmly established its power, the writers were not allowed to devise their own forms and make their own discoveries; they had to abide by the rigid principles of Socialist realism. The spiritual universe had to be subordinated to a militant social creed. But if the Russian writer lost much of his freedom under Party restrictions, he enjoyed a number of advantages denied his professional brethren in the capitalist West. He was, or believed he was, part of an epic undertaking to transform the nature of mankind. He participated actively in the fulfillment of production plans and was thus made to feel useful. Since he worked for the State, he did not have to compete with his wares in the commercial market.

He does not feel himself a slave since he adheres to the ideology which unites the people, the party and the government. He is protected against isolation, against the difficulties and hardships of earning a living by his pen. . . . All that is asked of him in return is just one sacrifice: to say yes to the regime, to say yes to its day-to-day interpretations – an inescapable concession which yet carries the germ of of a total corruption.[8]

[7] Paul Valéry, *The Outlook for Intelligence*. Translated by Denise Folliot and Jackson Mathews. New York and Evanston: Harper & Row, 1962, pp. 205-210.

[8] Raymond Aron, *The Opium of the Intellectuals*. Translated by Terence Kilmartin. Garden City, New York: Doubleday & Company, Inc., 1957, p. 300.

A number of committed writers outside Russia refused to make this one sacrifice and thus escaped the danger of total corruption. They revolted against Party domination of literature. The reason for their repudiation of Marxist aesthetics and Party control is given by Stephen Spender, who could not accept that

> it was necessary to deny to others the freedom to say what they believed to be true, if this happened to be opposed to the somewhat arbitrary boundaries to freedom laid down by the Proletarian Dictatorship.[9]

Nor was Spender convinced that the dictatorship of the proletariat was bound to give way to the classless society. His declaration of faith articulates the belief held by many modern writers that to concentrate exclusively on politics would spell the death of art:

> Because I do not believe that the central organizations of the Communists are capable of making a classless society, or indeed of doing anything except establish the rule of a peculiarly vindictive and jealous bureaucracy, I do not feel that I should surrender my judgment to theirs. . . .[10]

This does not mean, of course, that the writer thereby disqualifies himself from facing up to the crucial problems of his time. Henry James did so in *The Bostonians* and *The Princess Casamassima*. H. G. Wells excoriated the profit-seeking motif in England in his novel, *Tono-Bungay*. Joseph Conrad, the least politically-minded of novelists, touched on the vagaries and passions of politics, though that was not his main concern, in *Nostromo* and *Under Western Eyes*. But in each of these cases and in others that we might mention the writer did not bind himself to a given political doctrine and not only shape his work accordingly but attempt to convince the reader that it offered a solution for the world's ills. It is not the purity nor intensity of his dedication to the Social Muse that will count for him in the end but the depth of his insight into the moral heart of man – one thinks of the *Heart of Darkness* in this connection – and the universality of his vision. In the final analysis, his literary contribution will be judged not by "the rightness" of the cause he defends nor by his ideological commitment.[11]

The socially committed writer, however, especially if he is a Communist,

---

[9] Richard Crossman (ed.), *The God That Failed*. New York: Pocket Books, 1951, p. 243.

[10] *Ibid.*, pp. 273-274.

[11] As T. S. Eliot declares: "Of course, the writer has other responsibilities *qua* human being, not purely as a writer. It is not good enough for a writer simply to sign letters drawn up by someone else. That is a cheap way out. But there are occasions when a writer should accept any opportunity to express his views." Quoted by C. L. Sulzberger in *The New York Times*, January 9, 1965.

dismisses such talk as defeatist and decadent. Brecht, as we shall see in a later chapter, strove to establish an epic theater which would produce plays informed with a Marxist content. His dramas would teach "the truth" of social relations. Once men fully understood the class structure of the society they live in, they would know how to change their world. Instead of trying to call forth empathy or furnishing a purely "aesthetic" illusion, Brecht endeavored to emphasize the need for rational revolutionary praxis. Consequently much of Brecht's dramatic work, as in *The Good Women of Setzuan* or *The Caucasian Chalk Circle,* takes the form of political allegory.

This pseudo-scientific aesthetic in defense of a politically "engaged" or "committed" literature leads to the production of plays, novels, and poems that are for the most part baldly didactic. Essentially the call for commitment engenders a spirit of ideological righteousness, if not fanaticism, that is alien and inimical to the literary enterprise. As Henri Peyre well says:

The value of commitment has been misunderstood and exaggerated. The espousal of a cause (which may, in good faith, be a practical or a narrow or a criminal one) cannot in itself be a mark or a guarantee of talent.[12]

If all value in some measure reflects the life of society, it is not, as we have contended, the reflection that identifies its special or distinctive value as art. Nor is literature directly an agent for social reform or a proper medium for political propaganda. As André Gide declared: "I prefer not to write anything rather than bend my art to utilitarian ends." [13] Marxism, as Silone discovered for himself, is not primarily interested in the way the creative imagination functions but in determining the precise political effects it ought to achieve.

[12] Henri Peyre, *Literature and Sincerity.* New Haven and London: Yale University Press, 1963, p. 341.

[13] André Gide, *The Journals of André Gide.* Translated by Justin O'Brien. New York: Alfred A. Knopf, 1949, III, p. 252.

CHAPTER XVI

IGNAZIO SILONE: THE REVOLUTIONARY
TURNED SAINT

Can society be explained, defined, and "saved" solely in terms of the history of man's relationship to nature? In the effort to prove secularism equal to the task of an independent human history, Marx and his interpreters have had to give materiality to many of the images characteristically ascribed to the spiritual state. Secular order begins with the assumption that morality is completely and infallibly understood in the forms of adjustment man makes to nature's requirements.[1]

Silone is an example of the socially committed writer at his best. No one among his contemporaries has taken more seriously his duty to society, his responsibility to his fellow man. In all his writings, from his initial ardor as a Communist to his later quasi-religious identification with his people, this concern is paramount. After leaving the Communist Party and casting off the shackles of Marxist dogma, his social commitment took a new turn. He found a new sustaining faith. He would follow not the directives of the Party but the promptings of his conscience, and these led him to emulate the example set by Christ. His protagonists are resolved to live with the poor and share their life of hardship and suffering.

Silone, like Auden, shifts the universe of metaphoric discourse from the secular to the sacred. The sterile abstractions of Marxist ideology are supplanted by the viable redemptive symbols of Christianity. After his "reconversion," however, it is not the Christian doctrine that his novels embody, but the miracle of the divine presence manifesting itself in the human and the finite, especially in the sacrifices of which the humble and the lowly are capable. Frederick J. Hoffman makes this point explicit in *The Mortal No:*

Much of the social revolution of our age has been an attempt to secularize the system and to redefine the advantages, even the metaphysics, of Christian grace. Silone's novels repeatedly describe the corruption of the divine by the secular,

[1] Frederick J. Hoffman, *The Mortal No.* Princeton: Princeton University Press, 1964, p. 98.

the channeling of absolutistic energies into secular ways, finally the startling conjunctions of secular aspirations and spiritual yearnings.[2]

The human is thus interpreted in terms borrowed from the divine. Silone portrays within a social context the struggle for transcendence, the mystery of the sacrifice made in the name of brotherhood, without, like Graham Greene, playing emphatic variations on the theme of sin and damnation. This leads him to bring up the eschatological issue, the question as to the ultimate goal of human striving.

Silone speaks with the voice of primitive Christianity, seeking a new basis for human solidarity and a new conception of the nature of man. What he struggles to articulate is the pure religious impulse that is embodied in the fate of poverty, the affirmation of love. Unlike Arthur Koestler, he has not, in his disillusionment with Communism, reverted to the pole of denunciatory hatred nor has he withdrawn from the life of action. In his efforts to make literature an instrument for social betterment, he has simply resorted to the use of different weapons, that is all.

If he makes the attempt to justify the reasons why he seceded from the Communist Party, he is not, like a number of literary ex-Communists, afflicted with a bad conscience. He ceased to worship the God of collective power, just as he ceased to believe in the dream of social justice to be instituted by the dictatorship of the proletariat. Both are essentially evil, for they ignore the problem of the proper relation that should obtain between means and ends. Silone considers it a major disaster of modern civilization that it has been forced to pursue wrong goals,

while the true end, which is man himself, has become a means.... Speaking generally, one may say that every means tends to become an end. To understand the tragedy of human history it is necessary to grasp that fact. Machines, which ought to be man's instrument, enslave him, the state enslaves society, the bureaucracy enslaves the state, the church enslaves religion, institutions enslave justice, academies enslave art, the army enslaves the nation, the party enslaves the cause, the dictatorship of the proletariat enslaves Socialism.... Hence the saying that the end justifies the means is not only immoral; it is stupid. An inhuman means remains inhuman even if it is employed for the purpose of assuring human felicity.[3]

The experiment in Communism conducted in Russia, Silone concludes, did not result in the elimination of classes and the establishment of democracy but in the capitulation to another system of human enslavement.

In the early thirties, however, when he wrote *Fontamara*, Silone was still an earnest, dedicated Communist who practiced the art of fiction as a means

[2] *Ibid.*, pp. 96-97.

[3] Ignazio Silone, *The School for Dictators.* New York and London: Harper & Brothers, 1938, p. 214.

of propagating the Marxist creed. One critic complains that the purpose of the novel is clearly to preach the doctrine of Leninism. Though it is interestingly told as a story, *Fontamara* is accused of being "a mere dramatization of a doctrine that can be stated conceptually in a more precise manner. . . ." [4] In his revision of the first edition Silone remedied these defects. It now offers his present interpretation of the human condition. Berardo Viola, the hero, is accorded greater prominence and made a more convincing character. His sacrifice – he overcomes his self-concern and dies for his brethren – becomes exemplary.

Even in its revised version *Fontamara* is at bottom a militant call to action, but it is conspicuously different from the general run of proletarian fiction or novels produced under the auspices of Socialist realism. The protagonist is no "positive" hero; in his spirit of self-sacrifice he is governed not by Marxist theories of the will of the Party but by the Christlike ideal of brotherhood. In *Fontamara* the peasants come to an awareness of their oppressed condition and a dim but growing realization that something must be done, though they have not acquired sufficient insight to espouse revolutionary means. The story is told by a few peasants in the village who give their naive version of events in Fascist Italy under Mussolini. They are superstitious and illiterate but they cling to their human dignity and fight desperately for the right to survive. Though they are incredibly ignorant and can be taken in by the machinations of officials and property owners, they know when they are being fleeced; they know the difference between starvation wages and what they should receive; they know the meaning of hunger and want. Since the peasants are the narrators, Silone presses home no revolutionary message, no epiphany of the aroused will of the agricultural proletariat.

This novel has withstood the test of time because, as Silone says, the really important things it treats of – birth and death, work, love and suffering – are universal. He is painting a picture of men who cultivate the earth, endure poverty and hunger, and dwell in huts that are exposed to the elements, living huddled together with their animals. This village of Fontamara is a miniature universe. "The obscure story of the people of Fontamara is a monotonous *Via Crucis* of hungry and unsuccessful peasants who for generations have worked from dawn to sunset, sweating blood over a minute and sterile patch of dust." [5] Then Fascism came. Silone had to leave his country and he wondered what had become of Fontamara where he had grown up. His

[4] Eliseo Vivas, *The Artistic Transaction and Essays on Theory of Literature.* Columbus: Ohio State University Press, 1963, p. 104.

[5] Ignazio Silone, *Fontamara.* Translated by Harvey Fergusson II. New York: Atheneum, 1960, p. 9.

curiosity is satisfied when three peasants from Fontamara arrive at his door and tell the story of what happened in their village.

Berardo Viola, resolute, strong as an ox, had no faith in the authorities or the law; the law was rigged against the poor farmers. The peasants of Fontamara are reported as being subversive and a curfew is imposed, though these peasants go to bed anyway at dark, but they must be up long before dawn if they are to work the fields where they hire themselves out for pay. Another decree is promulgated that there must be no political discussions: no talk about prices or wages or taxes. And Berardo, who believes in direct action, agrees that argument is useless. The peasant is cheated shamefully because he does nothing but argue whereas the unreasoning donkey insists that he must have his fodder and cares not in the least about methods of persuasion. They, too, must be unreasoning, adamant in their refusal to work without food.

When the time comes for diverting the water of the spring, the peasants perceive how completely they had been swindled. They had been robbed of the water on which the life of their small holding of land depended. They were being defrauded by the very men whom they had trusted. They learn they can trust no one. They will have to rely on their own strength. Berardo, who is eager to marry and settle down, is busy trying to find work so that he can buy a small plot of land. He goes to Rome in quest of a job. His quest is fruitless, but he sees the light when he meets the young man who tells him about the activities of the Solitary Stranger, who goes wherever the peasants rise up in revolt. Berardo's life now takes on a new meaning when he is imprisoned and self-sacrificingly declares that he is the Solitary Stranger.

Despite the relentless questioning, the beatings to which he is subjected, he will reveal nothing. He dies in prison and in dying discovered his destiny. The villagers decide to bring out a clandestine newspaper, which they call *What Can We Do?* For every grievance they cite they add the pointed question: What Can We Do? The novel ends with a series of challenging questions:

> What can we do?
> After so much suffering, so many tears, and so many
> wounds, so much hate, injustice, and desperation –
> WHAT CAN WE DO? [6]

After leaving the Communist Party, Silone changed his conception of the function of literature and of the most effective way literature can influence

[6] *Ibid.*, p. 240.

the life of society. A lifelong habit of introspection led him to examine the motives that prompted him to join the Party. He had to free himself from this ideological obsession. He had not given his allegiance to the revolutionary movement as a political gesture, a matter of mere intellectual assent; it meant "a conversion, a complete dedication." [7] Though it was painful for him to abandon his activities in the underground organization of the Communist Party, his faith in Socialism remained unshaken. In its essence, he maintained, it represented "an extension of the ethical impulse from the restricted individual and family sphere to the whole domain of human activity, a need for effective brotherhood, an affirmation of the superiority of the human person over all the economic and social mechanisms which oppress him." [8]

The spiritual revolution that Silone records is religious in tone without offering any of the rewards that Christianity accords the believer. Silone's hero shares the life of the poor and participates in the struggle for the improvement of their lot and the recovery of their buried sense of self-respect without expecting to be blessed, in heaven or on earth, for his pains. The political battle is henceforth to be waged in the arena of conscience, and the outcome is a saintly dedication which seeks no otherworldly recompense and none of the benefits to be derived from the seizure of power. The revolutionary saint whose career Silone celebrates is not an instrument of history or a pawn in the vast and inexorable class conflict that is being fought. He is free and yet bound to his mission, which is nothing less than to affirm his solidarity with all suffering mankind.

Silone's aesthetic of social commitments thus takes a new turn. He ceases to be a political novelist in the strict sense of the term. As George Woodcock points out, "his writing proceeds steadily towards a conclusion that the regeneration of human society is governed by moral rather than political laws." [9] He is not concerned with disseminating propaganda or revolutionary doctrines. His protagonist is an heroic humanist, giving of himself freely, even to the point of emulating the sacrifice of Christ. Silone believes in man, his innate goodness, his potentialities for growth and development. The ethic of love takes the place of the abstract and inhuman revolutionary dialectic. "His quest is, and always has been, religious, ethical." [10]

The Seed Beneath the Snow marks a symbolic break with the monolithic

[7] Richard Crossman (ed.), *The God That Failed*. New York: Bantam Books, 1950, p. 99.
[8] *Ibid.*, pp. 114-115.
[9] George Woodcock, *The Writer and Politics*. London: The Porcupine Press, 1948, p. 156.
[10] Paul West, *The Modern Novel*. London: Hutchinson & Co., Ltd., 1963, p. 369.

rule of the Party and emphasizes the need for spiritual honesty and truth. Man must not live by abstract principles or be deluded by dogma. He must first undergo a change of heart. Pietro Spina, the saint who lives among the poor and humble in the village where he was born, is the voice that sounds this vision. The police are hunting for him; he has spent considerable time hiding in order to avoid capture, and this period of enforced solitude contributed to his spiritual rebirth. What obsesses the mind of Pietro Spina is the question whether the love of justice is completely extinguished among men caught in the grip of two evils: Money and the State. The only alternative left open to those who are true Christians is to revolt against both idols. Silone is convinced that the roots of self-respect, which nourish rebellion, cannot be torn up and destroyed. The attempt is made again and again but it invariably fails, for in some unsuspected place new seeds are already beginning to push their way upward beneath the snow. "There will always be men who are hungry not only for food but for justice, and in order to endure this sad life, they must have a little self-respect." [11] The struggle to win human dignity for the most degraded and oppressed of men is invested with a religious meaning.

The class conflict is no longer the motivating element in the plot. Simone, another character who, like Pietro, lives in poverty, is endowed with a spirit of noble generosity. Though he grants that mankind are divided into two classes, the rich and the poor, he believes that there are men

who do not lack for food and yet who cannot endure to see others go hungry; there are men who are ashamed to be well-off so long as others – most others – fare badly, men who cannot resign themselves to the oppression and the humiliation suffered by other men.[12]

This is the humane creed he tries to live by, a creed which Marxists would consider an example of bourgeois sentimentality. But Silone introduces Simone in order to point out that economic determinism has its limits, and that the division of mankind according to strict class lines often breaks down.

Pietro is revolted by party fanaticism and by the type of petty bourgeois intellectual who has turned revolutionary out of feelings of personal resentment. What animates this type principally is the desire to lord it over his fellow men. It was Communists of this stripe who had driven Pietro away from the revolutionary movement. What the Communist Party left out of account in preaching the necessity for revolutionary action was the essential solitude of fate which each man must learn to face alone. In the suffering of solitude Pietro had learned, what Hawthorne had set forth in "The Celestial

[11] Ignazio Silone, *The Seed Beneath the Snow*. Translated by Frances Frenaye. New York: Harper & Brothers, 1942, p. 154.

[12] *Ibid.*, p. 248.

Railroad," that before a man can hope to transform society he must first come into possession of himself.

A man who is spiritually a slave cannot work for true freedom. . . . When all is said and done, there is no better and more necessary occupation than man's effort to know himself and the meaning of his life on this earth.[13]

The present iniquitous social order must be rejected, but what is the best way of getting this done? It is incumbent on the revolutionary saint to attach himself personally to the people, to love all those who struggle and suffer. If he is to understand the real condition of society, he must live among the poor and become one of them in a community of brotherhood. Having thrown off his old dogmatic self, Pietro decides to lead a simple life among his people. At the end he willingly bears the cross for his poor brethren. What one must contribute to the cause is one's life.

The Seed Beneath the Snow develops the theme that the revolution must be waged by the power of a faith that is lived in all sincerity. The poor peasants of the land become the incarnate symbol of God. The revolutionary saint is the tragic figure who, while living with the people, is prepared, if necessary, to surrender his life for their sake. This is the redemptive myth that is shadowed forth in the symbol of the seed struggling to break through the crust of snow.

The symbolism of the seed beneath the snow also appears in *Bread and Wine*.[14] Pietro Spina, a revolutionist whom the police had hounded from country to country, returns to his own land though knowing full well that, if caught, he faces prison and possibly death. He cannot resist the call of his native soil. Experience has taught him that liberty cannot be bestowed as a gift. One must refuse to submit to the established order of things. Only those who have the courage to fight for what they believe is right are free men. In order not to be arrested by the police, Pietro assumes the disguise of a priest and retires to a small village. He still suffers from the conflicts between the ideals of his adolescence when he had yearned to become a saint and the disciplined knowledge of the man who had devoted himself to the revolutionary cause. Was it morally right, he asks himself, to adopt a life of contemplation while the masses were sunk in the muck of poverty? He recalls that

---

[13] *Ibid.*, p. 300.

[14] See Silone's play, *And He Hid Himself*, which was inspired by *Bread and Wine*. In his foreword Silone discusses the impact of Christianity on the modern drama. "The rediscovery of a Christian heritage in the revolution of our time remains the most important gain that has been made in these last years for the conscience of our generation." Ignazio Silone, *And He Hid Himself*. Translated by Darine Tranquilli. New York and London: Harper & Brothers, 1946, p. v.

originally he had been drawn to Socialism by his love of righteousness, his hunger for the absolute, but then gradually his love of the people had died out and he had succumbed to the pressures of a political party, instead of living for justice and truth alone. Though the revolutionary faith still burns strongly within him, the acid of doubt has already seeped into his system. Now he has time for reflection. He looks back on his years of service as a professional revolutionary and, like Rubashov in *Darkness at Noon*, feels appalled. He had set out to save the world and – therein lay his tragedy – wound up by losing himself. The return to his native region represented a desperate effort to throw off the bondage of his revolutionary past, to recapture the purity of vision that had first brought him to the movement.

The questions he asks himself reach to the heart of Communism. Could one remain loyal to the Party without compromising his sincerity as an idealist? Could truth and justice be identified with the directives issued by the Party bureaucracy? Had not Communism, in effect, dismissed all moral distinctions as petty-bourgeois prejudices? The fact that Pietro raises these heretical questions reveals the conflict of conscience that is raging within him. It was not the scientific analysis of society that had in the beginning attracted him to Communism, and yet through the years his moral idealism had been steadily subordinated to practical politics. That is the conclusion to which he is irresistibly led: power politics, whether of the right or the left, culminates in every instance in the degradation, if not disappearance, of moral values. Pietro sees now what a divided being he has become. He cannot recover the religious faith of his adolescence nor can he retire into solitude and ignore the needs of the poor. He discovers that he must first come to terms with himself and formulate a faith that will lend meaning to all his actions. Not by slogans or manifestoes or propaganda will the masses be won. What will finally gain their allegiance is the example set by a revolutionary saint who is willing to sacrifice himself in behalf of the cause. Some sparks of revolt still remained in the hearts of the people, which could be fanned into a great fire of liberation, but not under the corrupt auspices of the Party dictatorship. There was no exception to the rule, Pietro realizes, that every revolution began as a movement of liberation and degenerated into a tyranny.

That is the message this novel, like *The Seed Beneath the Snow*, sends forth: more persuasive than words, however inflammatory, is the life of a man who is sincere, genuinely disinterested, generous, free. It is a mistake to substitute logic and ideas for the deeper forces of the spirit. Pietro is convinced that a true revolution could be consummated if only a hundred were ready to renounce all safety, defy all corruption, free themselves from obsession with private property, sex, and their careers, and unite on the basis of absolute sincerity and absolute brotherliness. . . . [15]

The masses would follow such leaders. That is the only way of saving one's soul: by overcoming the claims of the egocentric self. It is the spiritual life rather than the pressure of economic determinism that will provide the dynamic power of the revolution.

Silone has, of course, been severely criticized on the ground that he interprets the conflicts of society in the light of purely moral and spiritual values. He had adopted an ethic of commitment that ran counter to the tenets of Socialist realism. In the eyes of his former comrades-in-arms he was not only a heretic but a renegade. In a letter addressed to friends, Silone sought to clarify his position as a writer, especialy his new treatment of the class struggle. What he finds lacking in professional Marxists is a sensitive awareness of the demands of the inner life. Marxism, he charges, has become a dogma, "a sort of drug, a sedative, a sop to one's conscience. Perhaps one day we shall reach the formula: 'Marxism is the opium of the people.' " [16] He now holds the belief that history is made "by men, not by social determinism." [17]

A better example of the politically committed writer is Bertolt Brecht. Though too gifted as a poet and possessed of too original a creative imagination to follow slavishly the ideological dictates of the Party, he never wavered in his allegiance to the Communist movement. After his conversion he devoted all his energies to the development of a type of drama that has a socially constructive influence on the audience in accordance with Marxist doctrine.

[15] Ignazio Silone, *Bread and Wine*. Translated by Gwenda David and Eric Mosbacher. New York: Penguin Books, Inc., 1946, p. 292.

[16] Ignazio Silone, "The Things I Stand For." Translated by Malcolm Cowley. *The New Republic*, November 2, 1942, p. 583.

[17] *Ibid.*, p. 583. See his recent book of essays, *Emergency Exit*. Translated by Harvey Fergusson II. New York and London: Harper & Row, 1968.

THE EPIC THEATER OF BERTOLT BRECHT

CHAPTER XVII

The phantoms formed in the human brain are also, necessarily, sublimates of their material life-process, which is empirically verifiable and bound to material premises. Reality, religion, metaphysics, all the rest of ideology and their corresponding forms of consciousness, thus no longer retain the semblance of independence.[1]

For man's fate has become man himself.[2]

1. The First Stage of Development

Brecht is perhaps the most talented and challenging exponent of the Marxist aesthetic of social commitment. Outside of Russia, he is the most notable and daring practitioner in the field of politicalized drama. His work, however, proves better than his theory. His creative vision reveals much in life that is not included in the philosophy of dialectical materialism. He is part of a German literary tradition that has long been concerned with the relation of man to society. From the beginning of his career he was violently opposed to the established order, but not until he embraced Marxism did he hit upon a militantly expressive form for his ideas: the epic theater, as he called it. In his early plays, particularly in *Baal*, he portrays, like Ionesco, the desolating lack of communication in the world. He begins his assault, characteristically, by removing "God from the theater. . . ." [3] In his later development as a dramatist his aim is to make the members of the audience keep their distance and retain their lucidity of perception in order that they may more effectually gain insight into the dynamic structure of society. The Brechtian dramaturgy of commitment is based squarely on the Marxist thesis that character is shaped by the pressure of the social environment and the force of

---

[1] Karl Marx and Friedrich Engels, *The German Ideology*. Edited by R. Pascal. New York: International Publishers, 1947, p. 14.

[2] Bertolt Brecht, *The Messingkauf Dialogues*. Translated by John Willett. London: Methuen & Co Ltd., 1965, p. 31.

[3] David Grossvogel, *Four Playwrights and a Postscript*. Ithaca: Cornell University Press, 1962, p. 6.

historical circumstances. There are no absolutes; everything in the universe of experience is subject to the dialectical process of change. The epic theater Brecht experimented with presents a demonstration, a timely lesson, a thesis replete with rational argument and supporting evidence. Brecht exploits the resources of the drama as a means of producing what he considers scientifically warranted conclusions, all bearing on the central theme of the need for revolutionary change. The experience in the theater is meant to call forth critical reflection and the will to join actively in the class struggle on the side of the embattled proletariat, instead of empathy and illusion.

The Expressionist writers in Germany protested vehemently, as we have seen, against those forces in industrial society which reduced the individual to an occupational function, an appendage of the productive apparatus. They denounced the entrenched system of capitalist exploitation, the oppressive profit-system, which gave rise to periodic outbreaks of catastrophic wars, but they had no clear-cut solution to offer for the grievous social ills and miseries that afflicted mankind. To the widespread, inhumanly efficient system of economic and technological exploitation of the masses, they opposed a vague mysticism, the life of dreams and intuitions, the cultivation of a primitivism, rooted in instinct, that would undo the evils wrought by a mechanized civilization. They would tear off the mask of hypocrisy worn by socially conditioned man; they would arouse him from his sleep of habit and overcome his fearful submission to convention, his wretchedness, his abject feeling of futility and despair. The way out of this impasse was for man to rediscover and reaffirm his biological heritage, his oneness with the rhythm of the earth and the primal energy coursing through the cosmos. The Expressionists were simply carrying to an extreme the aesthetics of romanticism.

The early Brecht turns out to be an Expressionist whose work expressed a mood of nihilistic despair as he contemplated the inhumanity of man to man. In *Baal* (1918) he creates a hero who is always alone, even in his sexual excesses. He cannot communicate. He can assert himself only through homicidal violence. Trapped in a world that is chaotic and ruthless, he is driven to irrational extremes and breaks out in irrational rages. Even at this stage of his development Brecht is aware of the disastrous implications of his nihilistic *Weltanschauung*. He is assailing society as fundamentally responsible for the wasteful lives his early heroes are forced to lead, but his criticism of the social order is not yet harnessed to a revolutionary program. He is not yet politically committed.

In *Baal*, he draws the portrait of the poet – a prototype of Dylan Thomas – who is alienated from society. A rebel by nature, he refuses to compromise with the honorific values of a culture geared to the cash-nexus. He knows, and fiercely exposes, the worst features of our civilization: its callousness, its greed, its crass disregard for human suffering. Bourgeois society is deadly; it is characterized by the spirit of boredom. One can be cured of this malaise of ennui in only one way: by releasing the spontaneous life of instinct. Sensuality, without benefit of moral restrictions, is more important than the accumulation of money or advancement in a career. Baal indulges orgiastically in sex not because he is endowed with a superabundance of energy but because he realizes that there is nothing else in the bourgeois world worth living for. The universe is without ultimate meaning and sex offers one means of revolting against this intolerable knowledge. He drinks heavily in order to drown his sorrow, to blot out the knowledge he has gained of the emptiness of existence. Angrily rejecting Christianity, the religion of asceticism, he clings to love as his sole refuge against the obliterating dark of the night. "The sky is black, and we are on a swing with love inside us, and the sky is black." [4] Baal blasphemously calls the world "the Lord God's excrement." [5] Once thrust into the light and the cold, man continues to seek "the country where there's a better life." [6] At the end Baal dies, but the world rolls on, indifferent and uncaring. [7]

Brecht comes closer to the social theme in his play, *In the Jungle of Cities*, which presents a conflict between two opposed attitudes to life: one represented by the honest worker Garga, an idealist, and the other by the gangster Shlink. The two are well matched. The drama focuses on the horror of life in the social jungle of our time. Brecht shows that there is no possibility of escape from the dehumanizing pressure of society, but his diagnosis does not lay bare the economic roots of the evil inherent in capitalism. As Garga points out: "Man is destroyed by trivial causes alone." [8] Garga finally reaches a stage of defeatism where all higher values are stripped of significance; the spiritual yearnings of men are trampled in the mire.

A Man's a Man (1925) is a farcial exposé of the folly of war. The comic incidents in which Galy Gay is involved (he is made to serve as a substi-

[4] Walter H. Sokel (ed.), *Anthology of German Expressionist Drama*. Garden City, New York: Doubleday & Company, Inc., 1963, p. 330.

[5] *Ibid.*, p. 353.

[6] *Ibid.*, p. 360.

[7] One critic interprets *Baal* not as a nihilistic work expressive of the irremediable absurdity of life; "the play depicts an anarchistic attempt to create personality in a depersonalized world, and death becomes the metaphor for Baal's failure." Gerald Weales, "Brecht and the Drama of Ideas," in John Gassner (ed.), *Ideas in the Drama*. New York and London: Columbia University Press, 1964, p. 139.

[8] Bertold Brecht, *Seven Plays*. Edited by Eric Bentley. New York: Grove Press, Inc., 1961, p. 47.

tute for a missing soldier in a British regiment) are designed to show that almost anything for good or evil can be done with a human being. Galy Gay is a victim sucked into the maw of the military system; he puts on a soldier's uniform and thus is caught up in a series of events that change his whole life. He loses both his name and his identity. But in this extravaganza Brecht is sharpening no Marxist axe.

In *The Threepenny Opera* (1928), Brecht uses the deadly weapon of satire to unmask the guilt of the lower middle class, to reveal "the close relationship between the emotional life of the bourgeois and that of the criminal world," [9] but it is done light-heartedly to the accompaniment of rollicking songs and outbursts of cynical laughter. The organization of thieves, Brecht makes us realize, parallels that of the sanctimonious middle-class business operators. Though the opera draws no flattering portrait of the working class, it stresses the motif that it is the economic system which makes men wicked. It pictures a society that is graft-ridden, corrupt, at war with itself, one in which only the cunning and the unscrupulous manage to survive. As Mrs. Peachum says, voicing a motif that looms large in Brecht's work: "Money rules the world." [10]

The extravagant satire, enriched by music, lyrics, and scenes of swashbuckling melodrama, conveys Brecht's bitter lesson in the established techniques of worldly morality. Peachum, an enterprising businessman who specializes in the fine art of fitting out his crew of beggars in disguises that will melt the flintiest heart and extort some alms, sings a song called "On the Uncertainty of Human Circumstances":

> The right to happiness is fundamental:
> Men live so little time and die alone.
> Nor is it altogether incidental
> That they want bread to eat and not a stone.[11]

It is an excellent idea to give charity to the poor and bring Kingdom Come that much nearer, but the facts of life unfortunately work havoc with this ideal. Bible in hand, Peachum bursts out in a realistic strain:

> But there's the little problem of subsistence:
> Supplies are scarce and human beings base.

---

[9] *Brecht on Theatre.* Edited and translated by John Willett. New York: Hill and Wang, 1964, p. 85.
[10] Bertolt Brecht, *Plays.* London: Methuen & Co., Ltd., 1961, I, 128.
[11] *Ibid.*, pp. 129-130.

> Who would not like a peaceable existence?
> But this old world is not that kind of place.[12]

Macheath or Mackie the Knife, leader of a gang of thieves, states the moral of the opera by singing that those who wish to reform him and his kind must take good care to feed them. Morality, in short, can function smoothly only on a well-fed stomach. In his "Notes to 'The Threepenny Opera'," Brecht remarks that his work critically examines the bourgeois conception of society. Though he is a gangster by profession, Macheath, like Peachum, represents the bourgeoisie, the only difference between them being that Macheath is no coward. Otherwise their interests and methods of procedure are fundamentally alike. Macheath, too, is an exploiter. As Brecht puts it:

The Threepenny Opera presents a picture of bourgeois society (and not only of the "lumpen-proletarian" element). This bourgeois society has, for its part, produced a bourgeois order of the world, and therefore has quite a distinct "Weltanschauung" without which it could probably not carry on.[13]

Evil is a powerfully active principle in Brecht's version of the world of men. In *Saint Joan of the Stockyards* Brecht delineates the adventures of a dedicated, idealistic girl who joins the Salvation Army but later discovers the nature of her mistake. In Brecht's dramatized world, the quixotic hero or heroine is bound to come a cropper when he encounters the inimical force of social reality. The scene is laid in the stockyards of Chicago. Joan, at the head of her shock troops of Black Straws, makes her first descent into the inferno of proletarian misery and there beholds how capitalism breeds industrial unrest and creates "a world like a slaughterhouse." [14] She has come to prevent the threatened outbreak of violence and make God's word effectual in the sphere of real life. It is not poverty, she is convinced, that oppresses the benighted masses but their blindness to higher things. Joan soon finds out that her vision of redemption does not correspond with the truth of economic reality. It is the evil of capitalism that drags these workers down. She becomes aware of the cutthroat competition that goes on all the time, stifling every altruistic impulse at its source. No gospel of salvation through the sacrifice of Christ can relieve the wretched plight of the workers. Joan finally gleans this bit of "true" wisdom:

> Oh, let nothing be counted good, however helpful it may seem,
> And nothing considered honorable except that

[12] *Ibid.,* p. 130.
[13] *Ibid.,* p. 188.
[14] Bertolt Brecht, *Seven Plays,* p. 155.

> Which will change this world once for all: that's
> what it needs.[15]

In the industrial jungle where force prevails only a countering revolutionary force can liberate the enslaved portion of mankind.

Gradually Brecht became convinced that man is the architect of his own misfortunes. But if bad social conditions are man-made, then it follows that they can – and must – be changed. Once Brecht became a Marxist, he ceased to strike a defeatist note. A transformed society would make it possible for mankind to achieve a decent sort of life. As a playwright Brecht took seriously to heart the injunction Marx set himself as a philosopher: namely, to change the world. Hence he formulated the aesthetic principles that make his theater revolutionary in content. The individual must recognize his impotence as an individual and sacrifice himself for the sake of the future by joining the ranks of the working class. In short, Brecht was one of the leaders in the effort to adapt the theater to political ends. Instead of providing the pabulum of entertainment, he would jettison the entire cargo of purely aesthetic effects and hammer home the thesis that society can be rationally and humanely reconstructed. "The theater then has no other goal for Brecht than to present us with the objective image of a given society." [16]

2. The Social Theory of the Epic Theater

By 1929 Brecht saw the economic crisis of the world come to a head. The structure of capitalism seemed to be collapsing of its own internal contradictions. The battle would now be fought to a finish between Fascism and Communism. Together with others who shared his Marxist faith, Brecht plunged into the political fray, crusading for Communism. The plays he composed from then on were charged with revolutionary motifs. The class war, though not thrust in doctrinaire fashion into the foreground, is always present. Converted as a writer to a creed of secular messianism, he now had an urgent and timely eschatological message to preach. Henceforth he identified himself closely with the cause of the aroused workers and deliberately attempted to employ the theater as an influential means of transforming the social order. The plays he wrote are the product of his intense social commitment. In his dramas he would expose the arbitary and iniquitous rules that govern the rigged game of capitalism; he would enlighten his audience

---

[15] *Ibid.*, p. 251.
[16] Walter Weidell, *The Art of Bertolt Brecht*. Translated by Daniel Russell. New York: New York University Press, 1963, p. 72.

by making them understand the basic principles of social causation, by familiarizing them with the science of society. And the science of society was best summed up in the teachings of Marxism.

Here, then, is the central clue to Brecht's dramaturgy: the belief that the world can be changed. The poor must not accept the ideology of the ruling class that all is right with the world and that nothing is to be questioned. The individual must be prepared to sacrifice himself on the altars of society. All morality is socioeconomic in its genesis and function. The fate of man is primarily controlled by his place in the system of productive relations. Hence Brecht's characters are not individualized; they are often stock types, bloodless but articulate abstractions, the embodiment of collective ideals or victims of the Moloch of capitalism. Applying strictly "behavioristic" criteria that are in accord with the philosophy of dialectical materialism, Brecht eliminates metaphysical speculation and psychological ingredients from his interpretation of human nature; his basic aim is to demonstrate that man need not be subjected to the iron hand of fate. Though he repeatedly revised his conception of the epic theater, he never abandoned the idea of using the drama for the purpose of rational exposition and the analysis of social processes in the light of Marxist doctrine.

Nor did he make the slightest effort to disguise his political convictions; in fact, he boldly proclaimed them in his work. For thirty years he was fairly consistent and comparatively orthodox in his Communist sympathies. As a dialectical materialist, he tends to simplify the life of man in terms of a Manichaean dualism: reaction and progress, good and evil, capitalism and Communism. Capitalism, he insists, is doomed. He relies on the mystique of the class war to resolve all conflicts. The results is that the theory frequently takes over and directs his dramatic imagination, though on a number of occasions, as in *Mother Courage*, his creative instinct leads him to disregard the requirements of political orthodoxy.

So Marxism often degenerates into a means of stylizing the actual course of events, facing the reader with gross over-simplifications, and leading to awkward intellectual shuffles whenever what was White ... has abruptly to be reclassified as Black.[17]

Thus at the outset of his career as a militant Marxist playwright Brecht faced a formidable problem: if his dramas were to be devoted to the task of dealing with the dynamic realities of the class conflict, they would have to do away with the anachronistic concept of the individual hero. This is precisely what Brecht endeavored to do. In *The Measures Taken*, the agitators

[17] John Willett, *The Theatre of Bertolt Brecht*. London: Methuen & Co., 1959, p. 197.

wear masks to indicate their depersonalization as members of the Party. The myth of the individual is bound to disappear. Brecht is therefore not interested in individual psychology or dream states or the arcana of subjective motivation. The emphasis is not on character analysis. Society is the protagonist and provides the plot, the *mise-en-scène,* the chorus and the commentary. As Brecht himself declares: "The continuity of the ego is a myth. A man is an atom that perpetually breaks up and forms anew. We have to show things as they are." [18]

In brief, the purpose of the new drama, epic in structure, is to liquidate the individual. The epic drama of commitment will concern itself with the pressing socioeconomic problems of the age. In contradistinction to the traditional fare of the theater, it will depend heavily on reportage. Brecht drew up a table to illustrate the contrast between what he called the dramatic and the epic theater. In epic drama the human being, the object of inquiry, is depicted as alterable, as part of an ongoing process of social change. Epic drama demonstrates the validity and relevance of the fundamental principle of Marxism: namely, that social life determines thought. Rational, unemotional, materialistic in its point of view, epic drama avoids heart-rending dissection of the individual, his feelings, his anguish, his estrangement – "as though the individual had not simply collapsed long ago." [19]

Here we begin to perceive the main draft of Brecht's aesthetic of social commitment and the ideological import of his dramaturgy. His so-called non-Aristotelian drama grew out of his conviction that the theater must dispense with the opiate of empathy and the "reactionary" technique of imitation or mimesis. By means of the marriage of film and play, Brecht hoped to utilize the new dramatic art as a pedagogic discipline. He welcomed the introduction of films on the stage because they made it possible to overthrow the theme dominant in bourgeois drama of the ineluctable working of fate, for it is not fate but social forces that act upon men. The film can be employed, as in the Soviet Union, to show that "morality is in fact determined by work." [20] Brecht declares that the new theater, by availing itself of the contributions of technology and the science of man, can, and must, devise an art that will influence the behavior of people. That is the nature of his ambitious program.

Once I've found out what modes of behavior are most useful to the human race I show them to people and underline them. I show them in parables: if you act

[18] *Brecht on Theatre*, p. 15.
[19] *Ibid.*, p. 46.
[20] *Ibid.*, p. 50.

this way the following will happen, but if you act like that the opposite will take place. This isn't the same thing as committed art. At most pedagogics.[21]

It is, however, more than a pedagogic demonstration that Brechtian drama supplies. The energizing force of his art lies in his revolutionary faith, his total commitment. If his dramatic work is grounded allegedly in science as a means of teaching men the underlying significance and the consequences of their behavior, the real aim, as Brecht frankly admits, is to induce them to change their pattern of behavior. Brecht enthusiastically hails the advent of the instructive theater. The stage would take up such challenging and edifying themes as inflation, war, the class struggle, religion, strikes, unemployment, the competition for commercial markets. The chorus would add enlightening commentary explicating the actual facts of the situation. Statistics would support the pedagogic purpose. Thus the social criticism of existing conditions depicted on the stage would make clear how and why the world had to be changed.

Brecht's dramaturgy deliberately subverts the traditional notion of what the drama is and what at its best it should be. Like the practitioners of Socialist realism in the Soviet Union, Brecht makes ideology the criterion of worth in literature in general and in the drama in particular. He makes no bones about his intentions of using the theater as a medium of social reconstruction. Brecht sees himself as the prophet of socialized drama that gives expression to new world values. As he himself says:

The concern of the epic theatre is thus eminently practical. Human behavior is shown as alterable; man himself as dependent on certain political and economic factors and at the same time as capable of altering them.[22]

Brecht is fervently conducting a crusade for an activist theater that will produce exemplary revolutionary plays. Epic drama will, of course, interpret man as a function of his environment. Each event will be traced to its roots in a determinate historical context which is shaped by the prevailing structure of society. If the dramatist wishes to picture the world as it is, he must view everything from a social perspective. A theater that is meant to exercise a decisive influence on the social behavior of the spectator must be based on Pavlovian psychology. The socially committed dramatist works on the assumption that the emotional reactions of the audience can be experimentally controlled. The new theater should do more than document the ugly fact of exploitation; it should do more than analyze and explain; it must be able to stir the masses to revolutionary action. It is the midwife of history;

---

[21] *Ibid.*, p. 67.
[22] *Ibid.*, p. 76.

it is a "religious" institution devoted to secular ends.

What we get is a type of what we call "magical" art, a direct and determined form of mass-conditioning. This bold conception of a class-oriented, Marxist art offers a striking example of the reductive fallacy. Society is enthroned as the all-inclusive category, the touchstone of value. Furthermore, this conception implies a profound faith in art as a potent weapon in the class war. "Art," declares Brecht, "is never without consequences. . . . [23] Just as the theater affects the sensibility and taste of an age, so, Brecht holds, it influences moral as well as political dispositions. What we have here, in effect, is the rehabilitation of the Platonic-Puritan evaluation of art made over in the Marxist image. Brecht is obviously in favor of the play with a message, but the "right" kind of message. That is why he contends that his theater

is in a naive sense a philosophical one; that is to say, I am interested in people's attitudes and opinions. . . . I wanted to take the principle that it was not just a matter of interpreting the world but of changing it, and apply that to the theatre.[24]

What makes Brecht's plays live and accounts for his popularity in England and the United States is that he wrought better than he knew. Or to put the matter differently, his work is not always in keeping with his theories. Though he was a confirmed Marxist, it is evident that he would have chafed under the administrative attempts of the Commissar to apply "the orthodox" principles of Socialist realism to his productions. A truly socialist art, he argued heretically, must not neglect quality in the interest of political indoctrination. The class character and educative function of dramatic art can be implemented without turning out ideologically resounding trash. In a note dated September 1954, Brecht states his own definition of Socialist realism. It means

realistically reproducing men's life together by artistic means from a socialist point of view. It is reproduced in such a way as to promote insight into society's mechanisms and stimulate socialist impulses.[25]

This is the theoretical program Brecht undertook to achieve, the ideal of scientifically uncovering "the mechanisms" of society and thus lead men, through critical insight and the stimulation of their socialist impulses, to the knowledge that they are capable of directing their own fate. It is this aesthetic program which is unworkable and which Brecht, despite all his casuistic

[23] *Ibid.*, p. 151.
[24] *Ibid.*, p. 248.
[25] *Ibid.*, p. 269.

theorizing, never succeeded in applying to his plays. When it came to the sticking point, when the issue of art versus doctrinal purity arose, Brecht sharply rejected the dogma that art could be brought into being by ideological fiat. No official in power should presume to act as the judge of excellence in art. "It's not the job of the Marxist-Leninist party to organize productions as on a poultry farm." [26] Art must not be brought under the blundering jurisdiction of some government department.

3. The Epic Theater in Action

When we come to the plays themselves we can see what a world of difference there is between the Socialist aims Brecht set for himself and the work he actually composed. The power of the imagination proves stronger than the siren seduction of ideology. Though Brecht presents many of his leading ideas and beliefs in a variety of dialectically posed situations, his plays do not incite to action nor do they appreciably endanger the established order of things, no more than *Ghosts* and *Mrs. Warren's Profession* were instrumental in eradicating syphilis, reforming the institution of marriage, or wiping out the evil of prostitution. Though his protagonists are not individualized, they do not act or talk like personified political attitudes. Far from creating "positive heroes" in the fashion prescribed by Socialist realism in Russia, he endows his characters with the saving grace of humor and a sense of irony. Though he reveals the tragic waste of war and focuses his lens on the wretched suffering that poverty causes, his *Lehrstücke* are not set pieces of Communist propaganda. Brecht was certainly a genuinely committed writer, but he was also a poet at heart and the poet in him triumphed as a rule over his political loyalties.

The theme elaborated in *Galileo* (1938) is scarcely revolutionary in import. The message the play ingeniously spells out, namely, that in the long run scientific truth banishes superstition and error, is one that a "bourgeois" dramatist like Ibsen would have given his blessing. Galileo knows that the earth is not situated at the center of the solar system; the cosmological picture will have to be radically revised, regardless of the damage it does to the colossal pride of man. At the beginning of the play he announces his belief in the dialectical value of skepticism. "The millennium of faith is ended," he declares; "this is the millennium of doubt." [27] Observation, experiment, *praxis* – these are the methods that bring the scientist closer to the heart of truth. But Galileo encounters formidable opposition when his views become

[26] *Ibid.*, p. 269.
[27] Bertolt Brecht, *Seven Plays*, p. 335.

known; his explorations of the heavens are considered dangerous by the Church authorities. If the earth is but a minor planet revolving around the sun, then where is God? Galileo is compelled to reply that God is not there. As a mathematician and astronomer he is convinced that God is either within man or He is nowhere.

The Church is determined to stamp out this pernicious heresy. Galileo, by removing man from his divinely appointed position in the center of the universe, has committed an act of treason against mankind. He is branded an enemy of God. Brecht skilfully dramatizes the forces in conflict by introducing a monk who is torn between his need to preserve the foundations of religious faith and his need to believe in the scientifically disclosed truth. How could the people bear it if they were deprived of their belief in God and were told that they are trapped on "a lump of stone ceaselessly spinning in empty space, circling around a second-rate star"? [28] Robbed of their celestial hope, they could then find no shadow of meaning or shred of justification in their earthly existence. Would it not be wise, in order to insure their peace of soul, for Galileo to keep silent? Galileo's retort is that the progress of truth cannot be halted, but that it marches steadily forward only if men persevere in making it known. The Little Monk is converted to the "New Philosophy." The subversive doctrine is spreading. It is then the Church strikes. Galileo must be taught a salutary lesson. Will he submit to the ecclesiastical authorities? Will he remain constant even in the face of death? He decides against the fate of heroic martyrdom. He recants and is permitted to live. He has no desire to be heroic.

Brecht views this act of recantation with ironic realism. Here is a scientist who is opposed to the priesthood and its superstitions, who doubts the Christian faith and yet prudently agrees to profess the geocentric theory. In order to save his life, he is prepared to confess his intellectual sins and renounce the truth he has discovered. Thus by this strategy of deception he gains time and wins the opportunity to write his treatise and make a genuine contribution to science. Hence even though he betrays his profession, his recantation stands justified. Brecht apparently approves of this ethical relativism, just as in *The Measures Taken* he seems to justify the murder of a comrade who in his humanitarian righteousness endangers the Communist cause.

Mother Courage (1938), Brecht's best play, is an effective exemplification of his dramatic method. It does more than denounce the horror and inhumanity of war. It exposes the underlying motives of those who declare war and

[28] *Ibid.*, p. 367.

those who wage it. Mother Courage, who is no Ma Joad, is defeated by forces beyond her control, but she is shown to be guilty just the same because she is willing to accept things as they are. Brecht explains that in composing this work his intentions were to demonstrate

That in wartime big business is not conducted by people. That war is a continuation of business by other means, making the human virtues fatal even to those who exercise them. That no sacrifice is too great for the struggle against war.[29]

As in his portrayal of Galileo, Brecht does not present Mother Courage in an heroic light, though her ability to endure in the face of adversity of the worst kind is nonetheless admirable. Instead, his object is to persuade the audience that she is incorrigible, unable to profit from her experience. He paints a stark, unrelieved picture of conditions during the Hundred Years' War. In scene after scene he reveals that war is no respecter of morals or persons. The brave are killed off equally with the cowardly. Mother Courage makes no vaunting display of courage. Like the masses of the poor, she works hard to support herself but she has no understanding of the meaning of the class struggle. Like Falstaff, she is not fooled by toplofty talk of honor or victory. When the troops of "the enemy," heralded by the roar of cannon, are approaching, the Chaplain declares: "We're in God's hands now." Her reply is: "Oh, I hope we're not as desperate as that!" [30] A defeat, according to her, is sometimes a victory for the little man, who has lost his honor, "nothing more." [31] And yet in the end, despite the tragedy that befalls her family, she fails to learn her lesson; she gamely puts up with conditions as they are because there is nothing else for her to do. It is this fatalistic philosophy which Brecht condemns.

Perhaps the best example of Brecht's epic theater is *The Caucasian Chalk Circle*, which is an ideological parable. It tells a story within a story, but it is the message that is accorded central importance. As a Marxist playwright Brecht zealously broadcasts the social faith to which he is committed, namely, that the world can be changed. The Prologue of *The Caucasian Chalk Circle*, which takes place among the ruins of a shattered Caucasian village, deals with the problem of mechanization and collectivization, the distribution of land and the use of tractors. It celebrates the age of the Commissar. The story teller then goes back in time, recounting his tale, in the shadow of Soviet tractors, of how the great ones in the benighted past lorded it over the earth like gods and how change finally came to free the masses from the curse of economic oppression.

[29] *Brecht on Theatre*, p. 220.
[30] Bertolt Brecht, *Seven Plays*, p. 284.
[31] *Ibid.*, p. 285.

To sum up: Brecht begins in *Baal* with a savage, nihilistic assault on bourgeois culture, sparing man none of his cherished illusions. Later in his career he proceeds to argue that individualism is an outlived myth. Huge forces, anonymous and implacable, govern the fate of man, but he has it in his power to change the world. We have shown that though Brecht was a socially committed writer, he never served as a compliant mouthpiece of the Communist Party propaganda machine. He nevertheless based his work on the philosophy of dialectical materialism. He removed not only God but the individual hero from his epic theater. Brecht's dramaturgy, rooted in and growing out of the Marxist synthesis, is concerned chiefly with the externals of action and "the moral" to be derived from exhibiting the inexorable play of economic determinism. He thereby sacrifices the complexity of character which emerges from the depths of the individual in his struggle with himself as well as his society.

Sartre, like Brecht, issues a call for a literature of social commitment, but limitations of space prevent us from offering a consideration of his work The contribution of both writers raises the difficult question: committed to what? How can literature as art be evaluated in terms of the canons of commitment? As Kaelin well says:

Is the work nothing but a means to some further end? the propagation of an idea, philosophical, social, or political? If so, the author never escapes his propagandist guise, even if his work shows all the stylistic excellence of a literary masterpiece.[32]

Much of Soviet literature falls within this area of interdiction as propaganda, as we shall see in the following chapter on the cult of Socialist realism.

[32] Eugene F. Kaelin, *An Existentialist Aesthetic*. Madison: The University of Wisconsin Press, 1962, p. 121.

CHAPTER XVIII

THE CULT OF SOCIALIST REALISM

What is the artist's duty in a time of struggle, supposing he wants to take part in the struggle? In my view the artist's duty is notably different from that of other participants who contribute to the struggle with arms and political action. The artist's first duty is to create art, for he knows that an art which is non-art can make no effective contribution to the cause in which he believes.[1]

No adequate judgment of Soviet literature is possible unless one is constantly aware of the fact that it is, like all other activities in Russia, an integral part of the whole mechanism of the State. Creative writing in the USSR is a public function and as such is controlled by the Party and the Government and is subject to pressure by their agencies. In times of crises, this pressure degenerates into disciplinary measures, such as banishment from the press and literary unions, or into such administrative forms of persuasion as arrest, exile, and concentration camps.[2]

The idea of party art becomes a slogan for all Soviet literature, one of the main principles of our views on art.[3]

The assertion that the artist is entirely subject to the world surrounding him – is a meaningless assertion. The world by itself is formless and the first task of the artist is to find a form, select the material he needs. This selection is determined by his ideology which, in this case, plays the role of spectacles through which the artist sees.[4]

The proletarian realist examining reality realizes that the fundamental, moving historical force in the past, at present, and in the nearest future is the class struggle.[5]

---

[1] Alberto Moravia, *Man as an End*. Translated by Bernard Wall. New York: Farrar, Straus & Giroux, 1965, p. 123.

[2] Marc Slonim, "Russian Soviet Literature Today," in Marc Slonim, Lin Yutang, Giose Rimanelli, and Arturo Torres-Riosco, *Perspectives: Modern Literature of Russia, China, Italy, and Spain.* Washington, D. C.: The Library of Congress, 1961, p. 1.

[3] E. Troschenko, "Marx on Literature," *International Literature*, March 1934, No. 6, p. 147.

[4] "An Interview with André Malraux," *Ibid.*, November 1934, No. 5, p. 146.

[5] A. V. Lunacharsky, "Problems of the Soviet Theatre," *Ibid.*, July 1933, No. 3, p. 89.

Not everyone who looks for a solution to the social and ideological crisis of bourgeois society – and this is necessarily the subject-matter of contemporary bourgeois literature – will be a professed socialist. It is enough that a writer take socialism into account and does not reject it out of hand. But if he rejects socialism ... he closes his eyes to the future, gives up any chance of assessing the present correctly, and loses the ability to create other than purely static works of art.[6]

1. Politics and the Novel in Soviet Russia

In the course of its half a century of existence Soviet Russia has applied a systematic policy of control over its native literature. Though the Government exercised its monolithic power arbitrarily during Stalin's reign, it could not altogether silence occasional pockets of opposition. The theory that justified the rigorous censorship and suppression of ideologically objectionable books was that the Revolution had to be safeguarded. Writers were expected to voice the needs and aspirations of the proletariat, and the Party was the best institutional exponent of proletarian values and political truths. Socialist realism, established as the officially approved aesthetic cult, was meant to celebrate the new social order. The writer had to become an engineer of human souls. His mission as a novelist is to educate the masses; his work has to be propagandistic in tone and optimistic in content. He must take good care to glorify the Communist ideal. The principles of Socialist realism ruled Russian literature with undisputed vigor from 1932 until 1953.

Not only Russian writers but a large, devoted band of leftist novelists and fellow travelers outside of Russia enthusiastically took up the struggle to implement the aesthetic doctrine of Socialist realism. Russian literature was supposed to be based squarely on Marxist-Leninist ideology and rooted in the proletarian mystique. It was the pure Marxist content, its politically correct world-view as prescribed by the Communist Party, that identified a work as distinctly "proletarian" in character. Literature, an ideological superstructure dependent upon and shaped by its economic base, was intended to function primarily as a medium for educating the masses in the fundamentals of Socialism. Proletarian culture was designed to fulfill the utilitarian aim of glorifying labor, denouncing the iniquities of capitalism, and depicting the heroic struggle of Communism to establish itself throughout the world, though there was little agreement among Party leaders as to how all this was to be achieved. Leon Trotsky insisted that proletarian culture could not in the years following the October Revolution be instituted in Russia.

---

[6] Georg Lukács, *The Meaning of Contemporary Realism*. Translated by John and Necke Mander. London: Merline Press, 1962, p. 60.

The population as a whole was too backward. Education would have to come first. But Trotsky was ousted from his position of power, and gradually the Party, controlled by Stalin, took over the responsibility of guiding the development of Soviet literature.

The Party vigorously maintained that Soviet literature could prove equal to its historic task by serving as a vehicle for socialist ideology, which correctly interpreted the *truth* of social reality. The Russian writer was not, however, allowed to discover the truth of reality (whatever that might be) for himself; he was categorically told what the truth comprised and how it could best be communicated in his work. Realism – that is, Socialist realism – was the way that led to the truth, but this truth had to be constantly supervised lest the writer, wittingly or unwittingly, fall into counter-revolutionary sin or concern himself overmuch with questions of form and technique and commit the heresy of "formalism." Politics ruled art. Stalin prescribed the nature of the literary themes to be chosen, how they were to be treated, and the character of "the positive heroes" to be idealized. "To make the people more submissive to Party exploitation, writers were urged to inculcate in their readers a new socialist ethics, new work attitudes, and a new respect for socialist disciplines." [7] The role of the Party and its leadership had to be depicted in glowing colors. Fiction and drama were lauded not for their intrinsic merit as works of art but for their degree of propagandistic effectiveness, the "correctness" of their political orientation. The strange thing is that Russian writers (the dissidents had been weeded out or exiled or "liquidated") accepted this formulation of Socialist realism, though they often disagreed about specific ways of applying it. On the whole, they believed that literature should be realist in form and Socialist in content. What is more, committed as they were to the Communist ideal, most of them believed that literature should do its share in helping to build up the Soviet commonwealth and ensure the success of the proletarian revolution the world over.

Unfortunately the relation between politics and literature has never been satisfactorily determined. Irving Howe defines a political novel as one "in which political ideas play a dominant role or in which the political milieu is the dominant setting." [8] This is a vague enough generalized statement. What is meant by political ideas or the political milieu and how do they function in the structured context of the novel? In Soviet Russia, however, no critical doubts arose as to the efficacy and importance of the genre: the political

---

[7] Herman Ermolaev, *Soviet Literary Theories 1917-1934: The Genesis of Socialist Realism*. Berkeley and Los Angeles: University of California Press, 1963, p. 163.

[8] Irving Howe, *Politics and the Novel*. New York: Horizon Press, 1957, p. 17.

novel. It was set a given task: it had to conform to Marxist theory and Party dictates. In his report, delivered on October 29, 1932 at the Conference of the Organizational Committee of the All-Russian Union of Soviet Writers, V. Kirpotin points out that adherence to dialectical materialism on the part of the writer is not enough; it provides too simplistic and mechanical a formula. He proclaims Socialist realism as the best method to follow for the future development of Soviet literature, and by Socialist realism he means

the reflection in art of the external world, not only in its superficial details, or even in all its essential details, but in all its essential circumstances and with the aid of essential or typical characterization. We mean the faithful description of life in all its aspects, with the victorious principles of the forces of the socialist revolution, we mean the anti-private property, anti-capitalist nature of our work fostering in the reader the spirit of the struggle for the better future of mankind, the strengthening and guarantee of the dictatorship of the proletariat. We set socialist realism against idealism, subjectivism, the literature of illusion in any form whatsoever, as an untrue and distorted reflection of our actuality against sympathy with the past, capitulation to bourgeois individualism.[9]

What this wordy, jargonic pronouncement means in practice is that Soviet literature must be actively enlisted in the struggle for the dictatorship of the proletariat (whatever this catchword may imply) and the triumph of the socialist State. In short, literature must be infused with militant class-consciousness so as to hasten the advent of the classless society and bring a new and better world to birth.

These are the commandments of Socialist realism which the Russian writer must perforce obey if he is not to be taken severely to task for his ideological sins. The proletarian as the positive hero represents a type, a class that is destined to be victorious throughout the world; his individual characteristics, his personal dreams and desires, his introspections and subjective vagaries, are of no importance. The categorical imperative reads: it is society as a whole that must be reconstructed in accordance with the fundamental principles of Marxism-Leninism-Stalinism as interpreted by the Party. The novel is not regarded as a distinctive art-form with its own structural and technical requirements, but rather as a means of disseminating Communist propaganda, for all art, it is held, is basically propaganda of one sort or another. Used in this sweeping, all-inclusive fashion, the term "propaganda" becomes, like the term "commitment," semantically meaningless. Bad or crude propaganda, according to this slanted criterion, is that which is hostile to Communism. All literature, whatever its motivation or high credentials, which does not fit into the framework of Socialist realism, belongs to the realm of

[9] V. Kirpotin, "Fifteen Years of Soviet Literature," *International Literature*, 1933, No. 1, p. 145.

illusion or narcotic falsification of reality and constitutes a betrayal of the cause of humanity. Judged in this light, *The Metamorphosis* is seen as a nightmare of introversion, a despairing confession of the aimlessness and impotence of the uprooted intellectual in the capitalist world.[10] The same politically harsh strictures are applied to the Surrealists, who are condemned for indulging their sterile aesthetic pleasures, their perverse dreams and eroticized fantasies, thus cutting themselves off from

the real world where war and Fascism threaten. They allow the reactionary elements within themselves to take the lead, elements which sur-realism, final form of bourgeois poetics always had latent within it. . . . For the revolutionary movement has no use for saboteurs and for people who regard the revolution as all over. . . . Their last weapon is psychoanalysis.[11]

As we have already indicated, what the Marxist critics during the stormy thirties not only in Soviet Russia but also in England, France, Italy, and the United States urgently called for was an end to "escapism" and "aestheticism," idealism and subjectivism, and the creation of a genuinely revolutionary or politically committed literature. The "engaged" creative spirit must penetrate to the root of the diseases and disorders of capitalist society: the chronic poverty and unemployment, the economic waste, the exploitation of the laboring class, the misery of alienation. The revolutionary writer must transcend the narrow limits of his ego (the ego that is but a "grammatical fiction") and endeavor in his work to anticipate the direction the collective society of the future will take, the model for which has already been established in Russia. He must be supported by a substantial body of belief, and this belief must grow out of Communism. For apart from Communism, as one English critic of the left declared with magisterial finality in

---

[10] Howard Fast accuses Kafka of equating men with insects in *The Metamorphosis*. He then goes on to say that this "equation of man and cockroach is a part of an enormous process on the part of the ruling class which may be quite simply defined as a confusion and distortion of the nature of the objective reality." Howard Fast, *Literature and Reality*. New York: International Publishers, 1950, p. 11. Marxist critics have been exceptionally harsh in their judgment of Kafka, the apolitical and asocial writer *par excellence*. Lukács regards *The Trial* as an exemplary portrayal of the contradictions and irresponsibility of bourgeois society, but he finds fault with the abstract character of Kafka's allegory, the nightmarish atmosphere in which his fiction is steeped. By using the allegorical method, Lukacs charges, Kafka drains life of its meaning, so that everything he presents is "annihilated by his transcendental Nothingness." Georg Lukács, *Realism in Our Time*. Translated by John and Necke Mander. New York and Evanston: Harper & Row, 1962, p. 45.

[11] Paul Nizan, "French Literature Today," *International Literature*, November 1934, No. 5, pp. 142-143.

1936, "our age offers no belief that a man can hold without insulting his intelligence." [12]

In Stalinist Russia no writer was given the opportunity to insult his intelligence. All writers without exception were not only expected but compelled to conform to the principles of Socialist realism. According to the critical precepts promulgated by the dogmatic law-giver, Zhdanov, Soviet literature, if it is to fulfill its high destiny, must inspire martial valor and radiate an affirmative, optimistic outlook. Art must not only spring from the people, it must also be imbued with the proper ideological content – that is, with the inspiring spirit of Leninism. Literature as a mighty weapon in the revolutionary struggle becomes, if rightly conceived, Party literature. Writers, in Stalin's telling phrase that Zhdanov quotes, are *engineers* of human souls. Hence the ideological front must be brought into line with the industrial front. Zhdanov sums up what he considers the duty of the Russian writer to be:

While selecting the best feelings and qualities of the Soviet man and revealing his tomorrow, we must at the same time show our people what they must not be, we must castigate the remnants of yesterday, remnants that hinder the Soviet people in their forward march. Soviet writers must help the people, the State, and the party to educate our youth to be cheerful and confident of their own strength. . . . [13]

Here the writer is told dogmatically what conclusions to accept; he is not entrusted with the creative task of discovering his own truth. The ruler of a totalitarian State must endeavor to make the expression of literature subservient to his purpose; he must neutralize its possibly subversive appeal. He must simplify issues and debase the language of art so that it will address the populace in predictable and acceptable ideological terms. What the Commissar ignores is that though art and society are related and interdependent, art remains at bottom an autonomous activity, not to be conscripted for aims and ends alien to its nature: service in behalf of society, the State, or the Party.

Social upheaval is inevitably reflected in the content and style of art, and in many instances the artist is extremely sensitive to the hidden pressures and secret storm signals that precede violent change. His seismographic response to the latent currents carrying within them the forces that will mold the destiny of man can reach the form and significance of prophecy. In this sense the artist may influence the actual course of events – at certain times and in certain situations. But this does not mean that every progressive artist seeks political in-

[12] Philip Henderson, *The Novel Today*. London: Bodley Head, 1936, p. 98.
[13] Andrei A. Zhdanov, *Literature, Philosophy, and Music*. New York: International Publishers, 1950, p. 43.

fluence or considers his creative activity as a direct means of effecting a social or political change. The artist is primarily concerned with his art, he has been, he still is, and he will be in time to come.[14]

The committed writer in Russia had to pay a costly price for his commitment: the loss of his freedom, and without this freedom he could not achieve authenticity in his work. The doctrinal ukases of the Commissar left their traumatic imprint on the body of Russian literature for a period of over thirty years, from 1932 to 1953, the time of Stalin's death. For the openly declared and enforced function of art in a dictatorship, under whatever kind of euphemism it parades, is nothing less than the complete subordination of the individual to the collectivity. Society is enthroned as the jealous, exclusive God whom all art is compelled to worship. Neither society nor the State nor its leaders must be subjected to negative criticism, since such "counter-revolutionary" sentiments tend to undermine the morale of the people. In short, complexity, symbolism, introspection, and experimentation in general are ruled out. As Lunacharsky declared:

The proletarian state seeks to elevate to the level of socialist culture the backward toiling masses. . . . All these measures we are employing to regulate creative art, both proletarian and the art of those following the proletariat, and to put a stop to artistic work among the direct enemies of the USSR – this entire school of influences, from repression to the greatest care of the artist, to comradely concern about him, to giving him support, to penetration of his laboratory – all of them are good and necessary.[15]

In other words, those writers who cooperate with the State will be encouraged and handsomely rewarded, while the direct enemies of the USSR will be sternly repressed.

Whereas the writer in the West is still free to tell the truth as he sees it and thus commit himself to any cause in which he happens to believe, Zen Buddhism, Surrealism, Existentialism, the writer in the Soviet Union is under the necessity of obeying the mandates of the Communist Party. If he kicks against the pricks, he knows in advance the kind of punishment that he will have to suffer for his contumacy. Compare André Gide's outspokenness in *Afterthoughts*, after his visit to the Soviet Union, with the declaration of Party loyalty of a novelist like Yuri Olesha. No party in the world, Gide announces, "will ever prevent me from preferring Truth to the Party. As soon as falsehood comes in, I am ill at ease. My rôle is to denounce it. It is to the Truth that I am attached. If the Party abandons it, then I aban-

[14] Hellmut Lehmann-Haupt, *Art Under a Dictatorship.* New York: Oxford University Press, 1954, p. 21
[15] Quoted in *Ibid.,* p. 228.

don the Party." [16] Such a spirit of independence is anathema in the Soviet Union. There the worship of the abstract Truth is an illusion, a species of bourgeois idolatry. There is only class truth, Party-prescribed truth. He who is not for the workers is an enemy of the Revolution and must be unmasked. Let us listen to Yuri Olesha recite his creed of submission:

If I do not agree with the Party in a single point, the whole picture of life must be dimmed for me, because all parts, all details of this picture are bound together and arise one out of the other, therefore, there must not be a single false line anywhere.

That is why I ... say that in this matter, the matter of art, the Party is as always right.[17]

The Party is as always right! Such a declaration, made in public of unconditional submission to monolithic Party control, was more or less taken for granted during the period of Stalin's repressive regime.

2. *The Thaw and the Emergence of Social Criticism*

In the bad old Stalinist days "socialist realism" meant a non-imaginative – as it were, statistically correct – representation of reality, plus the edification received from the spectacle of the positive hero with a positive attitude to socialism. Art, in short, had to serve the purposes of the party. There realism began and ended. It is now becoming a subtler and more flexible term.[18]

To forestall doubt, the Party fights any tendency to delve into the depths of a human being, especially in literature and art. Whoever reflects on "man" in general, on his inner needs and longings, is accused of bourgeois sentimentality. Nothing must ever go beyond the description of man's behavior as a member of a social group. This is necessary because the Party, treating man exclusively as the by-product of social forces, believes that he becomes the type of being he pictures himself to be. He is a social monkey. *What is not expressed does not exist.* Therefore if one forbids men to explore the depths of human nature, one destroys in them the urge to make such explorations; and the depths in themselves become unreal.[19]

The fact that the officially sanctioned cult of Socialist realism gave rise to no literary renaissance, need not detain us. Our concern is to show how the ethic of commitment, carried to extremes, begot a countermovement of

---

[16] André Gide, *Afterthoughts on the U.S.S.R.* New York: Dial Press, 1938, p. 70.

[17] Yuri Olesha, "About Formalism," *International Literature.* June 1936, No. 6, p. 88.

[18] A. Alvarez, *Under Pressure: The Writer in Society.* Baltimore: Penguin Books, 1965, p. 66.

[19] Czeslaw Milos, *The Captive Mind.* Translated by Jane Zielonko. New York: Alfred A. Knopf, 1953, p. 216.

protest. Stalin's death was followed by the relaxation of externally imposed standards. The thaw set in. Voices were raised demanding greater freedom for the writer, who now wished to exercise the right to criticize social life. For it was obvious that the Revolution had not brought about the perfect social order. The belief in the advent of a scientific utopia which will give man complete power over Nature has received a setback. The Russian population abounded in criminals, shirkers, thieves, perjurers, traitors, suicides, and evil people. How account for the existence of such perverse types in the Fatherland of the Proletariat? Why had human nature not been radically transformed according to expectations? In 1956, the moral and social protest issued by a number of Russian writers made itself felt. They were not disillusioned Communists, they had not abandoned their political faith; they merely desired for the most part to loosen the authoritarian controls to which the arts had been subjected. Since they believed that their first duty was to be sincere, to achieve authenticity, they questioned the role of the Party in the determination of literary values. They were no longer willing to accept the crude, ready-made formulas handed down by the Party. Social reality was far more refractory and complex than dialectical materialism made it out to be.

While visiting Moscow in the summer of 1964, the Yugoslavian writer, Mihajlo Mihajlov, found the literary mood there one of hopeful anticipation that all dogmatic restrictions on literature and art would be removed. Kafka's work, together with critical articles on his contribution, was being published. What he finds even more extraordinary is the open treatment of the concentration-camp theme in Russian literature. He is convinced that the results of the communist experiment in the Soviet Union show "that the solution to man's crisis is not to be found in the political, social or economic spheres. It lies much deeper, in the existential, universal crisis of the personality, in the metaphysical depths of human beings." [20] Alienation is as active in a totalitarian country like Russia as it is in the capitalist world. What was happened is that

The old dominant idea which motivates men, the idea of an "earthly paradise," does not work any more. This is not because it is unrealizable; quite the contrary. For although the contours of the economically and socially just society can already be perceived in many ways, it is being realized that this alone does not give spiritual sustenance.[21]

[20] Mihajlo Mihajlov, *Moscow Summer*. New York: Farrar, Straus and Giroux, 1965, p. 164.
[21] *Ibid.*, p. 165.

It is not enough to build the welfare state, to raise the standard of living. All this, it must be asked, is intended for what purpose. For that is the crucial question. "For man will never be satisfied with the idea that he is born in this cosmos and 'that's all,' that his only aim in life is to live well." [22] This strikes a note of metaphysical revolt, challenging the myth of materialism as Dostoevski had done in *Notes from Underground*.

Though some of the barriers erected against the expression of heterodox views were removed, the Government, still retaining its monopoly of the media of communication, could decide which writer was to be silenced. The Pasternak affair is a case in point. *Doctor Zhivago* was first published outside of Russia. Writers who were too outspoken in their criticism had to smuggle their work abroad and even had to resort to the use of a pseudonym. *The Trial Begins*, by Abram Tertz, a pseudonym for Andrei Sinyavsky, is a fictional satire of the totalitarian repression of thought and art in Russia during the last year of Stalin's life. It is a scathing exposé of the extent to which the country as a whole is governed by terror and its people brainwashed with Party-manufactured slogans. In its description of the way the secret system of terror operates – the universal spying, the psychotic fear lest "enemies" conspire to overthrow the "proletarian" commonwealth – the novel owes much to Kafka's *The Trial* and Zamiatin's *We*. Stalin is represented as usurping the role of God, a God of wrath and thunder, and the City Public Prosecutor is his prophet. In his efforts to disclose the nightmarish truth about life in Russia under Stalin, Tertz presents types rather than individuals, but he does succeed in raising a number of disturbingly unorthodox issues. Seryosha, the son of the Public Prosecutor, naively asks why some wars are considered just while others are condemned as unjust. Adultery goes on in Soviet Russia as in degenerate Europe. Yuri Karlinsky, in love with the Prosecutor's wife, thinks of dying and finds frightening the thought of forever ceasing to exist. *The Trial Begins,* like *Doctor Zhivago,* strikes a new note in Soviet fiction, the emergence of the metaphysical vision. Now that people were deprived of faith in the dream of personal survival, how could Communism hope to satisfy this persistent, if irrational craving for immortality?

The story of *The Trial Begins* provides a framework for caustic comments on the Stalin cult, the relation of means to ends, the casuistic jargon of the dialectic. No dangerous thoughts are allowed to take root in the mind of the citizens; they must be led to believe that the end justifies the means; in the name of Communism everything is permitted. New centers of spying

[22] *Ibid.,* p. 166.

activity are uncovered. Two detectives in the novel indulge in fantasies on how to invent a psychoscope that would infallibly betray what people think and feel. The masses do not want freedom; they want a Supreme Ruler. "And now there is no God, only dialectics." [23]

The trial of the author of *The Trial Begins* on the charge of smuggling his manuscripts out of the country in order to have them published under a conveniently assumed pen-name and the harsh punishment meted out to him for his "crime," gave proof that, despite the thaw, the Government had no intention of allowing unrestricted freedom of expression. The printed record of the trial showed that the powers that be in the Soviet Union were determined to keep a rigid control over literature and the arts. In this case it was not a question of literary defiance or political subversion. Andrei Sinyavsky is a believer in Communism; he loves his country and its people, but he also loves the truth and is therefore opposed to what is known in Russia as "the cult of personality": the abject worship of Stalin and the brutal excesses to which it led. The proceedings of the trial afford an instructive lesson in the politics of a totalitarian regime that posed as the guardian of proletarian liberty, and in the curious semantics of literary interpretation as practiced by the prosecutor and the presiding judge.

Tertz had written *On Socialist Realism*, a brilliant study of the method of Socialist realism in a society that is sure of its purpose even to the point of issuing commands as to how fiction, for example, should be composed. The method results in a number of internal contradictions, which Tertz had the temerity to point out. That was the nature of his "crime." He affirms the truth of reality that fantastic art shadows forth, the art of the grotesque supplanting the verities of pedestrian realism. In his book, *On Socialist Realism*, he declares:

Having lost our faith, we have not lost our enthusiasm about the metamorphoses of God that take place before our very eyes, the miraculous transformations of His entrails and His cerebral convolutions. We don't know where to go; but, realizing that there is nothing to be done about it, we start to think, to set riddles, to make assumptions. May we thus invent something marvelous? Perhaps. But it will no longer be socialist realism.[24]

In short, the crux of the problem is literary: whether deviations from the official dogmatic party line are permissible. But the Soviet authorities do

---

[23] Abram Tertz, *The Trial Begins*. Translated by Max Hayward. New York: Pantheon Books, 1960, p. 128.

[24] *On Trial*. Translated and edited by Max Hayward. New York and London, 1966, p. 11. Quoted from Abram Tertz, *On Socialist Realism*. Translated by George Dennis. New York: Pantheon Books, 1961, pp. 94-95.

not interpret the situation in this way. There is to be no wall of separation between literature and politics, for all of life is included in the sphere of politics. To disclose the facts in the plots and purges of the Stalinist past – that brings the Soviet image into disrepute and must therefore be condemned as treasonable and defamatory. Even the products of the imagination are not to be tolerated if there is the slightest suspicion that they are directed against Russian Communism.

One of the men on trial together with Sinyavsky was Nikolai Arzhak, a pseudonym for Yuli Daniel. Daniel had spoken out against the brutal purges that took place under Stalin. And in *Moscow Speaking*, published abroad but not in Russia, he had presented as his central theme the belief that men should not forfeit their humanity but remain true to themselves alone. Regardless of the pressures to which they are subjected, they should follow the dictates of their conscience. At the end of *Moscow Speaking* the hero says to himself: "You should not allow yourself to be intimidated. You should answer for yourself, and you thereby answer for others." [25] In the courtroom Daniel courageously voiced his conviction "that there should be no prohibited subject in the life of society." [26]

Sinyavski was equally courageous and outspoken in his own defence. He did not deny that his fiction had dwelt on the barbarism characteristic of the Stalinist period, though he recognized that this period had to be passed through as a stage in Russian history. When the prosecutor asked him about his political views, he replied by saying: "I am not a political writer. No writer expresses his political views through his writings. An artistic work does not express political views." [27] Such a statement was pure heresy, sufficient proof that the man was guilty as charged. He who is not with the State is against it. In his final plea to the court, Sinyavsky raised the question as to what distinguishes literature from propaganda. His work, he insisted, did not fall within the dichotomous framework of pro-Soviet and anti-Soviet propaganda. His writing was simply un-Soviet.

3. Further Voices of Protest in Soviet Literature

Russian writers have of late rediscovered, or rather dared to reaffirm, the importance of the inner life of man. In *The Bluebottle* Valeriy Tarsis pro-

[25] Niholai Arzak, *This Is Moscow Speaking*. Translated by John Richardson, in Patricia Blake and Max Hayward (eds.), *Dissonant Voices in Soviet Literature*. New York: Pantheon Books, 1962, p. 306.

[26] *On Trial*, p. 81.

[27] *Ibid.*, p. 101.

duces a novella that does not fit into the procrustean category of Socialist realism. It is not strenuously optimistic in tone and orthodox in its expression of ideology. It does not deal with proletarian champions of labor, positive heroes, who against great odds manage to build factories and dams, extract huge quantities of coal from mines, and surpass by prodigious effort the quota set for production. On the contrary, it is questioning, bitter, introspective, metaphysical in content, and defiantly satirical in its evaluation of the dominant political cliches and the quality of the Russian elite. What we get in these novellas, *The Bluebottle* and *Red and Black*, published in one volume, is an absorbing account of the protagonist's struggle to break away from the current Party control. He criticizes the cult of optimism and the wretched mediocrity of the art that is turned out under Party direction. Here is further evidence of the underground struggle of the individual during the post-Stalin period not to be reduced to a thing.

The title story relates the mishappenings, the misfortunes really, of a philosopher who revolts against the dictatorship of the Party. Yoan Bluefly had up to then praised the virtue of rational discipline. He had sincerely believed that the individual is strengthened and enriched by subordinating himself to the common good of the social order, but then one day he began to question the truth of his theory that rationalism must prevail, that man is predominantly a rational being. From that time on his mind proved a traitor to his former system of thought. All that he had once fervently believed he now came to doubt. What of the paradisal promises held out by the Socialist State? What about its insistence that there was an objective reality? Was there actually a reality that could be grasped identically by two people? The idealists were not fools and yet they contended that each man inhabited his own world. Did it not follow that utopian plans for instituting collectivism were sure to fail? Why assume that people would be willing to sacrifice the pleasures of the present for the sake of a glorious future that might never be realized?

The positive hero has turned negative and is guilty of heresy. He sees that intellectual life in Russia is at a standstill; original thought is considered dangerous and therefore taboo. Literature and scholarship are made up largely of quotations. And those who prate most learnedly of Marxism, those who maintain it is not a dogma, nevertheless betray it in practice. They are time-servers, ideological conformists, timid conservatives. It was unheard of that someone not connected with the Party hierarchy should deem it his right to revise the revolutionary gospel. Hence the Party bureaucrats and their henchmen when they encountered a deviationist, and a recalcitrant one at that, one who refused to listen to reason, was considered mentally ill and deserved to be incarcerated in a psychiatric ward – a theme that Tarsis takes up in his autobiographical novel, *Ward 7*. Obviously the true Party man was never disloyal in thought or speech; he accepted and repeated the sentiments and slogans the Party promulgated. "A man who thought differently from the rest, even if what he thought about was the quickest and best way of achieving communism, was an enemy." [28] Bluefly, the heretic, looks upon these Party stalwarts as standing in the path of Communism. Bureaucrats who treated people as commodities, they had no understanding of the human soul.

And it is against the entrenched bureaucracy that Yoan, far gone in the evils of heresy, rages. He has written a book that "maintained that Soviet socialism was not socialism in any true sense." [29] The State was not to be regarded as the crowning achievement of collectivism. Collectivism in Russia is a mythic fiction, a monstrous hoax, a game played with the aim of proving that Russia is the savior of mankind. The people are not consulted, though the myth is proclaimed always in their sacred name. As Yoan says:

Just think: the whole of Russia has been doing nothing but swearing by the people and deifying them. And we progressives, so-called intellectuals, have been talking our heads off in their name for over a hundred years, while they, the people of Holy Russia, have been laughing up their sleeves at us.[30]

The people need not labor to debunk the myth; they know what has happened; they are aware that nothing has been accomplished as far as they are concerned.

Yoan's friend, Ostankin, believes, however, that in time socialism will become truly scientific and its aims fully realized. The present is but a transitional stage. History must be taken as it comes; it is not finically concerned about subjective expectations and sentimental dreams. Time will usher in the collectivist millennium. "Our monstrous bureaucratic State has no intention of withering away, and it will be much harder to smash than the bourgeois State; but once that's done, communism will follow soon after." [31] Ostankin declares that the ideas now branded as visionary will eventually be vindicated in the future. Ostankin is, of course, cognizant of the oppressive evils of the present regime with its terroristic use of force to stifle all opposition. Party discipline means: "don't you dare to think

---

[28] Valeriy Tarsis, *The Bluebottle*. Translated by Thomas Jones and David Alger. New York: Alfred A. Knopf, 1963, p. 28.

[29] *Ibid.*, p. 38.

[30] *Ibid.*, p. 42.

[31] *Ibid.*, p. 45.

what you think; mind you approve whatever is done and repeat whatever is said by the higher-ups." [32]

The satire is reserved in particular for Ilya Apostolov, a mediocrity, a conformist, who is elevated to a high position in the Soviet leadership. He is a realist who knows that despite the preachment of Marxist doctrine, the people were not the initiators of events nor the makers of history. Apostolov reaches the highest place in rank (he is most likely a take-off on Khrushchev) because he has mastered the art of keeping silent. Because he does not commit himself, he does not expose himself to the danger of liquidation. Tarsis draws this witty and malicious caricature of the man:

Apostolov had never voiced an idea of the remotest originality and never – God forbid – written an article. Perhaps because of this, after the annihilation of many anti-Party groups of various sorts, he was counted as one who had never defied the purity of Marxism-Leninism (not surprisingly for he had always avoided contact with it), and he was given an important ideological post. Now he actually began to make speeches: if they were not original, they at least proved that he was thoroughly versed in the current Party terminology and that he had no intention of revising any article of faith. . . .[33]

Yoan Bluefly is determined to go ahead with his work and bring it to completion even if, as he realizes, it would not be published in Russia. His comrades believe that he must be ill, mentally unbalanced. He is advised not to create trouble for himself. If he is ousted from the Party, he will be rendered helpless. How can he help matters by broadcasting his subversive ideas that socialism in Russia is non-existent? Will this not lend weight and substance to the calumnies being spread by the enemies of the Workers' State? He is reprimanded, he is warned. He is unable to sleep; he suffers from hallucinations; he broods over his past, hunting for the clue "to the mystery of the unhappiness which was strangling him to death." [34] He perceives that the new world is in many essential respects worse than the old. In this poisonous atmosphere everything seemed unreal. He is now convinced that it is a disastrous mistake to try to improve the world by force. He decides to write his confessions and we are given the complete version of Bluefly's diary.

Through this device we learn of his inner torments. He had become a Communist on the principle that Communism insured happiness for all, but now he realizes that there are no happy men in Russia. He cannot abide the hypocrisy of Communist officials who foam at the mouth when they

[32] *Ibid.*, p. 47.
[33] *Ibid.*, p. 55.
[34] *Ibid.*, p. 76.

discuss the lynching of Negroes in the United States but remain strangely silent and unconcerned about the death of thousands of innocent Jews in Russia, the elimination of dissident nationalities, or the exile of non-conformist writers to do forced labor. In looking back over his past, he wonders what he lived and labored for. Who am I? he asks himself. He is not impressed by the philosophy of dialectical materialism. As for Socialist realism, no one understands what the cult really represents. If a Tolstoy or a Dostoevski were to appear on the literary scene, their work would be neatly tailored to conform to the current political ideology. But Yoan is confident that in the end he will be the victor. He tells Apostolov:

Think of the future. In a hundred years everything will be done by machines. Not only will they do all the work, but they will also govern, control, judge, decide, translate – anything you like. The only activities left for human beings will be to use their imagination and to reproduce their kind.[35]

The conclusion drives home the point that socialism is a grotesque, horrendous lie.

The second novella, *Red and Black*, is more autobiographical in tone and content. It reveals the spiritual torment of a sensitive and gifted professor of French literature as he becomes aware of his alienation from the people and the politics of his land. Like Yoan, he is a far cry from the doctrinaire image of the positive hero. A lover of Stendhal, he believes that the human soul possesses mysterious and incommunicable depths. He is not impressed by the techniques the masters of Russia use to change and control human nature. Out of touch with his age, he refuses to repeat like a parrot the ideological idiocies promulgated by the rulers. Mimicry, he finds, has become the most highly cultivated art in his country. "Admittedly it is more difficult to turn out properly milled, drilled, pressed, and polished souls than machine parts; yet perhaps more progress has been made in this technique than in mechanics." [36] This is the professor's protest against the cult of standardization, the growing power of behavioral science to promote the process of self-adaptation to political demands for conformity.

Korneliy Abrikosov, the dissenting intellectual, is not deceived by the messianic jargon of the Party spokesmen. He does not believe in the theory of inevitabilism as applied to history. A poet at heart who has been infected with the subtle skepticism of a Stendhal, he looks upon himself as the last scion of the superfluous people. He has reached a point where he is no longer sure of anything. He will not worship false gods, he is no idolater, and that is why he feels isolated and lost. He will not write panygerics (sheer

35 *Ibid.*, p. 126.
36 *Ibid.*, p. 146.

lies) about the superiority of the Soviet homeland to the rest of the benighted capitalist world. At the end he commits suicide.

Another autobiographical novel by Tarsis, *Ward 7,* contains appalling
political implications. We have for some time been familiar with the madness of politics and especially the madness of politicos. The madness of
these leaders masquerades as the height of wisdom, the quintessence of public idealism; their intentions, however disastrous in their outcome, are always high-minded, their hearts incorruptibly pure. And what a lunatic mess
they make of their power of leadership: war, putsches, purges, persecutions
for heresy, treason, and thought-crimes, imprisonment, brainwashing, exile,
liquidation. But now we get an equally sinister reversal of techniques, the
politics of madness: the use of mental institutions as disguised prisons to
house the dangerous dissenter. In the climate of opinion that prevailed in
the Soviet Union after the death of Stalin, such punitive measures are not
regarded as extreme. The guilty party is no longer branded an agent provo-
cateur, a hidden Fascist, an enemy of the State. Since he finds fault with
the government and conspires to publish his inflammatory libels abroad,
he must be mentally afflicted. Otherwise his eyes would behold the truth of
life in Russia, that everything is for the best.

Thus Valentine Almazov, a thin disguise for the author himself, finds
he is *persona non grata* in his homeland for venturing to criticize the Establishment in a work published abroad. For his "abnormal crime" he is
committed to a lunatic asylum, instead of, under the Stalinist reign, being
shot to death or sentenced to hard labor in a concentration camp. The authorities have become more cunning in getting rid of malcontents and potential trouble-makers. The incarcerated writer finds the mental institution
filled with other citizens who are in the same boat. Tarsis furnishes a vividly detailed picture of the mental hospital and the patients in it. To be kept
there has its decided advantages: one is free to speak his mind on any
subject; for the "insane" there are no interdictions or taboos. As for therapy, that is only a ludicrous pretense. Patients are fed on drugs that ad-
versely affect their personality, resulting in loss of memory and impaired
sexuality until they are finally reduced to a state of submissive indifference.
Here the delirious paranoiac fantasies of William S. Burroughs are strikingly confirmed.

What makes this revelation so shocking is that, unlike *Nineteen Eighty-
Four* or *We* by Zamiatin, it is no fantasy; it is a documented account, dres-
sed up as fiction, of historical reality. These political victims are shut up in
a so-called mental sanatorium for an indefinite period, without a trial. Tarsis describes how his protagonist had been apprehended for the crime of

smuggling his manuscripts out of the country. He had published *The Blue-bottle* in England in 1962, under the pseudonym of Ivan Valeriy, though he personally did not wish this to be done. He made no effort to hide the fact that he was its author. As a result he was arrested and placed in an asylum. When Western intellectuals interested themselves in his case and protested against the injustice of his punishment, he was allowed to go free.

He regarded the hospital in which he was confined as a "walled-in concentration camp." [37] He is assigned to Ward 7, but his imprisonment could not tame or darken his spirit. What sustained him through this difficult ordeal was the power of his imagination. His country would not forever be kept in bondage and he envisioned the restoration of his native land and its people to a free life. What he yearned for and dreamed of ardently was the blessed ideal of freedom. For having lived under the nightmare of Stalinist repression, he, like his friends, discovered that the boundary line which separated good from evil was obliterated. They saw only the proliferation and triumph of evil everywhere. He was now convinced that however important ethical considerations were in the management of collective life, "freedom must come first: the country must be liberated from its monstrous yoke, swept clean of the monsters who had imposed it – only then, by the light of freedom, could it discover its new ideals and follow them." [38] Concretely, this meant that the totalitarian tyranny instituted by Stalin must be overthrown. For Almazov, as for his creator, the issue cuts much deeper than that. For him

what is at stake is not a political régime or a system of balance of powers but the one all-important issue: whether man as an individual, as a person, is to exist or not. Personal freedom is the one unarguable good on earth. The communists have put forward another: not man but the collectivity, not the individual but the herd. But do you imagine that humanity will ever consent to be a speechless and mindless herd? – it would much sooner be destroyed! What the West and the whole free world is trying to prevent is *man* being turned back into a communized anthropomorphic ape. It took thousands of years for the individual to emerge from the herd. Now the atavistic instinct has revived – significantly, among the "proletarians," the spiritually destitute who, naturally, are led by blinkered fanatics.[39]

His hope is that man will conquer over the ape. Here is a voice crying out against the rise of barbarism, the evil of ideological coercion. It is only the fear engendered by the police state that has prevented the people from re-

---

[37] Valeriy Tarsis, *Ward 7*. Translated by Katya Brown. New York: E. P. Dutton & Co., Inc., 1965, p. 13.

[38] *Ibid.*, p. 19.

[39] *Ibid.*, p. 20.

volting against all the pernicious nonsense preached in the name of Communism.

Ward 7 was crowded with three types of "patients": first, those who attempted but failed to commit suicide; such cases were classified as lunatics "because it was assumed (by doctors and politicians, writers and ideologists) that anyone dissatisfied with the socialist paradise must be a lunatic. . . ." [40] Then came those who were guilty of trying to get out of the country. Finally came the non-conformists, the outsiders, the malcontents, the haters of discipline and regimentation. The hospital was, in fact, run like a prison. Only one of the doctors in attendance knew the truth about what was wrong with the Russian people after passing through forty years of war, violence, counter-revolution, and oppression: they lacked a decent way of life. This doctor "thought it absurd to call 'persecution mania' the state of mind of people who had been persecuted for forty years and whose fathers had been shot or died in concentration camps." [41] What was urgently needed was the end of the campaign of repression, the recovery of the bracing air of freedom.

Almazov, we are told, is passing through a severe spiritual crisis. Now that his old political faith is gone, he does not know what to believe. "All he knew was that the only way of life offered him was intolerable, unworthy of men, fit only for insects." [42] Even the national language, prostituted by the servile purveyors of Soviet literature, had been drained of meaning; the Party had been transformed into an authoritarian Church. He had arrived at the conclusion "that Communism was a form of Fascism and that Russian literature had ceased to exist. . . ." [43] The West had no knowledge of conditions in Russia, the censorship, the lack of creative freedom. Filled with hatred for the prison that Russia has become, he declares that "A mental hospital is the only place for an honest writer in Russia nowadays!" [44]

The theme that Communism today is a form of Fascism is coupled with a profound distrust of collective societies; they are basically inhuman. The conflict takes place between the Mass and Man. Anyone who dares to criticize the ruling power in the State is either locked up in prison or consigned to a madhouse. The artist may be apolitical in his work, but that distinction will not save him. It makes him guilty just the same of the crime of "escapism" or "formalism" or whatever the pejorative label may be. After all,

[40] *Ibid.*, p. 22.
[41] *Ibid.*, p. 42.
[42] *Ibid.*, p. 34.
[43] *Ibid.*, p. 37.
[44] *Ibid.*, p. 45.

as Almazov says, "It was in Russia that a fascist totalitarianism was first set up." [45]

Another novel that reveals the shocking disparity between the utopian dream that originally animated the revolutionary struggle and the hideous realities of the Soviet dictatorship, is *One Day in the Life of Ivan Denisovich* by Alexander Solzhenitsyn. It shows how power corrupts and absolute power corrupts absolutely. After Stalin passed from the scene came the startling disclosure of mass purges, imprisonment, assassinations, slave labor camps, trials based on framed evidence and faked confessions. *One Day in the Life of Ivan Denisovich* describes with sober realism the conditions that existed in the concentration camps Stalin instituted for "the enemies" or the suspected enemies of the State – and such enemies were everywhere to be found. Now, at last, the Russian people were allowed to read of these enormities. The crimes of the past are brought to light, and it is made clear that these crimes are the natural and inevitable product of a totalitarian society. All Russia is pictured as a vast concentration camp.

The emergence of this type of social criticism in Russia points up the evils to which a literary ethic of commitment can give rise when it is taken over and managed with dogmatic and ruthless inflexibility by the State. Marxist literature, inside and outside of Russia, represents an ambitious effort to shape the nature of man as well as the structure of society. "Proletarian" literature is hailed as the voice of liberated mankind, the herald of social redemption. In the Marxist lexicon of aesthetics, the individual exists, even in his dreams and innermost feelings, only as a social being. "The conception of the private individual with his private consciousness is typically bourgeois." [46] But the individual perversely refuses to conform to the behavioral criteria set up by the lords of Communism for the politically adjusted citizen. Writers like Sinyavsky and Tarsis rebelled against the rigidly restricted version of reality formulated by Socialist realism. They demanded the freedom to explore the golden realm of fantasy, the world of dreams, the interior life of man: apolitical themes that could not be viewed through the ideological perspective of the class struggle.

---

[45] *Ibid.*, p. 105.
[46] V. J. Jerone, *Culture in a Changing World*. New York: International Publishers, 1947, p. 10.

PART IV

CONCLUSION

CHAPTER XIX

CONCLUSION

To suggest that poets tell men in crisis what to do, to insist that *as poets* they acknowledge themselves as legislators of the social order, is to ask them to shirk their specific responsibility, which is quite simply the reality of man's experience, not what his experience ought to be, in any age.[1]

Do books change opinions? Or do they merely activate opinions already held, or opinions for which predispositions are apparent (or can be considered after the facts have been apparent)? If so, under what circumstances? Is timeliness of content a determining factor, or can a book create its own right moment? To what extent does a book's persuasiveness depend on its force of argument? To what extent do manner, style, credentials and intent (or the concealment of intent), determine the effective response a book will get? [2]

I have spoilt most of my novels out of a sense of duty to some "cause"; I knew that the artist should not exhort or preach, and I kept on exhorting and preaching.[3]

When he [Sartre] renounced *being* and decided to *do,* to *make,* to *act,* he insisted that henceforth writing would always be a rallying cry, a commitment. This did not imply a contempt for literature but, on the contrary, the intention to restore its true dignity.... Commitment (*engagement*) ... is simply the writer's total presence in what he has written.[4]

The commitment Sartre talks of is not to a political doctrine, but rather to literature itself. To write is to be committed to a certain type of enterprise which makes certain demands on the author; if, I must add, he is to be authentic. Sartre's prescription is for an authentic literature; in most of the places where the word "committed" occurs, "authentic" could be substituted without changing the meaning.[5]

[1] Allen Tate, *The Man of Letters in the Modern World*. Cleveland and New York: The World Publishing Company, 1964, p. 32.
[2] Eliot Fremont-Smith, "The Effect of Books," *The New York Times*, November 7, 1966.
[3] Arthur Koestler, *Arrow in the Blue*. New York: The Macmillan Company, 1952, p. 107.
[4] Simone de Beauvoir, *Force of Circumstance*. Translated by Richard Howard. New York: G. P. Putnam's Sons, 1965, p. 41.
[5] Anthony Manser, *Sartre*. London: The Athlone Press, 1966, p. 252.

We have come a long way in trying to defend the truth of the paradox that while literature is deeply rooted in a social context and manifestly serves a social purpose, it cannot effectively be used to support the cause of morality, religion, or the politics of revolution. We have in the first section examined the work of some writers who are asocial and apolitical in their outlook. We then shifted our attention to the literature of social criticism and social protest and endeavored to show to what degree it was successful in carrying out its intention. Finally, we analyzed the motives which led a number of writers on the left to release their rage for commitment and disclosed the strange ways in which this rage was exploited by the bureaucrats of the Communist Party and the reaction to which this gave rise.

Though the writer is not a legislator of the social order, the literature he produces, in its exploration of the world of the imagination, is instinct with value. It expands the frontiers of consciousness, it deepens and refines the sensibility, it opens wide the gates of vision. It is able to do all this because, as an art, it confronts the world of social and existential reality without utilitarian designs or ideological preconceptions. Its primary and essential task is to interpret truly and fully the reality of man's experience on earth. In representing this reality as forever changing, forever new and different in the patterns of meaning it forms, inexhaustible and ambiguous in its protean manifestations, it envisages all possibilities of being, the comic as well as the tragic, the absurd as well as the sublime.

In working out of the logic of our central theme, we have included a critical discussion of productions by a number of representative modern writers from countries like France, Germany, Switzerland, and Russia as well as England and the United States. We have followed the comparative method in order to bring out the similarities as well as differences in modern literature as it comes to grips with the vital problems of our age. Despite the idiosyncratic features the literature of other lands display, differences caused by the genius of the language, the cumulative weight of a native tradition, and the force of historical circumstances, these features, these differences, are on the whole transcended by a striking similarity of pattern, a preoccupation with issues that go beyond national or geographic lines of demarcation.

The cause behind this phenomenon is not far to seek. The world has been unified in consciousness, though not in political fact. The battle that is raging today over the question which form of society, the open or the closed, shall rule the earth, is reduced in the imaginative literature of our time to a controversy, variously defined, as to the role of the individual in society. By virtue of his calling, the artist at work in the open society often

chooses to enlist in the ranks of the opposition. Even in a totalitarian regime, however, there is a saving minority of writers who refuse to abdicate
their function as the conscience of their race, preferring exile or imprisonment to the fate of prostituting their talent at the behest of the Commissar.
The writer as the voice of protest demands nothing less than the fullness of
self-realization and the right to reveal as best he can the truth of the human
condition. Though he is, of course, responsive to the pressure of social life,
he is concerned with values that are not summed up by the stresses and
strains of immediacy.

In the present world crisis there are those who would link art closely to
the life of action, but the fact remains that literature through the ages has
not served as an agency to promote revolution or social reform. Though
there are some seminal books that have a profound transforming effect on
the minds of a whole generation, these generally do not belong to the body
of imaginative literature. Effectiveness of response is measured by the
degree to which a book succeeds in changing the attitude of its readers on
a particular social or political issue. Despite such well-known examples as
Uncle Tom's Cabin, Hard Times, and *The Jungle*, literary works that produced such results are hard to find.

Nevertheless, the belief that literature is or should be a form of social
commitment has been accepted by a number of influential writers. Outside
of the Soviet Union, the most zealous propounder of this doctrine has been
Jean-Paul Sartre. Though Sartre is an impressive example of a writer who
in a time of trouble militantly takes his stand, concerned not simply with
his career as a writer but determined to utilize his art for the benefit of mankind, as an Existentialist dramatist and novelist he was obsessed by the
theme of subjectivity, a subjectivity from whose labyrinths there is no way
out. Even after his conversion to Marxism, he remained essentially inde-
pendent-minded. If he is outspoken in his support of Soviet Russia, he reserves the right to criticize it, as he did on the occasion of the Hungarian
uprising, when its policies run counter to the cause of the Revolution. He
turned to Communism because it brought home to him the truth of the
class struggle and correctly diagnosed the economic cause of misery and
oppression, but he quarreled with the Stalinist brand of Communism because it dogmatically played down the role of the individual and ignored the
reality of evil. The creative worker in this tragic era, Sartre feels, is faced
with the stupendous task of giving birth to "a literature which unites and
reconciles the metaphysical absolute and the relativity of the historical

fact. . . ." [6] Forced to live in the ambiguous context of history, the writer must effect a valid relationship between morality and politics. Art has ceased to be a luxury in a society that is disintegrating as it faces the prospect of a third world war. Hence, Sartre concludes, the writer must ally himself with the working class.

If Sartre voices his faith in the proletariat, it is a faith seriously flawed with reservations, and it is these reservations that have kept him out of the Communist Party. Such reservations raise a painful problem of conscience for the leftist writer. Can one become a Communist, Sartre asks, "and remain a writer?" [7] Sartre's answer at this time is firmly in the negative, though he later revised his political views. Since the social revolution has become conservative, he advises the writer not to lend his services to the Communist Party as a means of reaching the masses. "The politics of Stalinist Communism is incompatible with the honest practice of the literary craft." [8] If the work of art cannot accommodate itself to the dictates of bourgeois utilitarianism, neither can it afford to make its peace with Communist utilitarianism. It must categorically refuse to be exploited as an instrument of propaganda. The writer must be committed, but he must reject "solutions which are not rigorously inspired by socialist principles and, at the same time, stand off from all doctrines and movements which consider socialism as the absolute end." [9]

Though Sartre's call for commitment did not conform to the criteria prescribed for Socialist realism, his politicalized conception of authenticity in literature was not one other writers in France could endorse. His "Reply to Camus" [10] set forth the ideological differences, in their interpretation of Marxism and the question of loyalty to the Soviet Union, that separated the two men. And Alain Robbe-Grillet, in *For a New Novel*, demolishes the pretensions to literary value of didactic fiction and the thesis-novel. He is particularly effective in debunking the claims of the left with its battle-cry of commitment and its formula of Socialist realism. Whereas the Commissar is bent on utilizing literature as a weapon in the prosecution of the class war, the true artist believes that

art cannot be reduced to the status of a means in the service of a cause which transcends it, even if this cause were the most deserving, the most exalting; the

[6] Jean-Paul Sartre, *What Is Literature?* Translated by Bernard Frechtman. New York: Philosophical Library, 1949, p. 222.

[7] *Ibid.*, p. 253.

[8] *Ibid.*, p. 256.

[9] *Ibid.*, p. 278.

[10] Jean-Paul Sartre, *Situations*. Translated by Benita Eisler. Greenwich, Conn.: Fawcett Publications, Inc., 1966, pp. 54-78.

artist puts nothing above his work, and he soon comes to realize that he can create only for nothing. . . .[11]

The artist cannot respond to ideas and imperatives dictated from the outside, however worthy the motive, without damaging the quality of his work. Art must continue to function as art and in doing so it will have a decidedly "revolutionary" effect. Confusion is worse confounded when literature is judged solely by its political orientation; "the very notion of a work created *for* the expression of a social, political, economic, or moral content constitutes a lie." [12] Art starts with no antecedent beliefs, no panoplied ideology. For the novelist, in his portrayal of reality, does not deal with something ready-made and finished once and for all. Robbe-Grillet concludes that the only legitimate commitment for the writer is to literature itself. "It is not reasonable, henceforth, to claim in our novels to serve a political cause, even a cause which seems just to us, even if in our political life we advocate its victory." [13]

Literature is not in a position to offer solutions to practical problems; it raises questions about the world and man's place in it but presents no categorical answers. Whatever his personal views as a citizen may be on the stormy issues of his day, the writer is not qualified to act as a social prophet or volunteer his services as a social engineer. His work, however, is not of negligible importance. His contribution leads men to face themselves and their involvement in the human condition. It summons them to full awareness and authenticity of being by questioning all that is, including the problematical character of man himself. The writer is the bearer of a paradox which comforts while it mocks: in being critical of the society of his age, in angrily exposing its evils and abominations, he is holding up for its emulation nothing less than the image of the ideal. He has no need to engage in preachment or propaganda. His work speaks for itself in disclosing the ambiguity which surrounds the human adventure, the conflict, never completely resolved, between illusion and reality.

In the beginning was the Word, and the Word was made flesh. This sums up, in a way, the history of literature in the Western world. The breakthrough responsible for the transcendence of the animal level, the rise of letters, the efflorescence of art, all this was made possible by the discovery and progressive development of language. Through the increasing mastery of this unique symbol-forming faculty, man became a time-binder, a creator,

[11] Alain Robbe-Grillet, *For a New Novel*. Translated by Richard Howard. New York: Grove Press, 1965, p. 37.

[12] *Ibid.*, p. 38.

[13] *Ibid.*, p. 141.

a maker of history. By means of the living word he could arrest the inexorable flow of time, communicate with his kind, and leave behind him memorials of his experiences, feelings, and thoughts. Gradually he came to manifest a respect for words to a point where he tried to invest them with magical power, seeking like the shaman to use language to coerce reality. The belief in the magical power of language sustains the writer in hours of travail and imbues his work with a dynamic sense of purpose. But it is difficult for him to keep up such a faith at fever pitch. The recalcitrance of social reality, the knowledge that political power is wielded by rulers who are indifferent to, if not contemptuous of, the literary brotherhood, the sobering realization that poems, novels, and plays, even if warmly applauded by the cognoscenti, reach but a limited audience, and that for only a brief period of time – all this forces the writer to revise drastically downward the estimate of his putative influence on the world. He publishes book after book and perhaps insures a place for himself in the history of his native literature, but he is subject to dark troublesome moods when he wonders what effect the totality of his contribution has had on the social life of his age. Simone de Beauvoir, in her autobiography, *Force of Circumstance*, tells how as she grew older writing lost much of its enchantment but none of its urgency.

Despite this undertow of disenchantment, though all idea of duty, of mission, of salvation has collapsed, no longer sure for whom or for what I write, the activity itself is now more necessary to me than ever. I no longer believe it to be a "justification," but without it I should feel mortally unjustified.[14]

Simone de Beauvoir is filled with ontological terror as she contemplates the human condition. She continues to participate in the social struggle of her time, she signs manifestoes and protests, and this activity makes her feel that she is still a meaningful part of humanity, but she knows now that literature is without ulterior justification. Every writer belongs to a given society, but what does that prove? Literary forms and literary values often come to fruition apart from the determinations of the social milieu. Art forms rise to dominance in a particular age but why they do so is largely unpredictable. The same age gives birth to a Genet and a Sartre, a Dostoevski and a Chernyshevski, a Bertolt Brecht and a Samuel Beckett, a Wolfgang Borchert and a Peter Weiss. There is no ground for assuming that *all* literature is an expression of social forces and that its greatness depends on the degree to which it faithfully mirrors the truth behind these forces. As Wellek and Warren cogently point out:

---

[14] Simone de Beauvoir, *Force of Circumstance*, p. 650.

There is great literature which has little or no social relevance; social literature is only one kind of literature and is not central in the theory of literature unless one holds the view that literature is primarily an "imitation" of life as it is and of social life in particular. But literature is no substitute for sociology or politics. It has its own justification and aim.[15]

There have been influential critics as well as writers in the nineteenth and twentieth century who held diametrically opposed views. In the present world crisis, some believe that it is impossible for the writer to remain above politics. Koestler confesses that out of an urgent sense of duty to some "cause" he spoiled most of his novels by preachment or exhortation. As George Orwell declares: "In our age there is no such thing as 'keeping out of politics.' All issues are political issues. . . ." [16] If Orwell dwells so insistently on politics and its close relation to culture, it is because he is convinced that politics is the inescapable destiny of twentieth-century man. For Orwell the right upon which all other rights depend is the right to speak out freely, without fear of reprisal, and for that condition to obtain it is necessary to insure the survival of the open society. Orwell sharply rejects the Communist thesis which argues first, that freedom is a bourgeois illusion, and second, that unrestricted freedom is undesirable. According to him, it is not a question of obedience to the collective will as opposed to the reign of irresponsible individualism, but of truth versus plain lies. If the writer is prevented from telling the complete truth about his experiences and insights, if he is required to suppress or distort his subjective feelings so that they conform to the ideological dictates of the Communist Party, then he has prostituted his mind and debased his talent. And yet Orwell contends that there can be no resolution of this conflict by steering entirely clear of controversial issues.

There is no such thing as genuinely non-political literature, and least of all in an age like our own, when fears, hatreds, and loyalties of a directly political kind are near to the surface of everyone's consciousness.[17]

It is possible, of course, to define politics in such a way as to make it affect, directly or indirectly, all of life, but if the distinctions we have drawn in this book are valid, then it is precisely in such a destructive age as ours that writers and artists (and this was true of the Dadaists, the Surrealists, and the members of the Beat generation) would be strongly tempted to with-

[15] René Wellek and Austin Warren, *Theory of Literature*. New York: Harcourt, Brace and Company, 1949, p. 106.
[16] George Orwell, *Shooting an Elephant and Other Essays*. New York: Harcourt, Brace and Company, 1950, p. 89.
[17] *Ibid.*, pp. 112-113.

draw from what they consider to be the fraudulent and futile world of power politics. A point of view more or less similar to Orwell's is advanced by Raymond Williams, an English novelist and literary critic, who maintains that aesthetic judgments are closely related to moral and social values.

An essential hypothesis in the development of the idea of culture is that the art of a period is closely and necessarily related to the generally prevalent "way of life," and further that, in consequence, aesthetic, moral and social judgments are closely related.[18]

Thus the battlelines are joined between the social-minded critics and those who believe that literature, which has its own justification and aim, is no substitute for politics or sociology or economics. Paul Valéry, for example, denies that aesthetic, moral, and social values are necessarily related. He interprets the issue in a way that seems to support our conception of the asocial aesthetic. The mind wishes to preserve its freedom, its individuality, while society demands some measure of conformity.

On the one hand, the mind is opposed to the mass; it wants to be itself, and even to extend, endlessly, the domain in which the *self is master*. On the other hand, it is forced to recognize society, a world of wills and human hopes all limiting one another; and sometimes it wants to perfect, at other times to destroy, the order it finds there.[19]

When Valéry speaks of the mind he is referring to the creative mind of the intellectual, and that type of mind usually shies away from political parties or finds itself in fundamental disagreement with them. The distinguishing mark of this type of mind is its craving for freedom and independence; it thinks for itself and is not to be intimidated even by a show of facts; "it is, above all, the rebel, even in the act of bringing order." [20] A despoiler of myths (the economic, the political, the proletariat), a relativist in his outlook on life, Valéry rejects all absolutes. The evil that flourishes rankly in the human heart will be found under any form of government. Valéry's inveterate distrust of logical systems of thought and particularly of ideologies leads him to look upon politics as a lost cause. He dedicated his book, *Regards sur le monde actuel* (1931), "to those persons who have no system and belong to no party and are therefore still free to doubt whatever is doubtful and to maintain what is not." [21]

---

[18] Raymond Williams, *Culture and Society*. New York: Columbia University Press, 1959, p. 130.

[19] Paul Valéry, *The Outlook for Intelligence*. Translated by Denise Folliot and Jackson Mathews. New York and Evanston: Harper & Row, 1962, p. 102.

[20] *Ibid.*, p. 102.

[21] *Ibid.*, p. 3.

The complex problem of the relationship of literature to society is intimately bound up with the problem of the relationship of the individual to society. Actually there is no dichotomy between society and the self. Society provides the stage and the script of the drama in which all must participate, from the time of birth, in a variety of ways. But in another sense, society is an abstraction; only the individual, the social microcosm *par excellence,* is real. For a collectivity, as Simone Weil says, has no existence, it is only a fiction; "it has only an abstract existence and can only be spoken to fictitiously." [22] According to the Russian philosopher, Nicolas Berdyaev, society is by its very nature hostile to the development of human personality. "The realization of the value and primacy of freedom and personality sets man, alone and apart, over against society and the mass processes of history." [23] Society is necessary but it cannot serve all of a man's inner needs. The individual, especially the artist, works together with others and yet apart; he is essentially alone, though even when he secludes himself he never leaves the society of men. It is in his hours of creative isolation, essential for his work, that he brings all things into question and thus resists the conformist pressure of his culture. He focuses attention on the dilemma of the individual caught in the maelstrom of social forces and portrays the metaphysical struggle of his *persona* to impose some order of meaning on the universe. He is of necessity the enemy of bourgeois society and finds life under its auspices intolerable.[24] In this stance of alienation, in his steadfast opposition to the *status quo,* he takes upon himself the role of prophetic outsider, sedulously cultivating his eccentricity as the mark of his uniqueness. The inner struggle of the modern writer reveals the nature of the struggle that takes place between society and the self. The artist is today "thrown increasingly in on himself by the sheer size and engulfing blankness of industrial society; as life becomes more mass produced, mass organized and statistical the arts become – proportionately, despairingly – more extreme and solipsistic." [25] Throughout the nineteenth and twentieth century the crucial problem the writer faced was one of self-definition.

Whereas the novelist of the eighteenth century could delineate with some measure of detachment and objectivity the place and character of man in a

[22] Simone Weil, *Selected Essays.* Translated by Richard Rees. London: Oxford University Press, 1962, p. 16.

[23] Nicolas Berdyaev, *Dream and Reality.* Translated by Katherine Lampert. New York: The Macmillan Company, 1951, p. 52.

[24] See Cesar Graña, *Bohemian versus Bourgeois.* New York and London: Basic Books, Inc., 1964, pp. 43-44.

[25] A. Alvarez, *Under Pressure: The Writer in Society.* Baltimore: Penguin Books, 1965, p. 186.

fairly stable society, the modern novelist has had to experiment radically
with the established forms of fiction in order to picture the flux and fluidi-
ty of his social order; the traditional norms of caste and class, morals and
manners, have been swept aside. The writer as rebel now responds to and
records contradictions and discords in the social complex that did not
exist, at least not to the same disturbing degree, in Victorian times. For
example, the Existentialist aesthetic views the world in its irreducible con-
creteness, through the direct response of the individual to the challenge of
experience. Man, a stranger on earth, is fundamentally concerned with his
own self, tensely aware all the time of his own contingency. Going beyond
intellectual or sociological abstractions, Existentialism stresses the interio-
rized view of the universe. An Existentialist aesthetic thus grows out of an
ontological commitment, not out of some theoretical science of man or
science of society. The Existentialist hero starts his quest for meaning with
a question but he is invariably defeated in his hope of finding an unequivocal answer;

we arrive instead, not at any answer, but at the questioner himself. For questions
are asked only by existing men. Except for a living man of flesh and bone, not
a question would be heard in the boundless ocean of being in which we are
cast. . . .[26]

Opposed to the innovations introduced by Existentialist fiction, the stream-
of-consciousness method, and the different representatives of the *Nouveau
Roman*, the social novel continued to hold its own. An eminent and proli-
fic practitioner in this genre is C. P. Snow. The attack launched by the
avant-garde writers has not shaken his belief that the novel functions best
when it is rooted in society. Sensibility, he declares, is not enough; "the
novels of the near future, the novels of the atomic age will make a new
attack on the relations of men to their environment." [27] The conflict between world and self persists in the literary arena, but society is generally
the dominant metaphor in the fictional and dramatic universe of discourse.
Though society provides the generative context of values, the individual is
free to accept them or reject them. (Within limits, of course, for within the
totalitarian regime that option may be denied him.) We have seen that the
self, as it is depicted in the body of modern literature, is essentially social
and at the same time asocial and critical of society. The all-pervasive
social metaphor does not – not even in the productions of Socialist realism

[26] Arturo B. Fallico, *Art & Existentialism*. Englewood Cliffs, N. J.: Prentice-Hall,
Inc., 1962, p. 12.
[27] Cited in Paul West, *The Modern Novel*. London: Hutchinson & Co., Ltd., 1963,
p. 45.

in Russia – remove all sources of existential ambiguity. Paradoxical as it may seem, the writer is most faithful to his sense of social responsibility when he is true to himself. Literature, whether it deals with society on a huge scale in the manner of the *roman fleuve* or with the lonely, anguished individual in the fiction of Kafka or Paul Bowles, whether it takes up the theme of leftwing politics or that of "nausea" and the myth of the absurd, must do so through the medium of symbols that shadow forth the character of the society in which the self must work out its destiny.

Literature is addressed to other men and is therefore social in content. But this truism throws little or no light on the outcome of the creative process. For the individual is not merely the behavioristically shaped product of the forces in his environment. In creating the drama of the self, the novel, like the play, shows how the individual struggles to preserve his integrity in a world that wages global warfare, exploits human beings on a mass scale for profit, utilizes power politics as an instrument of domination, and systematically kills off millions in death factories. The self, if it is to maintain its freedom, must resist being sucked into what Sartre calls "a utilitarian collectivity." [28] It must always be on guard against the danger of self-deception, the jesuitry of "bad faith." This, according to one American critic, is the primary direction of modern literature – to present in terms of a succession of instantaneous experiences, "encounters of the self with objects, the full nature of the self and its situational dilemmas." [29]

Nevertheless, despite repeated disappointments and defeats, literature cherishes the dream that what is finite and incomplete in the individual can be overcome if the social order is perfected. Man dies, society lives on. Secular utopias offer a symbolic version of immortality. The intoxicating vision makes the social ideal seem attainable in the near or remote future. The course of history will see justice done, abolish the evils of the present, and found the Kingdom of Heaven on earth. The revolutionary is the hero who voluntarily endures martyrdom for the sake of this blessed consummation. Turning their back on the Christian promise of redemption, Malraux's protagonists are sustained in their hour of death by the conviction that they have given their life for a worthy cause – the dignity of all men – that will triumph in the end. As a revolutionary, the hero glories in his anonymity, the annihilation of his private ego. The "I" is only a grammatical fiction. The Communist hero feels that he is part of a movement that is directing the forward march of history. It is this mystical sense of collective purpose

---

[28] Jean-Paul Sartre, *What Is Literature?*, p. 36n.
[29] Frederick J. Hoffman, *The Mortal No*. Princeton: Princeton University Press, 1964, p. 453.

which all literature dedicated to Socialist realism is expected to celebrate. This is the Earthly Paradise, this "the Purpose which Fate destined for mankind." [30] Writers who hew to the Party line have "but one aim – Communism; one philosophy – Marxism; one art – socialist realism." [31]

Commitment or alienation, society or self, the demands of the collectivity or the rights of the individual, loyalty to the State or Party as opposed to the call of conscience – these are the key terms in a drama of conflict that is characteristic of the mind of modern man as well as the literature he produces. The controversy hinges basically on the kind and degree of commitment expected of the writer. At one extreme we have heard the socially aroused critics urge the artist not to misuse his genius as a form of make-believe, an exercise in pleasurable illusion. He must not fiddle idle, if engaging, tunes while Rome burns. He must take his stand and speak for suffering humanity or at least for that class, the embattled proletariat, who will in time effect the regeneration of society the world over. He must broadcast his message of social salvation for mankind, proclaim the heart of his utopian vision. At the other extreme we meet writers (Surrealists, the playwrights of the theater of the absurd) who refuse to conform to these demands. Are they therefore to be condemned out of hand as the irresponsibles, concerned solely with their own private fantasies, convinced that these are incommunicable and relying on a "non-sense" language of their own? Is their work to be dismissed as pessimistic, nihilistic, morbid, solipsistic?

Such harsh judgments spring from a failure to comprehend the intrinsic meaning of their asocial aesthetic. One English critic, R. D. Smith, makes this spirited and perceptive defense of the creative contribution of the playwrights of the absurd:

Beckett, Ionesco, and Pinter, engaged in finding themselves or saving themselves, remove their characters from immediate social contexts. This does not make them Reactionary, Anti-Human, Pessimists or Non-Communicators; in my view they are more deeply committed than many writers who aggressively claim a virtue in being committed. All writers are men, all men are committed, like it or not. Artists have the special social value of helping each of their fellow-men in his personal commitment.[32]

[30] Abram Tertz, *On Socialist Realism*. Translated by George Dennis. New York: Pantheon Books, pp. 30-31.
[31] *Ibid.*, p. 51.
[32] *Contemporary Theatre*. Stratford-Upon Avon Studies 4. New York: St. Martin's Press, 1962, p. 135.

The artist, if any ultimate duty devolves upon him, must be true to his vision of man and the world, and to the art that mediates his vision. He is free, like the masters of realism in France, Balzac, Stendhal, and Flaubert, to paint the portrait of society in his day, and it need not be a flattering portrait he draws, but his work is more likely to last if he does not succumb to the vice of preachment or propaganda. The imaginative writer provides no dogmatic formulas or easy, optimistic solutions. He projects the archetypal conflict in man's innermost self between what he is and what he strives to become, a conflict which always takes place against the background of society.

Man exists only in society but he is not limited by its temporal horizons. Society is the matrix in which he finds himself and in which he must forge his destiny, but he is not the resultant of social or historical determinants. The world of fiction and the drama has never succeeded in presenting the class man or the economic man except as a mechanical abstraction. Most Communist writers, however much they may subscribe to the mystique of the proletariat, do not actually create characters in action according to the prescriptive tenets of dialectical materialism. Even the positive hero is on occasion tempted by the counter-revolutionary Devil of doubt. Man, in short, is not an object to be manipulated according to scientific or political theory. The philosophical or political position a writer assumes is not the essential factor that invests his work with artistic value. Instead of beginning with a body of preformulated ideas, he discovers what he has to say, and how to say it, in the process of creation. Literature, which constitutes an open universe of the imagination, is opposed to dogmatic exclusiveness. It may be asocial and apolitical in content, like the work of Kafka, Proust, and Genet, and yet be "revolutionary" in its impact.

The cry of the lost, impotent self in much of modern fiction and drama is the piercing cry of distress of a society that is falling apart. It is the sickness of society that speaks through its alienated prophets. If they stand apart and cry havoc, it is because they are at war with themselves. However painful the metaphysical malaise they suffer from, they do not, as artists, abandon society to its fate. Their persistent efforts to unveil the truth of being testifies to their commitment. Unimpressed by the mass-psychoses and clamorous ideologies of their age, they explore the dimensions of the inner life and reveal that the dream of material progress is shattered, that insecurity is the fate of modern man. It is his deification of reason, his idolatrous worship of the collectivity, that has brought man to this present impasse. As Daniel Aaron, the literary historian of the left, declared, the experiences of lonely seekers ultimately become social, "and in the fantasies of the writer we discover belatedly our private and public fates." [33]

Society and self, individualism and collectivism: these are the two extremes between which the literature of the modern age uneasily oscillates. It is dangerous to predict what the outcome of this struggle will be. It is safe to hazard the guess that those works stand the best chance of surviving the test of time which are not harnessed to some cause or ideology, but which open up endless possibilities of being as they disclose the grandeur and misery of the human condition.

[33] Daniel Aaron, "Self or Society?" *The New York Times Book Review*, February 14, 1965, p. 39.

INDEX